After Auschwitz

After Auschwitz

Radical Theology and Contemporary Judaism

by Richard L. Rubenstein

THE BOBBS-MERRILL COMPANY, INC.
INDIANAPOLIS

The author wishes to thank the editors of the following periodicals for per-
mission to use material published in their magazines: *The Reconstructionist*
—"Religion and the Origins of the Death Camps." "The Dean and the Chosen
People," "Reconstructionism and the Problem of Evil," "The Rebirth of
Israel in Contemporary Jewish Theology," "The 'Supernatural' Jew," "The
Symbols of Judaism and the Death of God." *Commentary*—"Symposium
on Jewish Belief." *Christian Scholar*—"Person and Myth in the Judaeo-
Christian Encounter." *Journal of Bible and Religion*—"The Meaning of Torah
in Contemporary Jewish Theology."

The author wishes to thank the following publishers for permission
to use material published by them: The Macmillan Co., Inc.—"Judaism and
'The Secular City' " from *The Secular City Debate,* edited by Daniel Callahan.
Copyright © 1966, The Macmillan Co., Inc. The Reconstructionist Press—"The
Making of a Rabbi" from *Varieties of Jewish Belief*, edited by Ira Eisenstein.
Copyright © 1966.

The Bobbs-Merrill Company, Inc.
4300 West 62nd Street
Indianapolis, Indiana 46268

First Edition
Ninth Printing—1976
Designed by Quentin Fiore
Library of Congress catalog card number 66-27886
ISBN 0–672–61150–3 (pbk.)
ISBN 0–672–50604–1

To my children, Aaron,
Hannah and Jeremy.

Contents

Preface

The Jewish community has experienced more monumental changes in the twentieth century than at any other time in its very long history. The uprooting involved in the emigration of millions of Jews from eastern Europe to the United States and Canada, the death camps, and the rebirth of Israel each represent enormous alterations. Any one of these by itself would have been enough to create extraordinary problems in Jewish life; their occurrence in relatively rapid succession has created religious and cultural problems of unparalleled magnitude. Furthermore, the upheavals must be seen in the context of a world radically in flux. The loss of the religious dimension in secular society, the rise of technopolis, the revolutions in mass media, and the loss of the remnants of a stable moral order after the wars of this century have all contributed to the unprecedented upheavals in Jewish life.

In the face of so radical a change, some men romantically turn to an irretrievable past, yearning for a restoration of its virtues. They see the terrible flaws of the present and are most persuasive in delineating them. Unfortunately it is easier to be aware of the evils of our time than it is to be quit of them. It is better to recognize the irretrievability of the past and to explore the potentialities inherent in the present, regardless of the radical hiatus with accepted traditions this may imply. I am convinced that this latter approach will be forced upon us if we do not accept it willingly. It would have been better had six million Jews not died, but they have. We cannot restore the religious world which preceded their demise nor can we ignore the fact that the catastrophe has had and will continue to have an extraordinary influence on Jewish life. Although Jewish history is replete with disaster, none has been so radical in its total import as the holocaust. Our images of God, man, and the moral order have been permanently impaired. No Jewish theology will possess even a remote degree of relevance to contemporary Jewish life if it ignores the question of God and the death camps. That is *the question* for Jewish theology in our times. Regrettably most attempts at formulating a Jewish theology since World War II seem to have been written as if the two decisive events of our time for Jews, the death camps and the birth of Israel, had not taken place.

A religious community has some resemblance to a living organism. It is impossible savagely to rip out half of its substance without drastically affecting the surviving remnant. The first reaction to such a wounding must be shock and numbness. I do not believe the period of shock has entirely spent itself. It is only now that a tentative attempt can be made to assess the religious meaning of the events. This book represents one such attempt.

The time may come when the Jewish community can formulate its religious response as a community to what took place. That time remains a very distant prospect. For the foreseeable future, theological response will be private and subjective. Contemporary theology reveals less about God than it does about the kind of men we are. It is largely an anthropological discipline. Today's theologian, be he Jewish or Christian, has more in common with the poet and the creative artist than with the metaphysician and physical scientist. He communicates a very private subjectivity. Its relevance lies in the possibility that he may enable other men to gain insight and clarify their religious lives in the face of a common experience.

There are decided affinities between the theological insights expressed in this work and those of the contemporary Christian radical theologians. We have had some of the same teachers and we react to the same moment in history. Nevertheless, we react differently because our experience of the world has been so very different. I suspect that we part company most radically over what I regard as the Christian radical theologian's inability to take seriously the tragic vision. The tragic vision permeates these writings. How could it have been otherwise after Auschwitz?

The theologian writes out of his own experience and out of his own tradition. He addresses himself to all men. This work rests on the conviction that the experience of contemporary Jews has a relevance which exceeds the limits of the Jewish community. Many of the chapters in this book are the fruit of encounter and dialogue with Christians, both at home and overseas. I have been moved and altered by these encounters. It is my hope that what I have written will in some way contribute to the self-understanding of Christians as well as that of Jews in our times.

There was a time, not very long ago, when religious thinkers enjoyed the luxury of a stable institutional framework which allowed them to devote their time to research, study, and writing with few intrusions. Today's theologian enjoys no such calm. His ideas are as likely to be formulated while he is waiting for a jet as in the few moments he can spend undisturbed in his study. Although this work represents a relatively unified approach to the problems considered, it bears the marks of the highly mobile character of the theologian's vocation in contemporary America. The chapters in this book largely originated either as papers delivered at scholarly conferences, as university lectures, or as articles contributed to religious periodicals. I regard it as significant that they were written while I was a participant in the life of two secular universities, Harvard and the University of Pittsburgh.

I write as an American theologian, but Europe has had a very great impact on my thinking. This is evident in the very title I have chosen, *After Auschwitz*. It is also evident in the decisive influence upon my thinking of such intellectual movements of European origins as existentialism and psychoanalysis. During the time I was engaged in writing the papers in this book, I spent relatively long periods visiting France, Spain, Holland, and Germany. A brief visit to Poland had an overwhelming impact.

No man can write unaided. I have been helped, encouraged, and challenged by many good men and women. Above and beyond all other help I have received, that of my wife Betty was the indispensable ingredient for the completion of this task. My editor, Lawrence Grow of Bobbs-Merrill, guided this effort with a rare combination of theological insight and literary sensitivity. My secretary, Frances Hirsch, helped to type some of the manuscripts. The most important job she has done has been assisting me to meet my responsibilities in Pittsburgh over the last eight years.

I also want to acknowledge the encouragement, assistance, the influence of the following men and women: Rabbi Benjamin Kahn of the B'nai B'rith Hillel Foundations; Charles and Mary Merrill of Boston; Professor Rudolfo Cardona of the University of Pittsburgh; Henry Koerner of Pittsburgh; Doctor Ira Eisenstein of *The Reconstructionist*; Doctor Steven S. Schwarzschild of *Judaism*; Professor David Bakan of the University of Chicago; Professor Harvey Cox of Harvard; Professor Thomas J. J. Altizer of Emory; Professor William Hamilton of Colgate-Rochester Theological Seminary; Professor Zalman Schacter of the University of Manitoba and the Advisory Board of the B'nai B'rith Hillel Foundation at the University of Pittsburgh.

Pittsburgh, Pa.
August 23, 1966

After Auschwitz

My first visit to Germany took place in August 1960. At the time, I was vacationing in Wijk aan Zee on Holland's North Sea coast. Most of the other vacationers were Germans. Every time I passed one on the beach, I wondered what he had been doing during the war. Undoubtedly, some of my fellow vacationers had been involved in murdering Jews. They were now well-behaved, courteous tourists whose children sometimes played ball with my children. Because of the Jewish tragedy, I was both enormously hostile and curious concerning the Germans. I had not planned to visit that country. My curiosity finally overcame me. I visited Düsseldorf, Cologne, and Bonn. Quite by accident, I was invited to attend briefings which were being held for American-Jewish leaders in Bonn under the auspices of the Bundespresseamt, *the Press and Information Office of the Federal Republic. I accepted the invitation and had my first contact with Germans as human beings. The contact was brief but important.*

When I returned home, I pondered the question of how the Germans could have perpetrated such crimes. My attempt at comprehension may seem extreme at times; it is hardly as extreme as the phenomenon it seeks to explain. There are still men in Germany and Austria today whose watchword is "Long live Auschwitz!" Many of the themes which predominate in my later theological writings are already present in this paper: the dangers of apocalyptic enthusiasm, the meaning of the death of God, technopolis and the secular city, and the problematics of the Judaeo-Christian encounter.

1 / Religion and the Origins of the Death Camps

A Psychoanalytic Interpretation

THE EICHMANN TRIAL is now a part of history. In fate and in substance, the killer has been reunited with his victims. The dreary rehearsal of the facts was perhaps important, but the trial always pointed beyond itself to the question of *why* Eichmann and thousands of others, often men of exceptional ability and education, were compelled to elect their gruesome careers as executioners. Once the defendant's legal sanity was established, psychological considerations were precluded by the nature of the judicial process. Nevertheless, the question of why the events took place remains of far greater consequence than the legal question of the guilt of the participants. Though the Germans initiated the extermination machine, they were by no means without the active support and sympathy of many of the people whom they had overwhelmed. To achieve a catharsis of insight into the origins of the death camps is by no means a solely German necessity.

Men will be trying to understand why it happened for centuries. No two explanations will entirely coincide. No single attempt at explanation, including this one, will be entirely adequate. There are, however, some aspects of the death camps concerning which we are now quite certain. Common-sense explanations simply don't explain. None of the ordinary hypotheses of lawlessness, lust, the desire for personal gain, utility, or even simple hatred is really plausible. In order to understand the Nazis, we are forced beyond the ordinary canons of common sense. Nazi motivations largely defied normal expectations or predictions.

Considerations of usefulness did not deter the Nazis. Had their primary interest been to win the war, they never would have made the death camps such a central concern. They would have utilized, rather than alienated, every available talent, Jewish or gentile. Toward the end of the war, the dazed and defeated Germans were promised that German science would produce a secret weapon capable of turning the tide. Not infrequently an atomic weapon was hinted at. Ironically one of the most important sources of talent available to Germany's enemies in creating nuclear weapons was German-trained scientists who fled their native land when anti-Semitism left them no alternative. The sheer need for a compliant labor force in wartime should have dictated an entirely different approach, not only to the Jews but to the subject nations as well. Had final victory really been the Nazi aim, their whole conduct of the war would have been different. The history of the period suggests that, for the diehard Nazis as opposed to the average German, the war was not a means to victory. It was an end in itself wherein the Nazis permitted themselves behavioral freedoms impossible in peacetime. The Nazis often seemed far more intent upon achieving irrational victories over defenseless Jews and Gypsies than a real victory over their military opponents. They won the war that really counted for them, the war against the Jews. Eichmann's alleged statement that, though all else fail, he would go to his grave content in the knowledge that he had helped to kill over five million Jews is very much to the point.

In dealing with a movement guided by so great an element of mystique and ritual, it is impossible to avoid the question of religious origins. Although the Nazis have been called pagans, they were never genuine pagans like the ancient Greeks. They were satanic anti-Christians, saying no to much that Christianity affirmed and saying yes to much that was absolutely forbidden in Christianity. There is a striking parallel between the diehard Nazi and the priest who celebrated the Black Mass in medieval witchcraft. The satanic priest was never an atheist or a pagan. His problem was that he believed too much. He celebrated the

Black Mass, not because of lack of belief, but because he hated God and wanted to invert normal religious standards. Had he really been an unbeliever, he would not have been so dependent upon religion to determine the character of his rebellion.[1] He would in all probability have found better and more constructive ways to occupy his time. The Nazis were religious rebels rather than genuine unbelievers.

In one area the Nazis took Christianity very seriously. They did not invent a new villain. They took over the two-thousand-year-old Christian tradition of the Jew as villain. Nor did the Nazis create a new hatred. Folk hatred of the Jews is at least as old as Christianity. The Nazis intensified what they found. They created very little *de novo*. Nevertheless, in their intensification of the old hatreds, the Nazis added a new and radical element which had never been present in Christianity. They transformed a theological conflict, normally limited in its overt destructiveness by religious and moral considerations, into a biological struggle in which only one conclusion was thinkable—the total extermination of every living Jew. Where Christianity usually rested content in seeking to convince the Jews of the error of their ways and to seek error's remedy in conversion, Nazism had no interest in regarding the Jews as anything but objects to be exterminated. Nothing the Jews could do by way of confession, submission, surrender, betrayal, or apostasy could have altered their destined roles in the Nazi system.

The roots of the death camps must be sought in the mythic structure of Christianity. This assertion must not be regarded as an imputation of guilt against Christianity for the death camps. The Nazis were rebels *against* Christianity. The religious rebel is far more demonic than the simple pagan or the genuine atheist. Myths concerning the demonological role of the Jews have been operative in Christianity for centuries without creating so dire an entailment. In addition to the religious background, the peculiar ambivalence of an influential part of the German literary and intellectual community toward Christianity in the nineteenth

[1] I am indebted for this insight to Jean Paul Sartre's *Baudelaire*, H. Martin Turnell (Norfolk, Conn.: New Directions Books, 1950), pp. 71 f.

and twentieth centuries, as well as the response of the German people to defeat after World War I, were necessary preconditions before the Nazis could utilize the religious myths with such explosive force.

The oldest origins of the death camps may be seen in the extremely complicated relationships of ancient Judaism and primitive Christianity. The rival faiths have never been entirely distinct and independent religious movements. The Church has always regarded herself as the fulfillment and the true successor of the Synagogue. This is very apparent in the writings of St. Paul, the apostle who first carried the message of Christianity beyond the confines of the Jewish community. For Paul, only a Christian was a true Israelite. The Jews who rejected the Christ, though Israelites by birth, could not be considered Israelites after the spirit. In making his point, Paul delighted in drawing a parallel between the rivalry of Christian and Jew in his day and the ancient rivalry between Ishmael and Isaac. In Abraham's times, not all who were of the patriarch's *flesh* became children of his promise. Paul drew the conclusion that only those who had faith in the Christ, as Abraham had faith in the Lord, would truly belong to the community of God's elect. Faith in the Christ, not membership after the flesh, was for Paul the *conditio sine qua non* of participation in the New Israel.[2] Paul never doubted that the Church was the fulfillment of the old Jewish community, because he was convinced that the revelation incarnate in the Christ was the fruition of the revelation originally given to Moses. From its inception, Christianity considered itself the successor of Judaism rather than an entirely different religion.

The conception of the Church as the true Israel necessarily involved a very negative evaluation of the old Israel. This is not yet explicit in Paul. He regarded the "unbelief" of the Jews as part of the divine plan whereby the gentiles were first to be brought to the Lord, and he was convinced that ultimately the Jews would accept the Christ. He felt a real sense of kinship with those whom he regarded as erring brethren.

Within a hundred years, the split had become bitter and

[2] Paul's fateful discussion of the place of Israel in the Christian dispensation is to be found in Romans 9–11.

irrevocable. The Jews had fought two wars against the Romans in C. E. 66–70 and 132–135. As a result of the first war, the Jerusalem Temple, the center of Jewish religious life, was destroyed. The young Church took this as a double sign. It was seen as confirmation of Paul's contention that those who lived in the Christ were dead to Jewish Law, a great part of which required the destroyed Temple for its observance. It was also taken as proof of God's punishment of the Jews for their rejection of the Christ and complicity in his death.

During the Second Roman War (132–135), a significant part of the Jewish community, including Rabbi Akiba, regarded Simeon Bar Kochba, the leader of the revolt, as Israel's true Messiah. The Christians, many of whom were still of Jewish extraction, naturally interpreted this as a compounding of Jewish vice. Not only had the Jews rejected Christ, the true Messiah, but they had gone astray after a false pretender. When the Romans defeated the Jews and inflicted their devastatingly cruel revenge upon the losers, the Christians took the event as further proof of God's rejection of Israel and the truth of Christianity.

The development of the bitter religious antagonisms is plainly visible in the writings of Justin Martyr, a Palestinian Christian apologist who flourished about one hundred years after Paul. Paul's mild doctrine of the Old and New Israel was altered by Justin into an extreme contrast between the Church as the New Israel and the Synagogue as the despised and rejected of the Lord. There is a remainder of compassion in Paul which is absent from Justin. In Justin's writings an old Jewish idea—God's punishment of sinful Israel—has been combined with a new sin, the murder of the Christ. This murder was soon regarded as the murder of God. As we shall see, the Christian conception of the Jew as deicide is a significant component of the religious origins of the death camps.

In his *Dialogue With Tryphon,* Justin frequently expresses the conviction that Jewish disaster is nothing more than what the Jews deserve. A frequently quoted passage indicates how violent these feelings have become. Referring to circumcision, Justin declared:

[It] was given for a sign . . . that you alone suffer what you
now justly suffer; and that your land may be desolate, and
your cities burned with fire; and that strangers may eat your
fruit in your presence, and not one of you may go up to
Jerusalem.[3]

This was the reaction of one of the earliest and most important
Christian theologians concerning the fate of the Jews after their
defeat in the Judaeo-Roman war of 132–135. Justin understood
that Judaism and Christianity are religions of history and that
a principal validation of their claims must be the evidence of
history. Few such evidences are as enthusiastically set forth in
Justin as the historical fact of Jewish defeat by the Romans. For
both Justin and his rabbinic opponents, the war is more than a
military contest. The Romans are the retributive instruments of
the Lord against a sinful Israel. They play the same role in Justin's
interpretation of history as did the Babylonians in the prophetic
interpretation.

Sigmund Freud has suggested in *Moses and Monotheism*
that envy of the Jew as the chosen of the Lord is an important
component in anti-Semitism. This envy would seem to be exemplified in the Church's claim to be the true Israel. In effect,
Justin claims that the Christians rather than the Jews are now the
well-beloved of the Father. The Jews made an extraordinary claim
about themselves—that they were in a special and decisive way
God's chosen people. Instead of ridiculing the claim, a very significant segment of the non-Jewish world took it seriously. Lacking power of their own, the Jews compensated by magically
claiming a pre-eminent portion of divine concern. To their ultimate disaster, the claim was met with neither scorn nor ridicule.
Once accepted, as it was in a paradoxical way by Christianity, it
aroused envy and the desire to displace the favored child.

Though the Jews were hated before Christianity, especially in Hellenistic Egypt, the special and frequently pathological character of the hatred for them under Christianity must be
seen as in part related to one of the oldest conflicts between Jew

---

[3] Justin Martyr, *Dialogue With Tryphon*, tr. A. L. Williams
(London: SPCK, 1930), II, 107.

and Christian, that of who had the right truly to be reckoned as the elect of the Lord. By insisting that it was the New Israel, the Church made the claim that only its adherents were truly Jews before the Lord. Those who prized this status were necessarily threatened by the real Jews, who challenged the claim simply by their continued existence. Apart from anything the Jews said or did to appease their more powerful rivals, the very existence of the Jews was a threat to the New Israel. This was underscored by greater Jewish familiarity with the world which had given birth to Jesus and their continued rejection of him. Even when the manifest dialogue between Jew and Christian was cordial, Christians could surmise that Jews regarded the Christ-tradition as an embellished fantasy on the career of another Jew. Soren Kierkegaard has commented that the faith of a Christian dwells over a sea of doubt seventy thousand fathoms deep. He has also suggested some of the hideous pain which such doubt can render. Through no one's fault, the unspoken denial of Jesus by the Jews was frequently the occasion of much pain and potential loss of personal moorings in the believing Christian.

In the concentration camps Jews were murdered, not for what they did, but for what they were. No possible alteration of Jewish behavior could have prevented this fatality; the crime was simply to be a Jew. Jewish existence and the tenacity of Jewish survival were in and of themselves an affront to the claims of the Church. Faced with this survival, the Church usually interpreted Jewish existence as did Justin—that is, as filled with deserved sorrow, thus establishing the greatest possible credulity for the Christian claim to being the true Israel.

In the nineteenth and twentieth centuries, the Church's claim to being the New Israel was better understood by Christianity's Teutonic enemies than Jews or Christians. Resentment against Christianity and its enforced displacement of the Teutonic gods has been a significant motif in German life and letters since the Napoleonic wars. This resentment had important roots in the peculiar historical and geographical situation of the Germans. One root can be found in the old tension between the Teutonic north and the Latin south, from which Catholic Christianity originated. Charlemagne's forced conversion of the Saxons and Luth-

er's break with Rome were in part manifestations of this tension.
Modern German nationalism was first aroused during the War
of Liberation against the French, 1806–1813. Many of the German writers of the day interpreted their war against the French
as a continuation of the age-old struggle of Teuton against Latin.
Christianity was regarded as the product and imposition of a
foreign Latin culture. It was resented in influential German
circles. Nazism was an outgrowth of this aspect of German cultural history. Few themes are as vulgarly persistent in the stenog-
raphic reports of Hitler's wartime "table talk" as his hatred and
contempt for Christianity.

Few German philosophers have been as influential as
Hegel. Though by no means an anti-Semite in the twentieth-
century sense, he gave one section of his *Early Theological Writings* the title, "Is Judea Then the Fatherland of the Teutons?"
Hegel complains that Christianity has emptied Valhalla of its
gods and forced the German people to accept Jewish gods and
fables in place of their own.[4] This observation presupposes the
Hegelian concept of *Volksreligion,* in which the religion, mythology, and social organization of an ethnic community *(Volk)* are
regarded as a single organic unity. When any element in the constitution of the *Volk* is displaced or discarded, the unity of the
whole is broken. Such a breach in *Volk*-unity occurred when the
indigenous Teutonic gods were displaced by the foreign gods and
myths of the Jews. For Hegel, the gods of a people are an objecti-
fication of the inner nature of that people. By rejecting their ancestral gods, the Germans were in the deepest sense rejecting
themselves. Hegel did not carry his own logic to its ultimate conclusion in action. He was, however, followed by others such as
Erich Ludendorff and Alfred Rosenberg who were more prepared than he to enter that realm. They concluded that German
alienation and self-estrangement could be terminated only by an
end to the Jewish gods of Christianity.

---

[4] G. W. F. Hegel, *Early Theological Writings,* tr. T. M. Knox
and Richard Kroner (Chicago: University of Chicago Press, 1948), pp.
145 ff. For a contemporary discussion of the importance of the conflict
between Teuton and Latin for the growth of German anti-Semitism, cf.
Erik H. Erikson, *Childhood and Society* (New York: W. W. Norton,
1963) pp. 347 ff.

This hankering for the simplicities of an indigenous *Volk*-community was to become part of the reaction against the distressing complexities of an evolving modern technopolitan culture, with its confusing mixture of morals, faiths, and peoples. The yearning figured very largely in Nazi ideology. It received one of its simplest formulations in the watchword of Hitler's Reich, *"Ein Volk! Ein Reich! Ein Führer!"* In such a community there could be no room for the disturbing dissonances of the Jews or even of Jewish Christianity.

There is a double irony in the claim of the Church that it is the New Israel. It was inconvenient for the Teutonists to uproot the powerful Christian Church. They did vent their anger on the infinitely weaker Jews, thus providing themselves with a cheap victory for Teutonism. It would have been infinitely more difficult for the Nazis to uproot the hold of Christianity on the German people. That, however, was their ultimate intent. The ancient Jewish-Christian quarrel over the true Israel led to the utilization of the original Israel as a surrogate victim for the presumed sins of the New Israel in effecting the alienation of the German people from their native traditions. There were times when the Nazis had a clearer image of what and why they were fighting than either Jews or Christians.

While this helps to explain the origins of the conflict, it does not explain the murderous hatred felt by the anti-Semite for the Jew or why only extermination was regarded as the "final solution." This can in part be accounted for by the accusation against the Jews that they are the deicides, the murderers of God. The Christian religion, alone among the religions of the world, begins with a murder—the murder of God. Since then, it has used the cross, the instrument of execution, as its decisive symbol. In Christian thought the Jews play a twofold role: they provide *both* the incarnate Deity *and* His murderers. The assertions that the Christian Church is the true Israel and that the Jews are the rejected ones are of a piece. Without the alleged special relationship between Israel and God, with its implied magic potency, the Jews could never have provided either God or His murderers. Furthermore, the very envy implicit in the assertion that the Christians are now the elect of God was bolstered by the accusation that those formerly chosen (the Jews) exhibited deicidal hostility, thereby compelling the Father to seek a new and truly beloved child.

The seemingly contradictory complex of claims and accusations is not at all unlike the dynamics of sibling rivalry. Even the accusation "You have murdered or wanted to murder the Father" has this element. In Christian theology, Jesus as the Christ is God, the Son of God. The violence done to His person is, however, equally a violence against God the Father.

The accusation that a rival has sought to do away with the Father is a mode of displacing one's own feelings of guilt for similar unconscious hostility. The anti-Semite could thus envy the Jew as the beloved of the Father and, at the same time, regard him as the despised rival who wanted to murder the Father. The entire system exaggerated the importance of the Jews out of all realistic proportions. They were not seen merely as the defeated and impotent people they were, lacking a normal political life of their own; instead, the very marginality of their existence elicited mythic interpretations. Those who were homeless *(heimatlos)* became uncanny *(unheimlich)*, the decisive actors in the drama of God and the devil, sin and innocence, salvation and eternal damnation. They were regarded as possessing a terrible magic potency, both as the people in whose midst God-in-the-flesh had been born and as His murderers. This helps to explain the irrational delusion, so persistently held, that the Jews must be destroyed lest they destroy the non-Jewish world.[5]

The terrible significance of the accusation of deicide cannot be overstressed. At the extremely important vulgar level, the cry of "Christ-killer" has, more often than not, accompanied the instigation of anti-Semitic violence. One of the most searing scenes in André Schwartz-Bart's *The Last of the Just* is the one in which the little German children anticipate the development of Nazism by almost murdering little Ernie Levy as a Christ-

[5] The parallel between the Jew and the witches of the Middle Ages is important. Bruno Bettelheim has suggested that an irrational fear of the Jew's capacity to do great harm provided the SS with the inner justification necessary to do their work in the camps. Cf. Bettelheim, *The Informed Heart* (Glencoe, Ill.: The Free Press, 1960). Cf. Norman Cohn, "The Myth of Jewish World-Conspiracy," *Commentary*, June 1966.

killer. In our own times, the deicide theme has been examined by Freud, Dostoevsky, Sartre, and others who have understood that the murder and/or displacement of God is mankind's most demonic fantasy.

According to Freud, civilization and religion began with a "primal crime" in which the father of the original human horde was cannibalistically murdered by his sons, in order to gain sexual possession of his females. The father proved more potent dead than alive. His son-murderers experienced intense regret at their terrible deed and tried consciously to suppress its memory. The unconscious memory of the deed continued to agonize the sons and their progeny, thereby causing the murdered father to be imagined as the Heavenly Father. For Freud, the supreme object of human worship is none other than the first object of human criminality. Freud maintained that a great deal that is irrational and opaque in the ritual and myth of both Christianity and Judaism can be traced back to mankind's unconscious memory of its earliest parricide and to the contradictory feelings of guilt and promethean self-assertion which the criminal deed engendered. In the sacrificial death of the Christ, Freud saw a "return of the repressed." Mankind was compelled to repeat, at least symbolically, its original crime against God, while attempting to atone for the continuing feelings of guilt which that unconscious memory sustained.

We will never know whether Freud's aetiological myth is historically correct. It is psychologically illuminating that Christianity depicts itself as commencing its independent career with such a crime. Freud also believed that the cannibalistic aspects of the primal crime are repeated in the Mass, which he regards as both a symbolic repetition of and a ritual catharsis for the original crime.

Freud's myth of the origins of religion is less important in terms of what it tells about human history than in what it suggests about the agonies and conflicts which continue to beset mankind.[6] Adult maturity is bought at a terrible price. Control

[6] Cf. my article, "Psychoanalysis and the Origins of Judaism," *The Reconstructionist*, December 2, 1960.

of one's deepest instincts is the precondition for all men of their continuing participation in the social order. This is brought about with neither ease nor good will. Every society hangs precariously over the precipice of mankind's conflicting feelings concerning. its instinctual life. There is something in all men which would destroy the slender fabric of personal and social control that makes civilization possible. If Freud's myth of original parricide tells us little about human origins, the myth intuits a great deal concerning the awesome ambivalence men feel toward those who symbolize authority and civilization. *The murder of God is an immensely potent symbol of man's primal desire to do away with his impediments to instinctual gratification.*

Very frequently Christians object to the assertion that they are taught that the Jews are the Christ-killers. They claim that they are taught that *all* men are responsible through their sins for the death of the Christ. This is the way in which the subject is dealt with in many church schools today. The attempt to share the blame is of doubtful efficacy. Though all men may have been responsible from the religious point of view, the actual deed was committed by a specific group of men. The New Testament is explicit as to who these men were. It is equally explicit with regard to the continuing involvement of their descendants in the affair. Pontius Pilate does not make the ultimate decision. He offers the Jews the opportunity to choose Jesus or Barabbas for release from the death penalty. The Jews chose Barabbas. Pilate insists that he finds no fault with Jesus. He washes his hands of the affair and permits the execution. The onus of guilt is clearly upon the Jews. In Matthew they reply to Pilate's protestations of innocence: "His blood be upon us and on our children" (Matthew 27:25). The murder of God is thus depicted as a continuing source of guilt of the Jewish posterity.

The explosive significance of the crucifixion story as the myth of the death of God is well illuminated by Ivan Karamazov's reputed remark in Dostoevski's *The Brothers Karamazov: "If God does not exist, all things are permitted."* In both Judaism and Christianity, all moral restraints are ultimately derivative of God's lordship over the created world. The wish to murder God is the terminal mythic expression of mankind's ineradicable temptation to moral anarchy. A world without God would be a world with no impediment to the gratification of desire, no matter how perverse or socially harmful. The perversity of the human heart finds its ultimate expression in the myth of the murder of God.

The death camps are one possibility in a world devoid of God. As Hannah Arendt has suggested,[7] the realm of the impossible ceases to exist in such a world; the limitations of reality become a parenthesis to be overthrown. By the same token, the desire for a world without limitation is a regressive hankering for the unrestrained gratification of the anarchic desires of childhood. There is an awesome fatality in Hitler's description of himself at the beginning of *Mein Kampf* as a *Müttersohnchen,* a little mother's boy. Though Hitler claimed that he outgrew this stage, many who knew him closely were convinced that he never did. In his hatred of his father, in his contempt for the limitation of moral as well as military reality, in his irrational intuitionism, in his utter failure to achieve an adult sexual relationship with a woman,[8] and in his final suicidal mania for himself and his country, the *Müttersohnchen* remained triumphant.

Leon Poliakov has suggested that the Nazi movement and its culminating expression, the death camp, were part of an anti-value explosion of the German people.[9] This is consistent with the idea of deicide. One wishes to murder God in order to be all that there is to be, all that one can be, and above all to do all that one wishes to do. The death camp was the place where the morally impossible finally became the commonplace and even the trivial for the Nazis; their desire was impeded only by the boredom of gratification.

The accusation that a people is deicidal implies that they are utterly beyond law. This may seem a strange accusation to make against the Jews, a people who were the creators of so vast

[7] In *The Origins of Totalitarianism* (New York: Harcourt Brace, 1951).

[8] Cf. Ernst "Putzi" Hanfstängel, *Hitler: The Missing Years* (London: Eyre and Spottiswoode, 1957).

[9] Cf his *Harvest of Hate* (Syracuse: Syracuse University Press, 1954).

a system of religious law. This seeming paradox did not escape Justin Martyr's attention. Unwittingly this basically decent philosopher helped to create the demonological interpretation of the Jews which was to result in so much bloodshed throughout the centuries. Justin maintained that only the excessive moral weakness of the Jews made it necessary for them to be placed under the discipline of the law. He interprets their outward personal and moral conformity as the fruit of a terrible inner lawlessness. In a sense, Justin was an excellent intuitive psychologist. Socially compliant behavior is achieved through an inner struggle against regressive anarchic tendencies. Unfortunately Justin turned his intuition of what is a universal conflict into evidence of a special Jewish proclivity toward evil. This contrasted, according to Justin, with those who experience the freedom of the Christ; they need none of the legal constraints of the Jews. Only the enormity of the temptations of the deicidal people make the special restrictions and inhibitions of the Law necessary.

A universal tendency toward moral anarchy was thus identified and displaced onto the Jews. During the Middle Ages, the identification of the Jew as the moral anarchist was intensified by his further identification with the Devil and the Anti-Christ. These identifications were already implicit in the crucifixion story and the rivalry between the two religious communities. The identification with the Devil is explicit in the Fourth Gospel, in which Jesus is depicted as saying to those who reject his mission:

> If God were your Father, you would love me, for I proceeded and came forth from God; I came not of my own accord, but he sent me. . . . You are of your father the devil, and your will is to do your father's desires. He was a murderer from the beginning, and has nothing to do with the truth, because there is no truth in him. . . . But because I tell the truth, you do not believe me. (John 8:42–45)

In medieval Europe, the only people who openly and successfully resisted Christianity were the Jews. The Germans tried and failed. Since the Jews were the one people resident in Europe who had seen the Christ and beheld His passion, their stubborn refusal to acknowledge Him was ascribed to the supernatural power of their satanic master. The only other group which continuously resisted Christianity were the members of the satanic witch cult. The Jews were depicted as openly worshipping the blackest of masters, whereas his non-Jewish devotees were depicted as at least having the decency to pay their homage in secrecy.[10]

The identification of the Jew with the Anti-Christ was implicit in the earliest Jewish rejection of the Christ. In medieval popular mythology, the final return and triumph of the Christ would be preceded by a battle waged between the forces of the Christ and those of the Anti-Christ. As the Christ was the son of God, born of a Jewish virgin, the Anti-Christ would be born of the union of a Jewish whore and the Devil. He would be raised in Galilee and trained by sorcerers and witches in the black arts. At the age of thirty he was to announce himself to the Jews in Jerusalem as their Messiah. His actual mission would last only three and a half years, the duration of Jesus' ministry. During this time he would unite all previous heresies, utilize the blackest of arts, and raise up a huge army to do his evil work. In some versions of the tradition, the army of the Anti-Christ is to battle against the legions of the Christ in a final armageddon in which Christ will ultimately be victorious. This was tied in with the myth of the ten lost tribes of Israel who were regarded as dwelling in prosperity somewhere in Asia in vast numbers. At the summons of the Anti-Christ, they would form a formidable host challenging the Lordship of the Christ over Christian Europe.[11] This is a medieval anticipation of the myth of "Jewish" Bolshevik hordes which the Nazis used so effectively. It was supported by the realistic dangers which stemmed from invasions and threats of invasions which Europe faced from the Huns, Turks, Mongols, and Arabs. Fear of the Anti-Christ's legions was a reflex of the folk anti-Semitism of European culture. The aggressive intentions of the anti-Semites elicited retaliatory anxieties which were embodied in the Anti-Christ myths.

It is interesting to note in passing that the identification

[10] Joshua Trachtenberg has gathered an impressive catalogue of such identifications of the Jew with the demonic in his book, *The Devil and the Jews* (New Haven: Yale University Press, 1943) .

[11] Cf. Trachtenberg, *op. cit.*

of the Devil with the Jews has survived even Hitler in the German theater. In the recording of Goethe's *Faust,* Part I, presented
by the Düsseldorf Schauspielhaus and recently released by the
Deutsche Grammophon Gesellschaft, Gustof Gründgens plays
Mephisto with distinctly Yiddish overtones. Gründgens popu-
larized this interpretation of the Devil under the Nazis and has
not seen fit to alter his Yiddish Mephisto nor apparently has
anyone strongly objected in spite of the terrible history of our
times.

The Anti-Christ was a sort of polar opposite of the
Christ. As the Devil's Messiah, he represented a demonic re-
versal of the value system normative in Christian Europe. Unfortunately the Jewish response was hardly ever relevant. Faced
with the Christ-killer accusation, Jews usually took the accusation
seriously at the *manifest* level and protested their innocence. Seldom if ever did they understand that the accusation was an attempt by the accuser to deny his own lawless temptations by
ascribing them to the Jews. The Jewish protestation of innocence
only made matters worse. One of the worst aspects of the two-
thousand-year-old Judaeo-Christian encounter has been their
mutual incapacity to understand what was vital to the other.
There was apparently no way in which Jew and Christian could
simply acknowledge the problem of overcoming inner lawlessness to be a universal one. Each side could only bolster its own
uncertain conviction of virtue by blackening the other. This
dreary procedure has yet to be terminated.

No motive other than indecent willfulness and dedica-
tion to the demonic was permitted to explain the continued Jewish rejection of Christianity. Trachtenberg points out that the
Jews were regarded as knowing the truth about the Christ but
deliberately rejecting it. They were more often regarded by the
Church as *heretics* than as *infidels.* No imagined crime was too
heinous to be ascribed to them. As they had been guilty of the
crucifixion, they were regarded as symbolically repeating the
crime by the sacrificial murder of Christian victims especially at
Passover time.

The blood libel accusation has persisted down to our own

times. It was utilized by the Nazis. In the light of what we know of the sacrificial mode of religious life, the continued utilization of the ritual murder accusation against the Jews is by no means inexplicable. Religious sacrifice had its origins partially in the ritual murder of a human victim. The purpose of the offering was to assure the continued well-being and prosperity of the community through the death of the victim. Vicarious atonement figures very largely in such practices. There seems to be something in most of us which, when we are sufficiently threatened, sees safety in the death of another. "Let him die instead of me" is an age-old cry of mankind.[12]

From a psychoanalytic point of view, the doctrine that the death of the Christ atones vicariously for the sins of mankind is an example of the *return of the repressed*. In Biblical Judaism, atonement was effectuated by the scapegoat offering on the Day of Atonement. The animal's character as a surrogate for an original human victim now seems indisputable. At some time in the past, the community or communities which had preceded Israel offered human victims to effectuate atonement and cleansing. When John the Baptist greets Jesus upon seeing him at the River Jordan, he is depicted as saying: "Behold the Lamb of God who taketh away the sins of the world" (John 1:29). John is depicted as reidentifying the intended human victim with the animal surrogate. The circle was thus completed. Once again the death of a divine-human victim brought forgiveness and security. The promise Christianity offers to its believers is that this once and for all human sacrifice has the power to save mankind from its sins. Many of the dynamic elements of ritual murder are present.

There are, however, significant differences between the ritual aspects of the crucifixion and other sacrificial deaths. In pagan ritual murder, the community accepts its own guilt for participating in the sacred violence. No outsider is blamed for the deed, which is regarded as a sad and bloody necessity. The community must choose between two unpleasant alternatives: a limited act of violence in which one dies for all, or the very real

[12] Cf. James George Frazer, *The New Golden Bough*, ed. Theodore H. Gaster (New York: Criterion Books, 1959).

danger that all will succumb as a result of the false mercy of omit-
ting the sacrifice. Faced with these alternatives, the pagan accepted
his own guilt and reluctantly committed the bloody deed.

In Christianity, the victim is no longer a pre-eminent
member of the community but the incarnate Deity. Furthermore,
the Church did not have to accept the guilt of the deed. The guilt
was ascribed to the Jews. Little attention, however, has been paid
to the fact that the death of Jesus was a once and forever act.
Insofar as the need for a scapegoat remained an urgent psychic
necessity, as it was in times of stress, the memory of the one
sacrifice was insufficient to satisfy the hunger for a victim. There
is real irony in the age-old anti-Semitic accusation that the Jew
practices ritual murder. The radical anti-Semite lives in a world
which remains endangered as long as it is uncleansed of Jewry.
For the anti-Semite, there is only one solution, the extermination
of the Jew. This is ritual murder, made infinitely less painful by
the Christ-killer accusation. The sins and the guilts which beset
his existence demand the death of the Jew. The Nazi "final
solution" represented one vast explosion of all of the repressed
forces which in paganism had been channeled into the controlled
and regulated slaughter of one victim at a time. When the anti-
Semite accuses the Jew of ritual murder, he accuses him of the
very crime which he himself intends to commit. What he fails
to comprehend is the inherent gratuity of the whole process. The
death of the victim never solves real problems. The only thing
the death of six million Jews may have taught some Germans
was that they had only themselves to blame for their own predicament. There were no longer any Jews available upon whom
to hang the onus of defeat.

As I have suggested, though Nazism has been attacked
as pagan, the movement was never really pagan. Such accusations
do an injustice to paganism. Nazism was an inverted and demonic
transformation of Jewish and Christian values, combined with a
Romantic hankering after a paganism it never understood. It
needed the Judaeo-Christian *yes* to assert the Nazi *no*. The
Greeks were pagan. For them the decisive misdeed was *hubris,*
the taking upon oneself of more than one's allotted portion in
the nature of things. *Hubris,* man's rebellion against his limits,

was always a limited self-aggrandizement. It was exhibited in the folly of Oedipus, seeking to avoid a fate which came closer with every step he took to escape it; it was also manifest in the desire of Clytemnestra, whose adulterous passion irretrievably furthered the fated destruction of the house of Atreus. *Hubris* never signified complete and total lawlessness, such as is implied in the notion of *deicide*. It was followed, as night follows day, by inevitable *nemesis,* which righted the wrong and restored nature's disturbed equilibrium. Good and evil were rooted in the very nature of the cosmos itself. Evil was in a sense unnatural; inevitably the fates would overtake its perpetrators. All things were measured out, and even the gods could not trespass their assigned limits.[13]

Nazism is the product of a negative reaction to the Judaeo-Christian world. As much as the nineteenth- and twentieth-century Teutonists wanted to rid themselves of Christianity, they were far more influenced by it than they imagined. In the end, the Nazis were able to *negate* Christianity and its values while using the Christian myth of Jewish villainy to their own purposes. They were never able to restore a genuine paganism. Perhaps Goethe foresaw the ironies of a German attempt to restore paganism when in *Faust,* Part II, he made the union of Faust, the German, and the Greek Helen of Troy result in the birth of Euphorion. Euphorion very quickly evaporates into nothingness. Nazism is Judaeo-Christian heresy, not paganism. It presupposes, though it overturns, both its *mythos* and its *ethos.*

The difference between the Judaeo-Christian conception of *sin* and the Greek conception of *hubris* is of decisive importance. In the Judaeo-Christian universe, good and evil are not rooted in the nature of things. The natural and the moral worlds are regarded as entirely dependent upon the omnipotent will of the Creator. He who created the natural world also created good and evil. *Sin,* in both Judaism and Christianity, is rebellion against the will of the Creator. Righteousness is conformity with that will. Furthermore, as Kierkegaard has suggested in *Fear and Trembling,* the particularities of God's will

[13] Cf. Martin P. Nilsson, *Greek Piety* (London: Oxford University Press, 1948).

are not subject to man's critical scrutiny, no matter how opaque
or puzzling they may seem. We are to conform because of the
ultimate authority of the Source, regardless of whether we understand why we comply.

*Only in the Judaeo-Christian conception of a divinely
created cosmos does deicide make sense as an anti-value explosion.* It did not make sense in paganism, for the pagan believed
that even the gods were governed by law and necessity. There
could be no comparable deicidal myths in paganism, because
riddance of the gods could not effectuate a riddance from the
norms to which even the pagan gods were said to be subject.
There are in paganism myths of the death of the gods. There
are dying gods aplenty, but no pagan could ever say as Ivan
Karamazov is reported to have said: "If God does not exist, all
things are permitted."[14]

Only in Biblical religion was the motive for deicide
meaningful, for only in Biblical religion were all norms derivative of a God who transcended them. *Murdering God makes sense
only when all values derive from Him.* In such a system the deicidal act is an assertion of the will to total moral and religious
license. This is the real meaning of the Christ-killer accusation
which has been repeated *ad nauseam* for almost two thousand
years. Though there were other social and economic conditions which were necessary before the theological antecedents
of anti-Semitism could be turned into the death camps of our
times, only the terrible accusation, known and taught to every
Christian in earliest childhood, that the Jews are the killers of
the Christ can account for the depth and persistence of this
supreme hatred.

In a sense, the death camps were the terminal expression
of Christian anti-Semitism. Furthermore, enough "I like Eich"
comments have been passed or inscribed on toilet walls since
the Eichmann trial to indicate that the enterprise still strikes
dark admiration in a great many people. Without Christianity,

---

[14] This analysis has some affinities with Albert Camus's comments on Christianity in his essay "Helen's Exile" in *The Myth of Sisyphus,* tr. Justin O'Brien (New York: Vintage Books, 1955), pp. 134 ff.
I am deeply indebted to Camus for many of my insights.

the Jews could never have become the central victims. Nevertheless, it would be a vast oversimplification to suggest that Christianity was responsible for the camps. Christianity provided an indispensable ingredient, the demonological interpretation of the Jews, but only anti-Christian heretics could use this material as did the Nazis. Psychologically speaking, one of the purposes of the deicide accusation against the Jew was to enable Christians to lead a decent life. The myth of Jewish guilt was an important element in the Christian moral universe. Unconsciously intuiting mankind's most demonic temptation, the murder of God and subsequent moral anarchy, the Christian often sought to ward off the temptation by projecting it on his stereotype of the Jew. This projection was realistically supported by the fact that the Jews were heir to similar moral struggles within their own natures. There was a kernel of truth to the accusation that the Jews wanted to kill God or had done so symbolically, insofar as all men are possessed of the same yearning for infantile omnipotence. Nevertheless, the crucifixion tradition sought to avoid murder and violence. It represented a very human attempt to come to terms with some terribly dark inner forces. Normally the system of Christian religious restraints worked. Though the average Christian seldom looked upon the Jew with the kindliest of vision, he was under no compulsion to extirpate the deicide in himself by the actual murder of the Jew.

The darker aspects of the myth came to the fore, united with the Teuton's resentment of Jewish Christianity, when the delicate balance of civilization was upset in Germany by the real or fantasied catastrophes which followed upon defeat in World War I. The shock of national defeat and the inability of the German people realistically to accept the fact that they had brought their predicament upon themselves were important ingredients in the witches' brew from which the death camps were ultimately spawned. Reality, symbolized by the defeated German political community and its external relations, became increasingly unacceptable. During the inflation of 1923, more than the currency was spurious. Increasingly the German method of dealing with this unacceptable reality was marked by regressive modes of action.

The very selection of Adolf Hitler by the German people and the demonic fascination he exerted upon them cannot be divorced from the radical rejection of normality and its restraints which took place under Nazism. Hitler was the man from nowhere, possessed of an all-consuming infantile fury, with nothing to lose. He offered the Germans the simplest and most infantile method of dealing with their real and imaginary enemies—extermination. His multiform abnormalities increased his fascination in a culture which was in despair over the political and social complexities of modern civilization. The relations between a leader and his community are in any event emotionally overdetermined, but never so completely as in the mysterious affair between Hitler and the Germans. He elicited from them something demonic, atavistic, and insane. The man, the people, and the hour were made for one another.

In recent times, much thought has been given to the terrible strains placed upon the average man by technopolis, the contemporary urban mixing of values, traditions, religions, moral standards, and ethnic inheritances in a single community.[15] Only in the more or less rural and isolated areas of Europe and America have the older, more homogeneous ethnic communities been able to maintain themselves. Linz, the community in which both Hitler and Eichmann grew up, was a relatively homogeneous community. By contrast, few communities have ever been as cosmopolitan as the pre-World War I Vienna which nourished Freud, the theoretical master of the irrational, and Hitler, the practical master of the irrational. There is probably in most of us some yearning for the simplicities and predictabilities of the older monolithic folk-culture which the contemporary culture of the cities has largely pre-empted.[16] In America this yearning is sometimes visible in a nostalgia for the simplicities of the rural Protestant culture of the nineteenth century. There is something disturbingly alienating, even for members of the majority ethnic group, in technopolis. Human relationships become anonymous; values are challenged rather

[15] Harvey Cox's *The Secular City* (New York: Macmillan Co., 1965), of course, comes to mind.

[16] Cf. Cox, *op. cit.*

than confirmed; men become strangers in the world their families created; above all, the dominance of the majority group is subtly challenged. One of the most disturbing aspects of super-culture is that the majority ethnic group, though remaining numerically superior, often becomes a cultural[17] minority in the most important cities of the nation it has created. The bitter complaints by the Nazis concerning the importance of Jews in the cultural life of Berlin and Vienna in the twenties reflected this phenomenon. Whether the modern experiment in super-culture will really work remains a question for the future. In times of radical stress, people tend to lose their capacity for cultural ambiguity. They seek to recapture lost simplicities. This is a phenomenon not limited to the German scene. In contemporary America, the growth of an irrationalist right-wing movement is an example of the same tendency. In super-culture, ties between group members are rational, nonemotional, and contractual. In ethnic or folk-culture, ties are emotionally determined. Rational and contractual ties are necessarily alienating. They involve primarily the legal status of the person. Folk ties, because of their emotional content, give group members a sense of mutual involvement. Each social arrangement has its advantages and disadvantages. However, lest the involvements of folk-culture be overestimated, the importance in super-culture of privacy, mobility, and anonymity for personal growth must not be forgotten.[18]

Whatever may have been the emotional advantages of folk-culture, the inventiveness of man has put an end to its viability. The sheer rapidity of transport and communications has ended the still remembered simplicities of the older cultures. Nevertheless, groups are not unlike their component individuals. They tend to regress in times of stress to more primitive and even infantile modes of coping with reality. At such times super-culture, with its rationality and coldly alienating indifference, tends to be forsaken. There are attempts, largely forced and artificial, to recreate the emotional ties and simpler morality of the older folk-

[17] I mean much the same thing when I use the term *super-culture* as Cox does when he uses the term *technopolis*.
[18] Cf. Cox, *op cit.*

community. There is a tendency to utilize elements in the group's cultural inheritance which are of great antiquity. These are seldom the most rational or the most enlightened aspects of that inheritance.

The shock of defeat in World War I led Germany to attempt to reorganize society along the lines of a homogeneous *Volk*-culture.[19] Insofar as super-culture was regarded by the Germans as the product of European liberalism and the French Revolution, there were, as we have seen, important German advocates of a return to *Volk*-culture throughout the nineteenth century. The shock of national defeat added immensely to their significance.

Sigmund Freud offered an awesomely prophetic analysis of the way in which groups are formed and individuals surrender their judgment and rationality to an all-powerful leader.[20] Freud pointed out that men permit themselves cruelties and immoralities as members of cohesive groups which they do not normally allow themselves as individuals. He maintained that *intensification of affect* and *diminution of intellectual functioning* are traits which radically distinguish the behavior of groups from that of normal individuals. In group behavior, there is a regression to the primitive, illogical, magical thinking and the immediate satisfaction of drives which characterizes the world of the infant. This remains an archaic inheritance of the unconscious throughout life. When the going gets rough, the sleeping infantile monster awakens to its career of destruction and cruelty.

Freud maintained that *identification with and absolute submission to the will of the leader (Führer)* is a third decisive aspect of group behavior. Writing shortly before Hitler was to compose the murky pages of *Mein Kampf* in Landsberg Prison, Freud suggested that unquestioning loyalty to the leader and *the identification of moral standards with his will* were indispensable features of group behavior. He maintained that the

[19] The conflict between super-culture and folk-culture was reflected in the conflict between the cosmopolitan and the introverted nationalist in Germany. Cf. Erik H. Erikson, *op. cit.,* 349 ff.

[20] In *Group Psychology and the Analysis of the Ego* (London: Hogarth Press, 1921).

group members identify the leader with their own *ego-ideal*. Since the *ego-ideal* is normally regarded as that mental faculty to which is ascribed self-observation, moral conscience, and censorship, the result is the complete suspension of the individual's normal moral judgment and an identification with the morals of the leader.

After the Nazis had established themselves in power, all German officials were compelled to take an oath of allegiance to the person of Adolf Hitler rather than to the constitution. Every German was bound by the closest of psychological ties to the Führer. The ties were reinforced every time two Germans greeted each other with *"Heil Hitler!"* One could not use the telephone without the Führer's presence being felt in the simple but demonically effective greeting. Elsewhere in Freudian literature, the *ego-ideal* is more or less identified with the *superego*, the faculty of criticism and moral judgment which makes for moral compliance in the individual. It derives from the introjection of parental authority in the psyche of the individual. For Freud, God is the projected *superego* of the community. By becoming the *superego* of a very significant part of the German people, Hitler acquired the God-like ability to determine right and wrong simply on the basis of his anarchic, archaic, and totally destructive will. The Germans were bound to Hitler by primal libidinous ties as members of a psychically, if not racially, homogeneous community. When Hitler took upon himself ultimate responsibility for the actions of those bound to him by solemn personal oath, he completed the transformation of the German moral system. Right and wrong were no longer defined by obedience to or rebellion against the will of God; right and wrong were defined solely in terms of obedience to or rebellion against the will of the Führer. Even the most casual remark of Hitler at the table could and did become the basis of an all powerful *Führer-Befehl*, an order of the Leader.

Non-Germans have frequently been puzzled by the disclaimer of responsibility put forth by German participants in some of the worst aspects of the Nazi crimes. Invariably the response has been, "I acted under orders. I did my duty." Eichmann's defense was hardly atypical. Few of those involved in major crimes had the courage to declare: "I was a Nazi. I still am. I'd do it all over again if I could." The recent film *Mein Kampf*, which depicted Hitler's career, ended very strikingly. After rehearsing the enormity of the Nazi crimes, it showed scenes of Hitler's major subordinates all disclaiming responsibility. The last image is a brief glimpse of Hitler as the narrator asks the question: "Did he do it all himself?"

More than one student of the war has wondered at the seemingly charmed life Hitler led in spite of the fact that the German General Staff[21] was largely aware that he was bringing Germany to ruin. Notwithstanding the obvious destructiveness and folly of Hitler's military leadership, especially after the failure of the 1944 *Putsch*, the generals were utterly incapable of bringing about his downfall. They later explained that they could not bring themselves to violate the oath of allegiance they had pledged to him. Honor had reduced itself to absolute fealty to the most dishonorable leader history has ever known. While I would not want to absolve anyone who played a significant part in the tragedy of his responsibility, I would like to suggest that fidelity to this oath was more than an insincere dodge. Although the Germans were willing to make and break promises at will in their dealings with others, they could not break their oath to Hitler, the leader of their *Volk*-community, without feeling that their entire moral universe, primitive and atavistic as it was, would fall apart. He had become their conscience and their source of moral judgment. Super-culture had been overcome. The burdensome pain of the inevitable loneliness and alienation of super-culture was at an end.

Alienation and individual moral responsibility are of a piece. If super-culture creates alienation, it also fosters the development of individuality and responsibility. A responsible adult does not make moral decisions solely on the basis of the values and expectations of his peers. There is a self-determining quality to his actions which is normally only possible in a person who has the capacity to set himself at a distance from his en-

---

[21] The O.K.H., the *Oberkommando des Heeres*, not the O.K.W., the *Oberkommando der Wehrmacht*, which was little more than a rubber stamp for Hitler's whims.

vironment. An integrated adult accepts a real measure of alienation as the price of autonomy. An atavist finds alienation intol-
erable. He is more than relieved to surrender his individuality
to the mystique of a primitive folk-community and the will of
its leader. Nowhere was this more apparent than in the monster
rallies the Nazis sponsored at Nuremberg, where hundreds of
thousands of individual identities blended into one another, and
one guiding, anarchic will became the will of all.

Once the oath to Hitler had been given and Hitler accepted complete moral responsibility for the actions of those
loyal to him, the German people had arrived at the point of no
return. No absolute monarch ever bound his people more completely or more primitively than did Adolf Hitler. The barbar-
ians had triumphed over the slender texture of civilization as an
external enemy threatening not at the gates, but within the
heart of the city itself. Henceforth there was only one real crime:
disobedience to the will of the Führer. It is not surprising that
the system could not outlive its leader. His will had become the
collective conscience of the German people in very much the
same way that the will of the Lord had been the standard of right
and wrong for the Jew and the Christian. While Judaeo-Christian
submission had normally been life-enhancing, the new German
submission became an instrument of mass-murder and national
self-destructiveness.

In Germany, after 1918, a form of mass psychosis ultimately destroyed the remnants of reason in political life. The
incapacity of the Germans realistically to accept defeat and their
subsequent regression under Hitler to a primitive *Volk*-commu-
nity were accompanied by the need to find a magic enemy of
omnipotent proportions upon whom the terrible happenings
could be blamed. Once the decision to form such a community
achieved a consensus, there was no longer a viable place for the
Jews in German life. If nothing else, their international connec-
tions, their involuntary cosmopolitanism, and the never-to-be-
forgotten fact that Jewish emancipation had first been brought to
Germany by Napoleon's foreign armies, all made Jewish participation in an increasingly introverted and embittered Germany
thoroughly untenable. It ought not to be forgotten that the

restoration of civic rights to the pitiful Jewish remnant after
World War II was also the work of foreign invaders in the first
instance.

The untenability of the Jewish situation in Germany was
already implicit in the sociological distinction Ferdinand Tonnies
made between *Gemeinschaft* and *Gesellschaft* (1887).[22]
Tonnies regarded *Gemeinschaft* as an organic group which shared
a genuine community of possession, morals, belief, and association; *Gesellschaft* was regarded as the rational and contractual
association of isolated, self-seeking individuals bound by no
such organic ties. *Gesellschaft* is typical of modern Western society. Even as important a Jewish thinker as Martin Buber compared *Gesellschaft* most unfavorably to *Gemeinschaft*.[23] By hankering after a *Gemeinschaft* of the German people, German high
scholarship contributed its sophistication, albeit not always with
malicious intent, to a movement which was ultimately to be utilized effectively by the Nazis, who were the only Germans to attempt to create such a community. In it, there could be absolutely
no place for Jews. Even without the war, had German life been
reconstructed on the basis of a *Gemeinschaft*, German Jews would
have had only the alternatives of complete assimilation or emigration. Hitler won his war against the Jews and, by doing so, eliminated a major obstacle to the formation of an organic German
community. The division of Germany and the expulsion of the
Germans from their homes in eastern Europe have proven that the
Jews were by no means the only, or even the most important, impediments to such a community. Nevertheless, today's German
intellectuals can drink their tea along Berlin's Kürfurstendamm,
imbibe their Löwenbrau in Munich's Schwabing, or gulp more
Kafe mit Schlag than is good for them in Vienna almost completely undisturbed by the intrusion of a Jewish mannerism or a
Jewish face. Hitler did not fail the Germans on the Jewish
question.

Perhaps it is no accident that the same Vienna which was
so influential in the careers of Hitler and Freud also nurtured

[22] Cf. Ferdinand Tonnies, *Community and Society* (New York:
Harper Torchbooks, 1965).

[23] Cf. Maurice Friedman, *Martin Buber: The Life of Dialogue*
(Chicago: University of Chicago Press, 1955).

Theodore Herzl, the father of modern Zionism. His vision of a reconstituted Israel was ultimately the result of a radical pessimism concerning the place of the Jew in a modern state.

In the end, more was required of Germany's Jews than expulsion or assimilation. An omnipotent enemy was needed to provide the raw material for what was to be history's greatest ritual murder. German popular culture had long ago designated the villain-enemy-victim. The medieval myths of the Jew as the Christ-killer, from which were derived the secondary myths of the Jew as Anti-Christ, Devil's spawn, Satan, sorcerer, magician, cannibal, and murderer, pointed to the existence of a demonic power equal to the task of sapping Germany's strength, of secretly causing her defeat, and of gloating in the triumph of the victors. The age-old Passion plays, such as the one still performed at Oberammergau, the liturgy of Holy Week, the religious instruction of little children, the habit of providing Mephistopheles with a Yiddish accent in the oft-repeated performances of Goethe's *Faust,* and even the turning of Hansel and Gretel's witch into a Jewish crone all reinforced an ancient hatred in a time of modern anxiety and bitterness. Just as the "demonic" Jews of the Middle Ages had supposedly brought about the Black Death by their midnight arts and had allegedly sacrificed innocent Christian children in order to drink their blood at Passover, so they were now regarded as a prime cause of the Fatherland's defeat. Not the open power of the known enemy but the hidden power of the satanic magic enemy had brought about the "stab in the back."

Wagnerian opera was all too frequently rehearsal for destruction. Peter Viereck has pointed to the influence of Wagnerian opera on the development of neo-Teutonic ideology.[24] In the opera house, it was possible to resurrect the old Teutonic gods and give to their *mythos* a ritual setting without the necessity of a frontal attack against Christianity. As the most sophisticated of the Teutonists know, a frontal attack on Christianity would never succeed. They also knew that, with proper encouragement, any people could be Christian on Sunday and something entirely different at other times. Viereck contends, with consider-

[24] Peter Viereck, *Meta-Politics—The Roots of the Nazi Mind* (New York: Capricorn Books, 1961), pp. 126 ff.

able justice, that the Germans saw themselves largely in Wagnerian terms. They regarded themselves as a nation of Siegfrieds, especially after the defeat in the First War. Just as Siegfried had his Hagen, the Germans had their Jews. As blond Siegfried was basely betrayed by Hagen, the Germans increasingly regarded the Jews as Hagen-like betrayers. The dramatics of Wagnerian opera became real as the Nazi leaders enacted their own *Götterdämmerung* with the collapse of the Third Reich. Nevertheless, the figure of Hagen as the betrayer is quite secondary and derivative. The Germans may have seen themselves as Siegfrieds, but they saw the Jews as Judases rather than Hagens. Surprisingly Viereck never mentions the Judas myth in which the betrayer is firmly and explicitly identified with the Jews. It was the intersection of the Judas and Hagen myths which finally fed the flames of German paranoia beyond the quenching point.

The paranoid myth of the Jew as the magic betrayer sufficiently potent to destroy Germany from within, as he had once destroyed the Christ, was vastly reinforced by the *kiss of Judas* tale. In the Gospels, Judas betrays the Christ for thirty pieces of silver. When the enemies of the Christ come to seize him, Judas identifies the divine-human victim *by a loving kiss.* The moral of the story is obvious: one can never trust a Jew. Even the most seemingly outgoing offer of friendship and affection by a Jew can never conceal the betrayer's curse. Furthermore, these stories are not told when the hearers are at an age at which they are capable of evaluating their applicability to flesh-and-blood Jews. They are first heard as bedtime stories for little children who have yet to separate the worlds of fact and fantasy. In later life, they are most operative in periods of stress when the individual is most likely to regress from his adult faculties of rationality and self-criticism to the infantile level at which he first experienced these tales. In the German regression from super-culture to *Volk*-community, we have a social analogue of this process.

Even without Hitler, the Judas story is destined to continue to play a vital role in unconsciously poisoning Jewish-Christian relations. The Judas tale is part and parcel of the Passion drama, which is retold and relived by every practicing Christian during Holy Week. From the cradle to the grave, few stereotypes are as consistently reinforced under the most emotionally potent environments as these. The high point of the Christian religious calendar rehearses, amidst utterly magnificent music, frequently aesthetically overpowering architecture and ceremonial grandeur, the terrible tale of the Jewish betrayal and the Jewish murder of the Jewish God!

The Judas story created the psychological ground which made it possible for Germans under stress to believe that the Judas-Jews had betrayed their country and caused her defeat in World War I. It was futile for Jewish defense and veterans' groups to point to Jewish sacrifices on behalf of the Fatherland during the war. After all, Judas had betrayed his Lord with a kiss. The appearance of loyalty in a Jew could not be credited, even when that appearance was purchased through death on the battlefield.

By accusing the Jews of demonic powers, fiendish temptations, and utter lack of trustworthiness, the Nazis were able to use the most demonic of instrumentalities against them. *The demonic was thus made licit for the Nazis.* Nazi literature continually harped upon the alleged immorality of the Jews and the danger they presented to civilization, though no one ever endangered civilization so much as the Nazis. *Undoubtedly we seek to destroy in others what we fear in ourselves.* Those who accused the Jews of demonic intent and power created the most demonic environment ever known to man, the death camp, an environment in which God was dead and all things permissible to the masters. Some who called the Jews Christ-killers did so out of envy.

Norman Cohn has stressed the role of the Jews as the castrating father in the paranoid fantasies of the anti-Semite. There is merit to Cohen's hypothesis. It does not necessarily contradict the point of view expressed here. I would agree with Cohn that the anti-Semite is afflicted with the paranoid delusion that the Jew can inflict great harm upon him. The irrational fear of the omnipotent, demonic, magic-betrayer, which I stress largely because of the history of Germany after 1918, can co-exist in a delusional system with the irrational fear of the castrating father, which Cohn stresses. Nevertheless, I do not believe that

Cohn takes either the Judas-tradition or the deicide accusation seriously enough. In my opinion the age-old Christian accusation that the Jews have murdered God is far more decisive than the fear that the Jew is the castrating father. In the final analysis the anti-Semite sees the Jew as the demonic, all-powerful sibling.[25]

The Nazis referred to Auschwitz as the *anus mundi*. Such associations are hardly ever gratuitous. Norman O. Brown has pointed to the significance of the anal characteristics of the Devil in his highly insightful book *Life Against Death: The Psychoanalytic Interpretation of History*.[26] The sulphurous fumes associated with the Devil were in reality a fecal stench. His color, like that of the SS uniforms, was black. The Black Mass included scatological rites in which offal of the worst sort, including feces and menstrual blood, were kneaded on the buttocks of the Queen of the Sabbath as a sacred host. Brown also points to Hieronymus Bosch's painting in which Satan is enthroned on a privy from which souls pass out of his anus into the black pit of Hell. Luther's encounters with the Devil are shown by Brown to have been overdetermined by anal and fecal considerations. Brown is very clear concerning the importance of the Devil as the decisive opponent of the German reformer. He omits, however, the portentous fact that in German folk-culture the Devil is either a Jew or the Lord of the Jews, who are supposed to exude a fecal odor.[27] The *anus mundi* was the habitat of the Devil. If ever men successfully created such a habitat on earth, it was at Auschwitz.

Only at the *anus mundi* could the Jew as deicide, betrayer, and incarnate Devil be turned into the feces of the world. Rudolph Hoess, the Nazi commandant at Auschwitz, was one of the many Nazis to note and complain of the hideous fecal stench of the camp.[28] The camp literally smelled of human decay. The

[25] Cf. Norman Cohn, "The Myth of the Jewish World Conspiracy," *Commentary*, June 1966. For a balanced evaluation of the attempt to understand anti-Semitism primarily in terms of castration anxiety, cf. Erik H. Erikson, *op. cit.*, p. 354.

[26] Middletown, Conn.: Wesleyan University Press, 1959.

[27] Trachtenberg, *op. cit.*

[28] Cf. Rudolph Hoess, *Commandant of Auschwitz: The Autobiography of Rudolph Hoess*, tr. Constantine Fitzgibbon (Cleveland: World Publishing Co., 1959).

SS wallowed in human stench to destroy what they regarded as the ultimate in human evil. As had so frequently occurred before, those who saw themselves as overwhelming a radical evil felt compelled to fight evil with evil. The Devil could be fought only with the Devil's weapons.

Adolph Leschnitzer has written extensively on the role of witchcraft in determining the ultimate German attitude toward the Jews. In the treatment of the witch, no mercy was to be shown because of her demonic powers and those of her satanic master. The parallels between the ascription of the ills of German society to the witches in the sixteenth and seventeenth centuries and the analogous imputations against the Jews in our own times are instructive. According to Leschnitzer, over one million unfortunates, most of them women, were killed as witches between 1500 and 1700. The vast majority of the executions took place in the Germanic lands. The witches were regarded as an anti-Christian force within the community. This was an attribute they shared with the Jews. Like the Jews in the death camp, their bodies were ultimately disposed of by burning.[29]

Fire consumed the bodies of both the Jews and the witches, but the Jews were first executed by an insecticide, Cyclon B. In both Eichmann's and Hoess's testimony, the use of Cyclon B as the exterminating gas was ascribed to the desire to find an efficient exterminant which would not have the debilitating effect on the personalities of the guards that outright shooting of the victims had had. Cyclon B was chosen because it could kill large numbers quickly and efficiently. It was a variant of Cyclon A, an *insecticide*. Cyclon was an abbreviation of the gas's most important ingredients, cyanide, chloride, and nitrogen. Perhaps it was only an accident that in *Mein Kampf* Hitler had already said that things would have been different in World War I if some thousands of those who were to "betray" Germany had been rounded up and gassed. In our world, where the actual has far outdistanced the fantastic in its gruesomeness, it is far more likely that the "final solution" was really decided upon by Hitler at Landsberg Prison in 1923, if not earlier, rather than at Wansee in 1941.

In Nazi propaganda the Jews are identified with lice, ver-

[29] Adolph Leschnitzer, *The Magic Background of Anti-Semitism* (New York: International Universities Press, 1956).

min, and insects, the very organisms for which an insecticide like Cyclon B was most appropriate. These were also the organisms most intimately associated with the Devil in medieval demonology. These insects and detestable animals were also thought to be the brood of fecal dirt and to find their nourishment and habitat by wallowing in the same fecal dirt from which they were spawned.

The basic project of the death camps was to turn the Jews into feces, the Devil's food, gold, and weapon. In his confessions, Hoess insists that those who died did so with a minimum of pain and that only under very special circumstances was death accompanied by involuntary defecation. His testimony has been contradicted by a more reliable witness, Dr. Miklos Nyiszli, the Jewish assistant to Auschwitz's infamous Dr. Joseph Mengele. His description of the way the bodies were found after the gas chambers were opened is instructive:

> "The bodies were not lying here and there throughout the room, but piled in a mass to the ceiling. The reason for this was that the gas first inundated the lower layers of air and rose but slowly towards the ceiling. This forced the victims to trample one another in a frantic effort to escape the gas. . . .
>
> The Sonderkommando squad (Jewish prisoners assigned to this task), outfitted with large rubber boots, lined up around the hill of bodies and flooded it with powerful jets of water. *This was necessary as the final act of those who die by drowning or by gas is an involuntary defecation.*"[30] (Italics mine.)

No matter how efficient the crematoria were, there were always mounds of corpses waiting for the final riddance. The pervasive smell of decay was always there. To this must be added the fact that the overwhelming majority of those who died in the camps before being gassed did so of diarrhea and dysentery. Only in the camps was Dostoevski's vision of a world without God in which all would be permitted nearly realized. This was really hell on earth.

The death camps have demonstrated that mankind's

[30] Miklos Nyiszli, *Auschwitz: A Doctor's Eyewitness Account* (New York: Frederick Fell, 1960).

perverted fantasies are more deeply rooted in aggression than in sexuality. In the relations between the Germans and their victims, there was an almost total withdrawal of affect. They regarded their captives more as inanimate objects than as human beings. Only on the rarest occasions did sexual feelings intrude. These were institutionalized through military brothels. In the camps the Jews were treated as dead long before the fatal moment arrived. That which the Christian myth of the Jew as Judas, Christ-killer, and deicide asserted to be the Jews' ultimate aim—the total withdrawal of all impediment to anarchic desire—was actually brought about by their German murderers. They were able to rid themselves of the last restraints against violence of their Jewish God and to avenge His death at the very same time.

The aim of creating a world in which God is dead (or, more precisely, in which the Judaeo-Christian God is *negated*) was at the heart of the Nazi program. That such a world would be dominated by a real devil like Hitler rather than a fantasied Devil followed quite necessarily. Two years ago when I visited Marienfelde, the refugee center in West Berlin, I could not avoid contrasting the fate of Germans in defeat with what would have been the fate of Germany's Eastern enemies had the Nazis won. The plight of the East German refugees was unenviable, but at least they had their health and, by and large, their families were intact. Few left Marienfelde without the assurance of a decently paying job somewhere in prosperous Western Germany. Had the Nazis won, their death machines would have been self-perpetuating. The demise of the last Jew would have been followed by the acceleration of an enlarged extermination campaign against the Russians, Poles, and other Slavs. Russia's harsh treatment of East Germany is a paradise of magnanimity compared with the German occupation of Russia or Germany's postwar plans for the Russians. There is no more reason to doubt Hitler's promise to find greater *Lebensraum* by exterminating Slavs than his promise to exterminate the Jews. In the long run, a Nazi world would have consisted of Nazified Germans and their Nazified clients. Even the German people would have offered their share of victims for the destructive projects of their Nazi masters.

The anal character of the camps was not a phenomenon

isolated from the larger German community or from important aspects of Western civilization outside of Germany. The creation of the camps was a regressive search for a paradise lost, for a time, remembered from infancy, when little or no restraint impeded human impulse. All of us are heir to such longings. They powerfully affect our psychic structures. We do not normally succumb because we are not prepared to jeopardize the gratifications of adult life for the sake of infantile yearnings. When the strains of the adult world are too severe or its disappointments too bitter, the impediments to infantile gratification become less intense. When infantile regression is validated by peer-group consent, as it was among the Nazis, there is little limit to what the group will permit itself.

The fantasy of a world without restraints, the world in which God is dead, can be imagined at many levels. It can be seen as a world without impediment to sexual or aggressive activity. Undoubtedly these freedoms were components of the world the Nazis sought to create—one might better say, recapture—for themselves. However, sexual and aggressive permissiveness are by no means the only infantile freedoms we secretly yearn for. In the Witches' Sabbath scene of *Faust,* in which Goethe paints a picture of the meaning of utter abandon, there is another freedom, related to aggression, the freedom to soil, evacuate, and pass wind at will.

Anal freedom and its relationship to the Devil and the Jews may not seem very important at first glance. Nevertheless, toilet training is one of the earliest and most trying aspects of the socialization process in the child. Only when the child achieves a certain retentive ability can he be permitted his first tentative ventures into the wider social community. Any attempt to overcome the restraints of the social order must carry with it the dimly remembered vision of the time in infancy when the child was closest to mother and soiling was permitted without limit or restraint. It is unlikely that Adolf Hitler, the *Müttersohnchen,* ever forgot this time.

Goethe was too great a literary prophet to have distorted the truth about limitless freedom. When he depicted the seductions with which Mephistopheles sought to tempt the German

Faust, the vision of excremental freedom was an important component. Satan's promise of freedom carries with it the freedom to soil at will.

In the death camps, the dimly remembered anarchic freedom of the child was combined with the terror of adult power, technical intelligence, and efficiency. In the adult world, the problematics of human relations involve compromise and the adjudication of interest. Doing away with the other person is the most primitive mode of social encounter. It hearkens back to earliest infancy when the child relates to the world primarily by means of the mouth, and eating and sleeping are its primal modes of activity.[31]

There is a psychologically cannibalistic element in regarding eliminating the other as the only possible mode of dealing with him. This was the characteristic mode of behavior of the Nazis in dealing with their opponents in the East both in and out of the camps. It finally became their characteristic mode of dealing with themselves. When it became impossible to envisage total victory, the real Nazis could envisage only total destruction as the other alternative. Some, like Goebbels, actually gloried in the thought of the total destruction of their country and welcomed the Allied bombers as bringing a necessary catharsis which would ruin the old and create the eventual conditions of a purified, truly Nazi Germany.[32] At no point did it occur to the most strongly convinced Nazis that there might be a way in which their country, if not their inner circle, could live in a world which was in any way resistant to their claims. This was the most archaic incorporative mode of dealing with limit and frustration—one seeks to do away with that which impedes. Of course, by the time the war had gone on many months, the Nazis had passed the point of no return in criminality and there was for them no alternative but to fight to the bitter end or escape to a sympathetic country like Argentina. In the end, when the Germans refused to follow Hitler's suicidal scorched-earth policy, he

[31] Cf. Bertram Lewin, *The Psychoanalysis of Elation* (New York: W. W. Norton, 1950).

[32] Cf. H. R. Trevor-Roper, *The Last Days of Adolf Hitler* (London: Macmillan, 1950).

bitterly complained that the German people, who had sacrificed so much in men, treasure, and honor to follow him, were unworthy of him.

In *Life Against Death* Norman Brown writes about the obsession of German culture, at least since the time of Luther, with the problems of anality. This obsession came to a head in the camps. As we have noted, the Nazis referred to the camps as the *anus mundi* and they were entirely willing to permit corpses to deteriorate in large numbers unburied. The smell of carrion is terrible, but there is little or nothing to distinguish it from a strong smell of feces. While the Nazis could not without incontinence give free rein to their own anal obsessions, they could and did turn the Jews, whom their folk-culture regarded as the satanic murderers of the dead God, into feces.

Sadism and anality are related. Since great pleasure is derived from excremental action, a pleasure preserved in off-color jokes, attempts to curb free evacuation, such as toilet training, may be bitterly resented by the child. If such toilet training is remembered to have been harsh, when the child becomes a parent, he may deal with his own children with a similar harshness, moved by his own unconscious resentment at having been curbed and intuiting how deeply rebellious the untrained child really is. The Germans have always been exceptionally proud of their orderliness and cleanliness in the home as well as in the wider community. They seem to have lacked the understanding that the most rigidly disciplined of men are often the most inwardly rebellious and resentful. Such men often make excellent disciplinarians with others, because they want to make sure that none escapes the bitter training which has been inflicted on them. Undoubtedly this discipline, with all its self-perpetuating harshness, begins with toilet training. By opposing toilet training, the child has ample opportunity to express his hostility to the restraining and law-giving adult world.

Judaism as a religion of law represented much that such outwardly disciplined, inwardly rebellious men resented most deeply. This resentment was enhanced by the Church's claim to have liberated men from the God of the Old Testament and His Law. One of the greatest ironies of Jewish-gentile relations has been the enormous resentment the Jewish stress on behavioral discipline has elicited among non-Jews. According to Erik H. Erickson, Hitler is reputed to have said that conscience is a blemish like circumcision and that both are Jewish blemishes.[33]

In his book *The Psychoanalytic Theory of Neurosis,*[34] Otto Fenichel discusses the child's ambivalent attitude toward his own waste products. They are both beloved object (i.e. feces as gift) and hated object, the dirty leavings which are sadistically "pinched off" one's own body. Fenichel comments that in later life the sadistic personality will frequently treat others as he has treated his own feces. Furthermore, the feces are the first part of one's own body to become dead, foreign, dirty, and alien. Elimination is the first process in which something human is turned into a dead object. As adults, the quantifying rationality of modern society affords men many opportunities to treat others as dead objects rather than live persons. The tendency to treat the human as the inanimate is inherent in the necessities of technical civilization. For most of us, the tendency is regrettable and unavoidable. For the Nazis, it became an end in itself. This characteristic of the Nazis was exemplified in the death camps, the stench of the corpses and the use of people as raw material to be turned into feces, which was the chief industry of the camps. There were, of course, subordinate industries, such as the turning of the fat of the Jews' bodies into *Reine Jüdische Seife,* "pure Jewish soap," their gold teeth into Reichsbank deposits and, occasionally, their skin into luminous lampshades. Nevertheless, the transformation of human beings into feces was the camps' principal industry. Even direct passionate sadism at the level of individual personal relations seems to have been exceptional though permitted. The whole enterprise was directed primarily to the manufacture of corpses. The decaying corpses represented the final transformation of human beings into feces. The people of the Devil were turned into the ultimate element of the Devil.

Regression normally represents an unwillingness or an in-

[33] Erik H. Erikson, *op. cit.,* p. 341. For a discussion of rebelliousness and submission in German identity, cf. Erickson, *op. cit.,* pp. 326-358.

[34] New York: W. W. Norton, 1945.

ability to deal with the ironic complexities of the adult world. Adult existence is viable only as long as one is willing to accept the necessity of renunciation, discipline, and regard for others. It implies a willingness to accept less than the totality of one's desires, knowing that the insistence of desire must be moderated by the need for social order. The quest for the millennium is one of the darkest of human temptations.[35] This quest is not an attempt to do in the future what has not been realized in the past and the present; it is an attempt to embody concretely the fantasied remembrance of paradise lost, the time in childhood before the restraints of the world and society were known to be a necessity. The reason why the Nazis' form of millennialism aroused deeper fanaticism than did their Soviet enemy's was that the Nazis understood that the lost paradise promised more than economic and socio-political fulfillment.

Perhaps the decisive turning point came for the Germans when they refused to accept the reality of their defeat at the hands of the Western Powers in World War I. On December 11, 1918, only one month after the Armistice, the returning German soldiers marched in review, as if they were victors, before Friedrich Ebert, President of the Provisional Government, at the Brandenburg Gate. Ebert greeted the defeated army with the words, "I salute you, who return unvanquished from the field of battle." As J. W. Wheeler-Bennett has succinctly stated: "The legend of the 'stab in the back' had been born; the seeds of the Second World War already sown."[36]

The Germans followed Ebert and Von Hindenburg's lead in a fateful turning away from a reality they themselves had wrought. Like the protagonist in a Sartrian tragedy, they were incapable of assuming responsibility for their own acts. They were unable to say to themselves: "We are neither invincible nor omnipotent. We have been defeated and now our business is to

[35] It is on this issue that my disagreement with Thomas J. J. Altizer is most complete—although we both start from the sense of the total absence of God.

[36] John W. Wheeler-Bennett, *The Nemesis of Power* (London: Macmillan, 1961).

accept a world very different from the one for which we fought and to make the most of it." The Germans had lost much, but they still retained a unitary state and a land area which the Germans of today, living in divided and diminished East and West Germany, can regard only as a lost paradise of territorial grandeur. Instead of accepting a peace which was far easier than the one they finally were forced to accept, they allowed their highest leaders to convince them that they had not really lost, that they had been stabbed in the back, and that victory would finally be theirs when they destroyed their betrayers. Only time, and not much of that, was needed before the betrayer label was firmly placed upon those who had in any event borne the Judas label for almost two thousand years. The myth of Jewish magic villainy provided the perfect object for this fantasy. In Sartre's language, the "stab in the back" legend was a decisive example of German *mauvaise foi;* in psychological language, it was a massive retreat from reality to fantasy.

Instead of facing facts, the Germans became increasingly unable to accept reality. The goal of German life under the Nazis was to reconstitute the world in such a way that it could conform to primitive German wish and fancy. This was done through propaganda, military enterprise, and above all the death camps. The wish to structure things after their deepest and most archaic wishes would have driven the Germans, had they won, to make the death camp into the authentic prototype of the future Nazi state. Hannah Arendt was the first to see this in her book *The Origins of Totalitarianism*.[37] The further insights available since the publication of her work have tended to underscore the significance of her conclusions.

In the long run, reality will always have the final say, if only in the grave. The retreat into fantasy has neither rational limit nor measure. Since the original turning away arose out of an incapacity to accept realistic limitations, one remains discontent as long as any residue of necessity intrudes upon desire. Ultimately the terminal expression of this rejection of reality must be deliberate self-destruction. The killer's final victim must neces-

[37] New York: Harcourt Brace, 1951.

sarily be himself. Even the Nazi world of unimpeded aggressive freedom is still not a world devoid of restraints. It is a recapture of paradise lost, but it is not the final recapture.

There is a fateful destiny implicit in the child's first encounter with the world of objects in the form of the mother's breast. Only emptiness and pain can arouse the sleeping infant from its womb-like bliss. In pain, the child accepts the intrusion of the world of objects—at first the mother's breast—in order to do away with the pain. The breast is not prized in itself. It is only a detour on the path to the end of painful hunger and a return to sleeping bliss. The goal of the child's primal contact with the world is riddance of reality. Only later does a fated contradiction arise in which the objects by which satisfaction is gained are prized in and of themselves.[38]

There is something in all of us which finds reality unbearable. Every retreat from a mature confrontation with the limitations of the real world strengthens this tendency. When, as in the case of the Germans after World War I, the adult fails to deal realistically with his environment, a path is initiated which can have only one end—self-annihilation as the terminal mode of ridding oneself of an unwanted world. This is very apparent in alcoholics. Alcohol is a narcotic; its purpose is not to stimulate but to deaden. Its ultimate end is the destruction of the alcoholic. Normally, if the alcoholic receives no skilled assistance, nothing can reverse the process once it is under way. The warning, "You are destroying yourself," never really stopped an alcoholic unaided. Self-destruction—the final evasion of a complex and only partially satisfying world—is precisely what he wants. Reality must be avoided at all costs.

The Nazis were frequently described as "drunk with power." The metaphor is peculiarly apt. The final irony of Nazism was its self-destructiveness. The death of God does not create a world of instinctual freedom; it has the power to unleash the death instinct, hitherto held in check by important and even indispensable safeguards. Thereafter, it can reign supreme. In the case of the Nazis, their love affair with death far exceeded their violence against the Jews. It was to be found in the SS

[38] This is well expressed by Fenichel, *op. cit.,* p. 66.

ring insignia, in the names which they gave some of their elite units, such as the Death's Head, and above all in the way they ended their Third Reich.

Ultimately the end to restraint has no other meaning than the end to existence, for, of necessity, to be something means to be something definite, concrete, and *limited*. Only death and nothingness are without limit. Scholars may debate the exact merits of William L. Shirer's *The Rise and Fall of The Third Reich*.[39] It has at least one superlative merit. The author makes it very clear that the *Götterdämmerung* ending was implicit in the enterprise from the very outset. The Nazi adventure must be seen as a psychotic affair in the sense that the psychotic abjures and rejects reality for his preferred world of fantasy. As one reviews the dreary history of the Third Reich, one gets the feeling that one is reading a Greek tale in which almighty *nemesis* must pronounce the final judgment. Perhaps a similar feeling moved Wheeler-Bennett to entitle his magnificent history of the German Army in politics from 1918 to 1945 *The Nemesis of Power*. When Adolf Hitler inevitably failed to make the real world conform to his archaic fantasies, he had no choice but to eliminate reality by eliminating himself. As he had decreed the cremation of others, he now provided for his own burning. In those flames, the *Müttersohnchen* at last returned to the peace he had sought ever since the cruel fates thrust him forth from the bliss of his mother's womb. He had revenged himself upon a world which had disturbed that peace. He had finally returned to it.

Apart from the fact that self-destruction was the inevitable climax, perhaps almost equally ironic was the fact that the whole business of moral anarchy soon lost its charm. The Nazis had failed to anticipate the problem of boredom. Goethe clearly understood the limitations of moral anarchy in the Witches' Sabbath scene of *Faust*. He depicts Faust as irresistibly drawn to a beautiful naked witch. At the instant Faust reaches out to kiss the seductress, a bloody mouse leaps out of her mouth at Faust. Goethe's point is that things seldom end as we anticipate. When, as in the world in which God is dead, all things are permissible, they are by no means necessarily enjoyable. On the con-

[39] New York: Simon and Schuster, 1960.

trary, even a limited reality has decided advantages over the pursuit of fantasy. The whole insane Nazi venture soon became a very dirty, dull enterprise which had to be rationalized into a quasi-business venture to be bearable at all. Thus we find Himmler, in a moment of self-pity, commending the SS for having had to take part in the mess and "still remain good fellows." God was dead, hell—the *anus mundi*—was established on earth, and yet, even hell had lost its fine savor. All that remained, then as well as now, was an ineradicable stench. Nothing real had been gained; even the SS had won only the fantasy war against the Jews while losing the real one against the Allies. They left their country occupied and divided for the foreseeable future. The death of God had hardly bestowed its promised boon. The final lesson may very well be that there is more realistic pleasure in the disciplines and norms of the Living God than in all the freedoms of the Dead God.

I returned to Germany in August 1961 as the guest of the Bundes-presseamt to make a two-week survey of religious and cultural trends. I was scheduled to enter Germany on Sunday the 13th, the day of the closing of the border between East and West Berlin. Because of the international situation, I changed my plans and proceeded to Berlin so that I could observe the crisis directly.

The Bundespresseamt was extremely helpful. They arranged a series of interviews for me with religious and cultural leaders. I shall never forget my interview with Heinrich Grüber, Dean of the Evangelical Church of East and West Berlin. He dramatized the consequences of accepting the normative Judaeo-Christian theology of history in the light of the death camps. After my interview, I reached a theological point of no return—If I believed in God as the omnipotent author of the historical drama and Israel as His Chosen People, I had to accept Dean Grüber's conclusion that it was God's will that Hitler committed six million Jews to slaughter. I could not possibly believe in such a God nor could I believe in Israel as the chosen people of God after Auschwitz.

In the spring of 1965, Dean Grüber wrote to Christianity and Crisis denying the words I had ascribed to him. I replied that I did not bear the Dean any ill-will nor did I have any reason to falsify his words. The significance of the Dean's assertion of God's Lordship over the death camps is precisely the fact that he was not a Nazi or an anti-Semite but a very decent human being who believed in the historic doctrines of the election of Israel and of God as the final author of the historical drama.

2 / The Dean and the Chosen People

THERE IS an enlarged photograph in the Jewish Historical Museum in Amsterdam which epitomizes much that Jews feel concerning Christianity's role in the "final solution." The picture was taken in Westerbroek Concentration Camp in the Netherlands at a Christmas party celebrated by the SS and their women. Those responsible for the death of over one hundred and ten thousand Dutch Jews took time out of their grisly labors to celebrate the birth of their Jewish God in the very place where they were sealing the doom of every single Jew they could find. The plain fact of the matter is that those who murdered the Jews were, if not believing communicants of the Christian faith, at least men and women whose only exposure to religion was derived from Christian sources. Furthermore, contrary to much supposition, the people directly involved in the murder enterprise were not gutter riff-raff. More frequently than not, they were men with university or professional training behind them. In some instances, former pastors were active leaders of the work of death.

Christian thinkers very frequently point out that Nazism was an anti-Christian explosion which departed utterly from Christian morality. This is undeniably true. It does, however, gloss over the difference between those anti-Christian feelings which are rooted in a competing value system such as Islam, and the anti-Christian explosion of Christians against their own value system. Nazism was an anti-Christian movement. It was, nevertheless, dialectically related to Christianity. It was the *negation* of

Christianity as *negation* was understood by Hegel and Freud. It could have as little existed without Christianity as the Black Mass of medieval satanism could have existed without the Mass of Catholicism. Assuredly the classic villains of Christianity, the Jews, became the prime objects of extermination of the anti-Christian Christians, the Nazis.

The more one studies the classical utterances of Christianity on Jews and Judaism, while at the same time reviewing the terrible history of the Nazi period, the more one is prompted to ask whether there is something in the logic of Christian theology, *when pushed to a metaphysical extreme,* which ends with the justification of, if not the incitement to, the murder of Jews. Though there is an infinitude of pain in the exploration of this question, neither the Christian nor the Jew can avoid it.

Given the question of the relationship between Christianity and the holocaust, I considered myself very fortunate when, during the summer of 1961, while I was on a visit to Western Germany, the *Bundespresseamt,* the Press and Information Office of the German Federal Republic, made it possible for me to visit and interview Dr. Heinrich Grüber, Dean of the Evangelical Church in Berlin, at his home in Berlin-Dahlem. It was my third visit to Germany in thirteen months. The first two visits were private and unofficial. On this occasion the Press and Information Office was extremely helpful in making it possible for me to come to understand something of the complex reality that is present-day Western Germany.

Thousands of Germans could have testified against Eichmann and offered relevant testimony. Only one actually made the trip to Jerusalem to testify. Dean Grüber is a Protestant clergyman with a very long and heroic record of opposition to the Nazis on Christian grounds, and of friendship and succor for Nazism's chief victims. In the end, his courage brought him to Dachau and near-martyrdom. His resistance was especially meritorious because it incurred the possibility of great danger to his wife and children as well as to himself.

Since the war Dean Grüber has devoted himself to the work of healing and reconciliation. He has been instrumental in creating the Heinrich Grüber Haus in Berlin-Dahlem, and old-age residence for victims of the Nuremberg laws. These included Germans who had married Jews, Jews who had converted to Christianity, and a few old Jews who, in spite of the fury which had disrupted their lives, wanted to end their days in Berlin. With public and government support, a very spacious and attractive home has been built for these people who were the very special concern of the Dean.

In addition to testifying at the Eichmann trial, Dean Grüber has been instrumental in fostering the work of reconciliation between Germany and Israel on the political level, and between German Christianity and Judaism at the religious level. At his suggestion, on his seventieth birthday his German friends and admirers contributed well over one hundred thousand marks for the planting of a forest in his honor in Israel. He rejected all gifts. He insisted instead that the money be given to build Israel. He is also active in a German-Israel organization devoted to the exchange of visits between the youth of the two countries. He has visited Israel three times.

The Dean is over seventy, but there is a healthiness and a heartiness to his person which is noticeable immediately. He has a very attractive and spacious home, something very rare in Berlin today where, of necessity, apartment-house living is all that most people can hope for. He met me at the door and brought me to his study which was lined with books, a rather attractive oil copy of Rembrandt's *Flora,* and all sorts of relics and souvenirs of a long and distinguished career. In one corner, there was also a very impressive sculpture of the Dean's head.

After many sessions of interviewing Germans in all walks of life, I had learned to expect the interviewee to undergo a warm-up period before the initial reserve wore off. In the case of the Dean, this was unnecessary. There was an admirable bluntness and candor to his manner which revealed that the man means exactly what he says. This thoroughgoing honesty was present to the point of pain throughout the interview. It was not a quality the Nazis valued.

The most obvious point of departure for the conversation was the Eichmann trial. He explained that he went to Jerusalem with the greatest reluctance, and only after his name had come up so frequently that he felt he had no decent alternative. He also asserted that he went as a German, a member of the people who had perpetuated the injustice, and a member of the Christian Church which had remained silent before it.

"Did testifying cause you any harm with your own people?" I asked.

He replied that it had not and went on to say that he did not really see much difference between himself and Eichmann, that he too was guilty, that, in fact, the guilt was to be shared by all peoples rather than by Eichmann alone.

"If there had only been a little more responsibility all around, things would have been different."

He complained bitterly of how the governments of practically every civilized country turned their backs on the Jews, making it impossible for them to leave. He spoke of his own efforts to secure immigration visas and complained of how seldom he succeeded.

I asked him about the Heinrich Grüber Haus. He explained that he had helped hundreds of people, many of whom were victims of the Nuremberg laws, to leave Germany. In recent years some wanted to return. Originally he had founded his home for twenty people, most of whom were Christians who had lost Jewish relatives during the persecutions. He felt that these people deserved a more comfortable life in their remaining years than most old people. It was also extremely difficult to place them successfully in the average German old-age home as many German old people were still bitterly anti-Semitic and would have objected. To meet these problems, he had built, with much public support, this very unique and very beautiful home.

Without being asked, the Dean informed me that he had never converted Jews and did not want to do so now. On the contrary, he wanted Christians to become better Christians and Jews to become better Jews. I quickly learned that the Dean had very decided ideas on what Jews ought to be and how they ought to behave.

Again continuing without being questioned on the matter, the Dean informed me that Germany's Jews today were in great danger. He said that once again Jews are influential in the banks, the press, and other areas of public interest. This surprised me, as I had been informed that there are only eight thousand employed or self-employed Jews in a nation of fifty million.

"The problem in Germany is that the Jews haven't learned anything from what happened to them," he informed me. "I always tell my Jewish friends that they shouldn't put a hindrance in the way of our fight against anti-Semitism."

In view of his long established friendship for the Jewish people, I asked him to clarify his statement. He replied that many of the brothels and risqué night clubs, for example, are now in Jewish hands, especially those in close proximity to the army camps.

"For hundreds of years, there has been a virulent tradition of anti-Semitism among the Germans. Hitler exploited that tradition for his own ends. It is very difficult for us to wipe it out. After the Eichmann trial, this is one of my tasks. I am involved in one or two meetings a week to help end anti-Semitism, but it is very difficult because of the Jews in prominent positions and those who are engaged only in seeking money no matter what they do."

In reply, I told the Dean of the feelings of many Israelis that one of the most wonderful things about Israel is that there Jews have the right to be anything they want without relating it to the Jewish problem. I put the problem to him in terms of the freedom of every man to make his own life-choices and to pay the price for his personal decisions.

"Look, I don't understand why you are so troubled about a pitifully small number of Jews in shady positions or being interested in making money rather than following edifying pursuits. It seems to me that every person pays a price for the kind of life he leads. Why should Germans be upset about the life-decisions of these Jews unless they are unduly envious or neurotically involved in other people's lives? Must every Jew make himself so pale, so inconspicuous, even invisible, that he will give no offense? Is that the lesson Jews must learn from the death camps, that they must prove to the Germans their pre-eminent capacity for virtue? Wouldn't it seem a far better solution for all Jews left in Germany to leave and go where they could be anything they wished, without worrying about what the Germans thought or felt about them? After what has happened, why should any Jew remain and worry about attaining the approbation of the German People?"

The Dean was not prepared to let go. He was disturbed at the thought of the few remaining Jews leaving Germany. He felt that I was correct that Jews had as much right to be anything they pleased as the Germans, but he also felt that, after what had happened, they ought not to do these things, as it made the work of ending anti-Semitism so much harder. It was evident that in his mind there was an objective relationship between Jewish behavior and anti-Semitism.

Having asserted that the Jews had as much right to produce scoundrels or scalawags as any other people, the Dean quickly retracted. He spoke of the ancient covenant between God and Israel and how Israel as the chosen people of God was under a very special obligation to behave in a way which was spiritually consistent with Divine ordinance.

"I don't say this about Israel; God says this in the Bible and I believe it!" he insisted with considerable emotion.

The Dean was not the first German clergyman who had spoken to me in this vein concerning Israel. I had previously met a number of others in Berlin and Bonn. All insisted that there was a very special providential relationship between Israel, what happened to it, and God's will, that this had been true in the time of the Bible and that the *Heilsgeschichte* of the Jewish people had continued to unfold to this very day. In fairness to them, it should be pointed out that this belief has been shared by the vast majority of religious Jews throughout history. The theological significance of the Zionist movement and the establishment of the State of Israel lay largely in the rejection of *Heilsgeschichte* and the assertion that Jewish misfortune had been made by men and could be undone by men. For the pastors the conviction remained—it should be said that the conviction has been strengthened—that nowhere in the world were the fruits of God's activity in history more evident than in the life and the destiny of the Jewish people. In each instance I very quickly rejoined that such thinking had as its inescapable conclusion the conviction that the

Nazi slaughter of the Jews was somehow God's will, that God really wanted the Jewish People to be exterminated. In every instance before meeting Dr. Grüber, I was met by an embarrassed withdrawal.

Countess Dr. von Rittberg, the representative of the Evangelical Church to the Bonn Government, a charming and learned lady, was one of the German religious personalities with whom I discussed this issue. She had offered the customary interpretation of Israel's destiny as being guided by a special Divine concern, but she partially withdrew it in the face of my objection.

"Theologically this may be true, but humanly speaking and in any terms that I can understand, I cannot believe that God wanted the Nazis to destroy the Jews," she said.

Her reluctance to follow the logic of her theology to its hideous conclusion, which made the Nazis the accomplices of God, was, humanly speaking, most understandable. I found a similar reluctance in the other clergymen with whom I spoke, though, because I was a rabbi and a guest, there is a distinct possibility that I did not get a random sampling of theological opinion.

The same openness and lack of guile which Dean Grüber had shown from the moment I met him was again manifest in his reaction to my question concerning God's role in the death of the six million, a question which I believe is decisive for contemporary Jewish theology.

"Was it God's will that Hitler destroyed the Jews?" I repeated. "Is this what you believe concerning the events through which we have lived?"

Dr. Grüber arose from his chair and rather dramatically removed a Bible from a bookcase, opened it and read: *"Um deine-twillen werden wir getotet den ganzen Tag* . . . for Thy sake are we slaughtered every day . . ."* (Ps. 44:22)

"When God desires my death, I give it to him!" he continued. "When I started my work against the Nazis I knew that I would be killed or go to the concentration camp. Eichmann asked me, 'Why do you help these Jews? They will not thank you.' I had my family; there were my wife and three children. Yet I said, 'Your will be done even if You ask my death.'

For some reason, it was part of God's plan that the Jews died.
God demands our death daily. He is the Lord, He is the Master,
all is in His keeping and ordering."

Listening to the Dean, I recalled Erich Fromm's descriptions of the authoritarian personality in *Escape From Freedom*.[1] All the clergymen had asserted the absolute character of
God's Lordship over mankind and of mankind's obligation to
submit unquestioningly to that Lordship, but none had carried the
logic of this theology as far as the Dean did.

The Dean's disturbing consistency undoubtedly had its
special virtues. No consideration of personal safety could deter
the Dean from total obedience to his Heavenly Master; this contrasted starkly with too many of his fellow countrymen who gave
lip-service to a similar ideal but conveniently turned the other way
in the crisis. Nevertheless, there was another side to this stance
which was by no means as pleasant. Eichmann also had served
his master with complete and utterly unquestioning fidelity. Even
sixteen years after the close of hostilities, not only Eichmann, but
apparently his defense counsel, seemed to feel that such servitude
was self-justifying. Furthermore, in both the Dean and his demonic antagonist, the will of the master, in the one case God, in
the other case Hitler, was unredeemed by a saving empiricism.
Neither man preferred an inconsistency in logic to the consistency
of accepting the gratuitous murder of six million. In neither
individual was there even a trace of personal autonomy.

When Dr. Grüber put down his Bible, it seemed as if,
once having started, he could not stop himself. He looked at recent events from a thoroughly Biblical perspective. In the past,
the Jews had been smitten by Nebuchadnezzar and other "rods of
God's anger." Hitler was simply another such rod. The incon-
gruity of Hitler as an instrument of God never seemed to occur
to him. Of course, he granted that what Hitler had done was
immoral and he insisted that Hitler's followers were now being
punished by God.

"At different times," he said, "God uses different peoples as His whip against His own people, the Jews, but those

[1] New York: Rhinehart and Co., 1941.

whom He uses will be punished far worse than the people of the Lord. You see it today here in Berlin. We are now in the same situation as the Jews. My church is in the East sector. Last Sunday (August 13, the day of the border closing) I preached on Hosea 6:1 ('Come, and let us return unto the Lord: For He hath torn, and He will heal us; He hath smitten, and He will bind us up'). God has beaten us for our terrible sins; I told our people in East Berlin that they must not lose faith that He will reunify us."

I felt a chill at that instant. There was enormous irony in the Dean's assertion that the Germans had become like Jews. I was listening to a German clergyman interpret German defeat as the rabbis had interpreted the fall of Jerusalem almost two thousand years before. For the rabbis, Jerusalem fell because of the sins of the Jewish people. For Dean Grüber, Berlin had fallen because of the sins of the German people. When he sought words of consolation with which to mollify the wounding of his imprisoned church he turned to the very same verses from Hosea which had consoled countless generations of Israel.

He pursued the analogy between Germany and Israel: "I know that God is punishing us because we have been the whip against Israel. In 1938 we smashed the synagogues; in 1945 our churches were smashed by the bombs. From 1938 we sent the Jews out to be homeless; since 1945 fifteen million Germans have experienced homelessness."

The feeling of guilt was very apparent; so too was the fact that for him German suffering appeased and ameliorated this feeling. Everything he said reiterated his belief that God was ultimately responsible for the death of the Jews. It may have been a mystery to him, but it was nevertheless taken as unshakable fact.

The Dean had asserted that God had been instrumental in the holocaust. He had not asserted the nature of the crime for which God was supposed to have smitten the Jews. During the Eichmann trial, Dr. Servatius, the defense counsel, had offered the suggestion that the death of the six million was part of a "higher purpose," and in recompense for an earlier and greater crime against God, thereby joining the modern trial in Jerusalem with one held twenty centuries before. Time was running short.

I did not have the opportunity to question Dean Grüber concerning the nature of the enormous crime for which six million Jews perished. His thinking was so thoroughly drenched in New Testament and Prophetic categories that there is little reason to think that he would have disagreed with Dr. Servatius. Stated with theological finesse it comes to pretty much the same thing as the vulgar thought that the Christ-killers got what was coming to them.

At a number of American Protestant seminaries, there have been attempts to study and tone down some of the more patently anti-Semitic teachings in religious textbooks and literature. Similar efforts are today being made within Catholicism. The Jewish declaration of the Vatican Council is the outstanding example. Many thoughtful Christians assert that *all* men, insofar as they are sinners, killed Christ and that the blame must therefore not be placed on the Jews alone. In the face of a crime so hideous as the holocaust, decent men recoil and attempt to do what they can to root out the incitement to further evil. These attempts have been rightly appreciated in Jewish circles. Yet one is forced to ask whether there is even the slightest efficacy to any of these efforts. The fundamental issue transcends the question of whether Jews are regarded as Christ-killers. At the heart of the problem is the fact that it may be impossible for Christians to remain Christians without regarding Jews in mythic, magic, and theological categories. Jews alone of all the people in the world are regarded as actors and participants in the drama of sin and innocence, guilt and salvation,, perdition and redemption. If the Jews are an utterly normal people like any other, capable of the same virtues and vices, then there is no reason to assert that Jesus had more than a human significance. The Christian Church must insist on the separate and special character of the Jewish people in order that its claims concerning the significance of Jesus may gain credence. As long as Jews are thought of as special and apart from mankind in general, they are going to be the object of both the abnormal demands and the decisive hatreds of which the Dean spoke.

It would seem that as long as there is Christianity, Jews will be the potential objects of a special and ultimately pernicious attention which can always explode in violence. Even were all the textbooks "corrected," there would still be the Gospels, and they are enough to assure the ever-present threat of a murderous hatred of Jews by Christians. Even when Christians assert that all men are guilty of the death of the Christ, they are asserting a guilt more hideous than any known in any other religion, the murder of the Lord of Heaven and Earth. On the Jewish side, we would say that not only are the Jews not guilty of this deicide, but that no man is guilty because it never happened. Here again there is an unbridgeable wall. The best that Christians can do for the Jews is to spread the guilt, while always reserving the possibility of throwing it back entirely upon the Jews. This is no solution for the Jews, for they must insist that this dimension of guilt exists for no man in reality, although they might be willing to admit that it exists for every man in fantasy.

What made the visit to Dean Grüber so memorable and so interesting was the fact that here was a Christian who had almost died because of his efforts on behalf of Jews—the Nazis kicked out his teeth and at one point he was left for dead in Dachau—yet he was incapable of seeing Jews simply as normal human beings with the same range of failings and virtues as any other group. It may be argued that the Dean's opinions prove nothing, that he exhibited a typically German incapacity to place the concrete, empirical facts of day-to-day life before an overwhelming ideology. There is undoubtedly some truth in this. Nevertheless, the Dean's attitudes, especially in view of what he has done, intensify the question of Christian theology and the death of the Jews.

My visit did suggest one element of hope. Most Americans and Britons simply don't think the way Dean Grüber does. There seems to be something in the German mentality which demands utter metaphysical consistency. This has often been productive of much good. It has resulted in some of the greatest and most imaginative uses of the human intellect. The system of Hegel comes to mind immediately. Nevertheless, the existentialist and pragmatic protests have a validity which can be justified at least on human grounds. Human relations cannot, must not be absolutely consistent with ideological necessities. When they are, life is lost and a dead, murdering logic destroys what it cannot countenance.

Out of my interview I came away with a question for the Jewish community. Can we really blame the Christian community for viewing us through the prism of a mythology of history when we were the first to assert this history of ourselves? As long as we continue to hold to the doctrine of the election of Israel, we will leave ourselves open to the theology expressed by Dean Grüber, that because the Jews are God's Chosen People, God wanted Hitler to punish them.

There is a way out and Reconstructionism has pointed to it. Religious uniqueness does not necessarily place us at the center of the divine drama of perdition, redemption, and salvation for mankind. All we need for a sane religious life is to recognize that we are, when given normal opportunities, neither more nor less than any other men, sharing the pain, the joy, and the fated destiny which Earth alone has meted out to all her children.

We began with a question, whether the Christian Church's attitude involves it in a process which in times of stress incites to the murder of Jews. To this question we must now append a further question, whether the way Jews regard themselves religiously contributes to the terrible process. The tendency of the Church to regard Jews in magic and theological terms encourages the view that the vicissitudes of Jewish history are God's will. If we accept his theological premises, there is no way of avoiding Dean Grüber's conclusion that God sent Hitler. But how can we ask Christians to give up these premises if we continue to regard ourselves in this light? No man can predict the way the matter will end. There is, however, no doubt that the simple capacity of Jew and Christian to accept their own and each other's humanity lies at the core of any possibility of reconciliation between the two great faiths of the Western world.

As a result of having published several articles on the Berlin border crisis in the Pittsburgh Press during August 1961, I became acquainted with Professor Herbert Mainusch of the University of Muenster, at the time a Visiting Professor at the University of Pittsburgh. Upon his return to Germany, he suggested that I be invited to lecture in Germany. I was invited to be a principal lecturer at the Fifteenth Annual Conference on Church and Judaism held in Recklinghausen in February 1963.

This invitation was one of the most disconcerting I had ever accepted. I had been asked to enter into a dialogue with German Christians as to the meaning of the encounter of Christian and Jew and German and Jew. By accepting the invitation, I implicitly affirmed my conviction that there is no extremity of human estrangement which is altogether lacking in the potentiality of reconciliation. I do not believe that reconciliation has as yet come between Germans and Jews, but I do believe that it is important that we converse together.

The English version of this paper appeared in the Winter 1963 issue of The Christian Scholar. At the time, I was not aware of the affinities between my own theological perspectives and those of Protestant radical theologians. Thus, I was surprised and challenged to read William Hamilton's article "The Death of God Theologies Today" in The Christian Scholar, Spring 1965. He cited the article which follows as an example of death of God theology. There are, of course, major differences between us, but there are affinities.

3 / Person and Myth in the Judaeo-Christian Encounter

FROM THE TIME of the first Jewish settlement in Cologne in the year 70 C.E. to our own terrible and barbaric era, crucial portions of the drama of Jewish history have been played on the German scene. For Jews, Germany is a bitter but an inescapable reality. Many Jews are tempted to avoid all German contacts, even those which are sincerely offered in friendship. I can understand such an attitude but I cannot share it. We have been too directly and too violently involved in each other's destiny for either side to permit murder to be the last word, if we can help it. As a rabbi, I find myself inescapably drawn to the study of German history, philosophy, and contemporary politics. No other European country exhibits a comparable fascination, for no other European people has affected the life and death of my people as have the Germans. I try to understand Germany the better to understand myself.

I wish to explore the meaning of two related, tragic encounters, that of German and Jew and that of Christian and Jew. For almost two thousand years, an honest Judaeo-Christian religious encounter was all but impossible in Europe. At best, the Jew was the dependent, threatened client of the Christian. The implicit threat of superior power and its entailments hung over such meetings. That is why they were almost always disputations, forced upon a beset and fearful Jewish community which could rarely, if ever, afford the luxury of candor. Jews knew that victories in such disputations were actually defeats, for such victories were bound to be followed by the punitive anger of their opponents. It is not surprising that, in the meetings of Jew and Christian, Jews were more concerned with avoiding affronts to Christian sensibilities than they were with genuine communication.

Only in modern times has a beginning been made toward real communication, toward the meeting of I and Thou between Jew and Christian of which Martin Buber has written so persuasively. Such a meeting requires equality. The fact that I am a foreigner helps to make it possible for me to speak to you as an equal. I am neither your dependent nor your client, as Jews have so frequently been in the past. By the same token, I hope that I am beyond the *ressentiment,* which is the secret revenge of clients against their protectors and persecutors alike. Neither you nor I are doomed merely to behold mirror images of our own beings in this confrontation. In this there is gain for both of us. What we behold in the mirror may be familiar and secure, but he who tells you only what you want or expect to hear, as well as he who sits in judgment, turns the I–Thou of encounter and meeting into I–It. He refuses you as a real person. He reduces you to a manipulated artifact within the domain of his projects. Thus inequality not only precludes genuine encounter for the client; it distorts and debases the protector as well. Were I a native, I could expect no more than a bestowed equality. As Kierkegaard has suggested in his parable of the King who would bestow his love on the servant girl, memory makes a bestowed equality impossible. A tolerated Judaism can never achieve real encounter with Christianity. In order to meet you at all, I must do so as a foreigner.

No one chooses the community, the nation, or the tradition to which he is heir at birth. There is an absurd facticity, not only to our modes of finding ourselves in the world, but to the ways in which we are thrust into our respective religious situations. Neither Jew nor gentile is entirely free to confront God's mysterious singularity as if no one had preceded him. Jew and gentile alike are thrown into historically, culturally, psychologically and religiously defined situations which are, in a certain sense, beyond choice. You were not asked whether you desired to be born German; I was not consulted about being born American. We can choose the relative degree to which we take seriously our inherited religious traditions. We can, if we want, deny them, but this denial will be dialectically related to the original fact of the givenness of our traditions. Our religious affirmations are very largely the ratification of what is given and the making explicit of what is originally implicit in our situations. Nevertheless, the more serious we become about the domain of that which Paul Tillich calls "ultimate concern," the more we find that we must utilize the sacred forms and traditions of the communities into which we have been thrust. After Kierkegaard, we know that Jew and Christian are more separated by conflicting and opposing spiritual wagers than they are by proven superiorities or certainties in either the moral or sacred domain. We are divided by the absurd "thrownness" *(Geworfenheit)* of our concrete, historically determined situations. There is no way for the Christian to confront the holiness of God save through the Christ and the paths of sanctity in which He is the decisive figure. For the Jew, no religious way exists save through the Torah as its traditions have been inherited, reflected upon, and transmitted throughout Jewish history. Only God knows who, if anyone, ultimately dwells in His Truth.

The absurdity of both situations is made the more agonizing because Christian and Jew are heir to and participant in a conflict which is no longer of either's making. While both Judaism and Christianity can ultimately dwell outside God's Truth, only one of the conflicting traditions could conceivably dwell within it, at least with regard to the question of the Christ. If each is true to his inheritance, he is veritably destined to deny much that the other holds to be central to his existence. We are locked in a conflict from which there is no way out.

Tragic encounters can lead either to murder or to moral modesty and mutual enrichment. The problem has ultimately little to do with the question of Jewish safety. Creon was hardly better off with Antigone dead than confronted with the terribly annoying presence of Antigone alive. The murderer does something to himself as well as to his victim. In some respects, his is the greater problem, for, unlike his victim, he must live with himself after the deed. Creon and Antigone were driven by forces of which they were in no sense the masters. The forces and loyalties constituent of Jewish and Christian identities respectively can be little altered by either Jew or Christian. There is the possibility that, with awareness into the explosive potentialities of our religious ideologies, we will be able to moderate their destructiveness. Above all, I want to emphasize that at this point in history the conflict is beyond blame. Neither Christian nor Jew can avoid or deny the religious traditions out of which he has come. In some very important respects, we are heirs to conflicts we did not create but which we cannot with dignity or honor entirely avoid.

There is a very important area in which both normative Judaism and Christianity agree, in common opposition to almost all other religious systems. As Oscar Cullman has suggested, both ascribe to time and history a decisive place in the divine economy which is quite foreign to non-Biblical religions. Judaism and Christianity differ in their interpretation of hisory, but not their basic conception that God's relation to the world is primarily historical. Hans Joachim Schoeps would seem to be correct in maintaining that Paul the Apostle was acting largely as a Pharisee who was convinced that Jesus was in fact and in truth the Christ. Neither Paul nor his rabbinic adversaries differed in their faith that God would send a Messianic Deliverer. They differed radically in their *assessments* of the historical facts of the career of Jesus. Similarly neither Rabban Johanan ben Zakkai nor Justin Martyr differed in their belief that God was omnipotently active in history and that the destruction of Jerusalem by the Romans had been effectuated by God's will; they differed in their assessment of the sins of Israel which prompted God so to act. Rabban Johanan ben Zakkai, moved by a strong sense of Jewish self-criticism, ascribed the fall of Jerusalem largely to the failure of his community properly to fulfill the injunctions of the Torah, God's expressed will. Justin, seeing history through the prism of the Christ-event, could not avoid the conclusion that Jerusalem had fallen because the Jewish people had failed to accept and had in fact betrayed God's most precious gift, the saving gift of the

Christ.What united Justin and Johanan also separated them most savagely. Both saw history as the unfolding of the Divine drama of mankind's salvation, yet this was the cause of a deep and persistent division which has by no means ended in our own times.

If one accepts this common view of historical providence, some very unpleasant conclusions necessarily follow. In August 1961, I had an unforgettable conversation in Berlin with one of Germany's religious leaders who had done most to oppose the radical program of the Nazis against the Jews and to help as many Jews escape from the consequences of this program as he possibly could. His humanity was ill-rewarded at the time, though his sufferings undoubtedly have done much to remind the world of what has been referred to as "the other Germany." In the course of our conversation, this gentleman who had done so much to alleviate Jewish suffering asserted that it was God's will that Hitler had exterminated the Jews. He drew a parallel between Hitler and Nebuchadnezzar and asserted that, while both conquerors had acted with malice and in pursuit of their own selfish ends, they nevertheless were unknowingly also acting as the rods of God's wrath in punishing his sinful people. After recovering from my initial shock, I recognized that there was nothing new or surprising in this argument, that it had been asserted by the Prophets of Israel, by the Rabbis, and by the Fathers of the Church alike. I had never heard the argument applied so insistently to the events of our own times, but its logic was such that there was no reason to exclude the world of the twentieth century. Given the Judaeo-Christian conception, so strong in Scripture, that God is the ultimate actor in the historical drama, no other theological interpretation of the death of six million Jews is tenable. The only domain in which debate could be pursued would be that of assessing the sins for which Israel was so sorely afflicted. Yet it is doubtful that there would be much to add to what Rabban Johanan and Justin Martyr had said on that point. If one views all time and history through the perspective of the Christ, one would ultimately have to assert that God caused the Jews to be exterminated by the Nazis because of their continuing failure to confess and acknowledge the Christ. If one shared Rabban Johanan ben Zakkai's view, one would be drawn to assert that

the Jewish people had been exterminated because of their failure
to comply with the Lord's commandments as these had been enjoined in the Torah. Of course, it would always remain a mystery
why the Good Lord had suffered the relatively prosperous and
religiously permissive American Jewish community to escape intact while consuming the Polish Jewish community which was the
most religiously compliant Jewish center.

Perhaps no twentieth-century figure has dealt so meaningfully or so feelingly with this problem in its universal form as has
the French thinker Albert Camus in *The Plague*. A plague of immense proportions which breaks out in the city of Oran very
quickly begins to consume thousands of people in utter indifference to every human standard of virtue, vice, age, status, or social
utility. The central issue of Camus's great work is the question
of the meaning of the catastrophe which is so unconcerned with
the innocence or guilt of its victims. In terms of the normative
Judaeo-Christian interpretation of history, the plague can have
only one meaning—it must represent the punitive anger of the
Lord visited upon the sinful city. Camus illustrates this perspective in the character of Father Paneloux, the Jesuit priest who
leaves the solitude of his scholarship to come forth to preach repentance to the stricken community. In the presence of a large
and anxious congregation gathered in the cathedral, the good
father interprets the disaster which has overwhelmed his community in the very same way that the forementioned German clergyman interpreted the modern Jewish catastrophe and Rabban
Johanan ben Zakkai and Justin Martyr interpreted the earlier
disaster. The plague had been sent by a just and angry God in
punishment of the sins of the wicked community. The plague
would be lifted only when the community truly heeded its meaning and turned from its wicked paths to the ways of the Lord. For
Father Paneloux, as for all Deuteronomists who have preceded
him, human suffering could be understood only as the emblem of
human guilt and its retribution. The tragedy of suffering was
aggravated by the conviction that, because men suffered, they deserved to suffer.

Almost a century before Camus, the Russian novelist
Fyodor Dostoevsky had dealt with very much the same issue in

The Brothers Karamazov. Ivan Karamazov, the atheist, rejects the normative Judaeo-Christian interpretation of history. He will not allow that any possible good which could issue forth from the Divine economy of history could be worth the suffering of even one innocent child. Camus shared Ivan's refusal to justify the Lord in the face of innocent suffering. Father Paneloux is capable of maintaining his interpretation of events from the pulpit. Later he is broken by the terrible sight of the painful death of a child. Something happens to him as a result. He is never again the same man. His life is too thoroughly committed to the Prophetic-Deuteronomic interpretation of history for him to retract. Nevertheless, something in him has seen its limitations. Camus wisely and compassionately describes the way in which he takes sick and dies, not because of the plague, but because his world has been shattered and he knows no way of reconstituting it. Human solidarity triumphs over the interpretation of events which equates human suffering with Divine retribution.

At every point of significance in Camus's thinking, human solidarity is preferred to ideology. When we finish *The Plague,* we are aware of the fact that this solidarity is the deepest root of Camus's atheism. He refuses, as does Ivan Karamazov, to see man as inevitably and inescapably guilty before God. He accepts the tragedy, the inevitability, and the gratuitous absurdity of suffering, but he refuses to consent to its justice. He would rather live in an absurd, indifferent cosmos in which men suffer and die meaninglessly but still retain a measure of tragic integrity than see every last human event encased in a pitiless framework of meaning which deprives men of even the consolation that suffering, though inevitable, is not entirely merited or earned. We know that Camus reacted with deep sensitivity to World War II. The plague of which he writes was in reality the same plague which consumed Europe's millions. It was Camus's genius to be able to universalize the problem.

Camus's inability to accept the God of the Judaeo-Christian tradition in the face of the suffering of the innocent and his choice of an absurd cosmos which at least preserves a measure of human solidarity and dignity is reminiscent of an earlier decision of the same sort taken by an apostate from Rabbinic

Judaism in the first Christian century, Elisha ben Abuyah. He also elected an absurd and meaningless cosmos rather than interpret the suffering of the innocent as divinely inflicted retribution of sin. In the face of overwhelming Jewish suffering during the Hadrianic War, he exclaimed *"Leth din v'leth dyan"*[1]—"There is neither judgment nor Judge." Anticipating Camus by almost two thousand years, he elected a world without meaning rather than accept the justice of human suffering.

We concur with this choice of an absurd and ultimately tragic cosmos. We do so because we share with Camus a greater feeling for human solidarity than the Prophetic-Deuteronomic view of God and history can possibly allow. We part company only with his atheism. It is precisely because human existence is tragic, ultimately hopeless, and without meaning that we treasure our religious community. It is our community of ultimate concern. In it, we can and do share, in a depth and dimension which no secular institution can match, the existence Camus has so well described. We have turned away from the God of history to share the tragic fatalities of the God of nature. It is no accident that this turning is concurrent with the return of at least a portion of the children of Israel to the earth of Israel.

Jewish theology has since earliest times been peculiarly sensitive to Jewish history. It will be impossible to enunciate a meaningful Jewish theology for contemporary Jewish life which excludes the decisive question of God and the death camps. In the face of so terminal an agony, it is very easy to understand the monumental indifference of most Israelis, for example, toward traditional Jewish religious forms. With better instinct than they can verbalize, they associate traditional Jewish ideology with the European experience and its degrading and catastrophic finale. They understandably want no part of it. Their own experience has not been one of defeat or the need for theological self-justification. Above all, they refuse to see the European disaster as a working out of God's retribution. Had this been their ideology, they would have been forced to accept Rabban Johanan ben Zakkai's other conclusion: Jewish alienation from the ancestral

[1] Cf. Hagigah 14b ff. for the principal rabbinic source on Elisha b. Abuyah.

home was caused by a want of Jewish piety; what a want of piety had destroyed, only a perfection of piety could restore. By this reasoning, the most realistic way of restoring Zion was that elected by the most extreme elements of Jerusalem's Orthodox quarter, *Mea Shearim*.

Jewish life in the twentieth century has known two moments of *kairos*: the death camps and the restoration of Zion. However, the restoration of Zion took place only because Israelis and other Jews deliberately turned their back on Rabban Johanan ben Zakkai's ideology. Though Jewish religious leaders may verbally reaffirm that ideology, their acts belie this posture. *The meaning of the restored Zion is that the normative theology of history traditionally identified with prophetic and Rabbinic Judaism has been effectively demythologized.* This is an awesome and momentous change in Jewish religious sentiment after two thousand years. Its full meaning will be understood only by generations yet to come. The demythologizing fact has yet to appear in most contemporary expressions of Jewish theology. These hardly ever seem to be written in the twentieth century after the death camps and the restoration of Zion. There is an understandable hiatus between religious ideology and explicit action where real Jewish interests are involved. I believe that what Jews have done since the war offers a better key to what they think than the continued reiteration of the older, discredited historical myth. It is very difficult for a people to surrender a myth which has infused its existence with meaning for over two thousand years until a way is found to incorporate the newer, demythologized *Weltanschauung* into its religious and institutional structure.

This demythologizing process is everywhere apparent in deed if not in explicit ideology, especially in Israel. After the experiences of our times, we can neither affirm the myth of the omnipotent God of History nor can we maintain its corollary, the election of Israel. After the death camps, the doctrine of Israel's election is in any event a thoroughly distasteful pill to swallow. Jews do not need these doctrines to remain a religious community.

After the death camps, life in and of itself, lived and enjoyed in its own terms without any superordinate values or special theological relationships, becomes important for Jews. One cannot go through the experience of having life called so devastatingly and radically into question without experiencing a heightened sense of its value, unrelated to any special categories of meaning which transcend its actual experience. This distrust of superordinate ideologies is increased immeasurably because of our knowledge of the role such ideologies played in the creation of the death camps. Life need have no meta-historical meanings to be worth while. In a world in which so much gratuitously insane fury has been expended upon the Jews, those Jews who have extricated themselves from this terminal threat have a duty at least to be sane about themselves, especially where others have lost that capacity.

Undoubtedly this need for sanity within the community has been underscored by our rediscovery of Israel's earth and the lost divinities of that earth. Once again we have come in contact with those powers of life and death which engendered men's feelings about Baal, Astarte, and Anath. These powers have again become decisive in our religious life. We cherish our hallowed, ancient traditions, not because they are better than other men's or because they are somehow more pleasing in God's sight: we cherish them simply because they are ours and we could not with dignity or honor exchange them for any other. By the same token, having lost the need to prove that what we are or have is better than what others are or have, we have gained a reverence for other men's sacred traditions. This is a corollary of our belief that these traditions are not matters of original choice but are part of the absurd givenness of every concrete, limited human perspective. As children of Earth, we are undeceived concerning our destiny. We have lost all hope, consolation, and illusion. We have also lost all *ressentiment,* that emblem of poverty of spirit, and we have found a renewed strength, dignity, and vitality. Jewish life must live beyond all ideology in the joy as well as the pain of the present, seeking no pathetic compensations in an imaginary future for a life unlived in the now. It is either this or a return to an ideology which must end by praising God for the death of six million Jews. This we will never do.

We will never again regard ourselves in the old mythic

perspectives. For Christianity, however, the doctrine of the election of Israel seems to be indispensable. Unless Israel is the vessel of God's revelation to mankind, it makes no sense to proclaim the Christ as the fulfillment and climax of that revelation. While Jews can, and I believe must, demythologize their religious ideology, I see no way in which believing Christians can demythologize Israel's special relation to God without radically altering the meaning of Christian existence. Nevertheless, the Christian will always encounter the Jew as myth rather than real person unless some way can be found for Christians to demythologize their conception of Israel. In this dilemma, the tragedy of the Judaeo-Christian encounter becomes explicit.

It has been said that English literature has portrayed the Jew as the best of saints and the worst of sinners but never as a simple human being. This characterizes more than English literature; it characterizes the Christian view of Israel. If we are to be accurate, we would have to insist that the demonological interpretation of Israel is by far the more potent.

There is a polarity of images in Christian thought on Jews and Judaism which extends from Jesus to Judas but knows no middle ground. After times of great hatred and slaughter, the Christian image of the Jew will stress the resemblance to Jesus, recalling the Jew's virtues and his contributions to mankind's spiritual treasury. This is inevitable in a time of reconciliation, but it may have about it more than a little of the fattening of the sacrificial lamb for another round of slaughter. In any event, philo-Semitism is as unrealistic and as pernicious as anti-Semitism, for it destroys our most precious attribute, our simple humanity. Jews are not, nor are they obliged to be, paragons of virtue or models of holiness. To expect us to be more than other men, to pay us the unwanted and unasked-for compliment of asserting that we are, is an unintended cruelty but a cruelty nonetheless. A superlative degree of virtue excludes from the human community at least as effectively as a superlative degree of vice. Furthermore, since most men are inwardly far more convinced of their viciousness than of their virtue, they will have little reason to honor or admire those who either assert themselves or are condemned to the assertion by others of an inhuman virtue.

Sooner or later the image changes. Usually the Judas-image of the Jew comes to the fore when the Jews attain a certain numerical strength within a country and then begin to compete effectively with a significant segment of the non-Jewish population. The image of the Jew as the giver of religion is superseded by another image, the image of Judas who betrays his Lord by a loving kiss for thirty pieces of silver. The potency of the image is magnified by the fact that it is reinforced by early learning and the sanctity of the institution which teaches it. Nothing so poisons Jewish-Christian relations as the Judas story. The moral of the tale is simple and direct. No Jew can be trusted. Even his seeming virtue is only a demonic disguise for the betrayer's role. He may seem like a good citizen, a valued intellect, an unselfish patriot, but one can never be sure whether beneath these postures there lurks a betrayer. It is impossible to tell this story to children, to rehearse it in the Passion, to celebrate it in song, drama, and religious ritual without its casting a black cloud over Jewish-Christian relations.

Normally this image will do its subtle work without becoming overt. However, in time of stress, the power of this image will be magnified. In place of rational, reality-oriented modes of relationship, men and communities tend to regress to irrational images in which people cease to be flesh-and-blood persons, mixtures of virtues and vice, and become unambiguous embodiments of principles which are never found anywhere in an undiluted state. In the language of psychoanalysis, there is a regression from the secondary-process to the primary-process level of mental functioning.

When regression takes place under extreme conditions, one of the most important casualties is an individual's or a community's sense of responsibility for its own destiny. A search begins for a magic betrayer who has been guilty of the "stab in the back," who is responsible for every imaginable ill which has befallen the community. Such accusations are always creditable when directed against the Jews in Christian lands, because they represent a contemporary restatement of the mythic drama. As Jesus was betrayed by Judas, so the Jew now is regarded as betraying his Christian hosts. There is always an element of truth in the accusations leveled at the Jew, for he participates in the same spectrum of virtue and vice as his neighbor. There is, however, a very different level of expectation in his case. Since he has been praised as like Jesus, his failure to measure up to this unattainable image makes the Judas accusation all the more plausible. When this image has been reiterated for millennia in every conceivable form of religious literature and ritual, it will afford the key to understanding why the host nation has fared badly, why its armies were defeated, why depression and inflation have supplanted prosperity. Furthermore, in defeat one can always wound the Jew with the blows which are meant for the victor but which can never safely be directed against him.

One can only dwell in the domain of the sacred by an act of condemnation, for it is the fated destiny of the sacred personality to die as the sacrificial offering. In ancient times, the final piety of the King-Priest was to be offered up as a human sacrifice. In Christianity, Jesus, the King-Priest-Saviour, redeems a sinful world through His atoning and sacrificial death. In sacrifice, the human predicament is dramatized most effectively. Men, who are unable either to abide the disciplines of society or to overthrow them, dramatize their ambivalence in this holy act. In a sense, sacrifice redeems and saves, because it contains men's homicidal aggressiveness within controlled limitations. Furthermore, sacrifice dramatizes the most important fact about men. We would, if we could, become deicides. Had we but the power, we would murder God, for we will never cease to be tempted by Ivan Karamazov's demonic fantasy that if God were dead, all things would be permitted. It is impossible to avoid a sense of amazement at Christianity's marvelous mythic power, for in the crucifixion we behold the symbolic acting out of this deepest wish.

There is, however, a difference between the pagan priest lifting his sorrowful knife to offer up the innocent sacrificial victim and the Christian. The pagan priest knows that the guilt for the holy murder is his and that of the community he serves. He can perhaps justify his deed by insisting that, were he not to commit the limited act of religious violence, his community would soon enough disintegrate into a cannibal group knowing no limits to aggressive violence save those nature herself finally imposes by sheer exhaustion. The Christian has a deeper insight into the meaning of the sacrifice. He intuits that it is God whom we would murder even in the moment of our most reverential homage. Unlike the pagan priest, he need not accept the guilt as his own. The actors in the mythic drama, the Incarnate God, His betrayer, and those who reject and crucify Him, all are Jews. One can hate God for the virtue He commands, yet displace one's murderous feelings onto the Jew as His murderer. Whether one sees the Jew as Jesus or Judas, it is all the same. He must ultimately be condemned to play his final role in the domain of the sacred, that of sacrificial victim.

Even where he is not destroyed physically, he who is condemned to the domain of the sacred is excluded from the community of men. This is perhaps a fate more bitter than actual death, for it is a death in life. Nor can we forget that the sacrificial victim is the scapegoat. As long as life is prosperous and undisturbed, people let things go on pretty much what we Americans call a "live-and-let-live basis." Under stress, the humanity of the other disappears as reality disappears. At this point the ritual-murder aspect of sacrifice predominates. Its essence is the primordial hope that, in the suffering and death of the victim, the community will avoid or forestall its hurts or dooms. The death camps were one huge act of ritual murder in which the perpetrators were convinced that only through the elimination of the Jews could Germany's safety be vouchsafed. The years since 1945 have demonstrated the extent to which the death of the Jews has contributed to the actual safety of the German people.

I want to stress that I draw this picture with no sense of blame or anger. Myths and religious traditions are not easily invented. As a Jew, I find myself in the peculiar situation of regarding myself as of absolutely no consequence or meaning beyond my own projects and those of my family and the larger community in which I am involved. I know, however, that, though I did not and would not have made the choice, I have an unwanted superordinate significance for others. I also recognize, to my very great sorrow, that I have this superordinate significance largely because non-Jews took my ancestors seriously when they claimed for themselves a special religious destiny. I desire no such destiny

either for myself or for my community. I have tried to demythologize my situation for myself and my community, but I can
hardly blame Christians if they refuse to follow me. I know how
difficult it is to persuade Jews to accept the demythologizing
process with regard to their own status. It would be far more
difficult to get others to do so.

The deepest tragedy in Jewish-Christian relations is that
true dialogue, the genuine meeting of persons, is impossible so
long as Jew and Christian are committed to the religio-historic
myths of their respective communities. For the Jew who holds
firmly to the doctrine of the election of Israel and the Torah as the
sole content of God's revelation to mankind, the Christian insistence upon the decisive character of the Christ-event in human
history must be at best error and at worst blasphemy. For the
Christian who is convinced that the Divine-human encounters
recorded in Scripture find their true meaning and fulfillment in
the Cross, Jews are at best the blind who cannot see; at worst,
they are the demonic perverters, destroyers, and betrayers of mankind's true hope for salvation. There is no way in which these
positions can be mediated or diluted if they are held to be absolutely and unquestionably true. Not only do the mythic contents
of our religious faiths impede meaningful community; they absolutely preclude it.

Nevertheless, meaningful and friendly relations do exist
between Jew and Christian. In spite of all the impediments which
we know too well, Jews and Christians have frequently lived
together in harmony and friendship. In my own country this is
due to the fact that the religious factor, while undoubtedly a
powerful influence, is by no means the predominating element
in most human relations. Americans lack a talent for ideological
consistency. This may be an intellectual flaw. It is, however, an
enormous human and interpersonal advantage. The simple pragmatic concern to find a way to make a social situation work is
extremely important. American society is neither ethnically nor
religiously homogeneous. A multiplicity of elements enter into
social relations, of which the religious factor is by no means pre-
dominant. To the extent that men are prepared to risk the openness of encounter with no preconceived ideological intrusions,

meaningful relations between Jew and Christian are possible. Let us, however, recognize that a dilution of the mythic factor is involved. One partial solution to the problem of the meeting of persons would seem to be the pragmatic approach of allowing ideas and myths concerning Jew and Christian which are not necessarily consistent to coexist. This approach is probably the most realistic. It reflects the fact that people confront one another in a multiplicity of roles and relationships, that they are probably better off when they develop a tolerance for ambiguity which allows them a freedom in encounter which utter theological consistency would withhold. This may be the best that can be expected. It is limited by the fact that the mythic element can always overwhelm the pragmatic in times of stress.

Another possibility which has held a great attraction for many Jews has been the commitment to secular society devoid of any contact with religion. I am convinced that the root of Jewish atheism and secularism in modern times was always the insight that Jewish suffering could not be separated from the Judaeo-Christian conflict. If only religion could be totally eliminated, no further problem of the alienation of brother from brother would exist. I cannot share this view, no matter how much I may understand the underlying pathos which motivated it. Because our religious myths preclude that genuine meeting of persons which is the essence of true community, it does not follow that we can place our hopes in a completely secularized society. Society will always exhibit characteristic flaws. In our times, the ever-widening extension of the domain of technical rationality in our secular society of contract presents its own special threat to the genuine community of persons. With the growth of urban communities and their characteristic anonymity of persons, with the increased specialization of labor and the concomitant alienation of the individual from a meaningful relationship to his own creative capacities, and with the proliferation of dehumanizing modes of competence in the management of human affairs, the religious factor tends to disappear. Here, however, the disappearance contributes to, rather than diminishes, the depersonalization and dehumanization of social encounter. The conflict between Christian and Jew seems to be minimized, because a society of myth is replaced by a society of calculation and contract. What is needed, however, is a society of persons.

The rational society of contract subjects personal relations to a very high degree of abstraction. In its terminal expression it is possible to forget that we dwell in a human world at all. The icy symmetry of the modern skyscraper harms no one, but it does express the distance we have come in one symbolic area of human expression from the world of the gothic whose genius it was to embody and objectify the unconscious of mankind in stone. The worst expression of this world occurs when the vocabulary of mass murder is so sterilized by terms like *"Lösungsmöglichkeit,"* *"Sonderbehandlung,"* *"Evakuierung,"* and others that it is possible to ignore the fact that human beings are being annihilated. This is, however, the final manifestation of a dehumanizing process which is everywhere apparent in some measure throughout the Western world.

In its less pathological forms, such an abstract society runs counter to our earliest and most decisive experiences of social encounter. Our earliest modes of relationship are emotionally determined. Let us go further and agree with Freud that they are erotic in character. We never really forget this paradigmatic experience of the primacy of *eros* in social encounter. The alienating rationality of so much of adult social organization is undoubtedly indispensable to the successful functioning of our highly complex civilization. Nevertheless, in a very deep sense, this complex world is experienced as an expulsion from Eden. To the extent that we have achieved sufficient personal competence to be self-actualizing, we can accept the social necessity of being treated abstractly and impersonally, without so regarding ourselves. The autonomous individual can recognize and accept the necessity of this loss of *eros* in social encounter without losing his sense of inner worth or identity. He knows that there is absolutely no way of turning back the clock either to the experience of childhood or to the earlier homogeneous ethnic communities which once predominated throughout Europe and America. The trend toward super-culture is irreversible. Yet when appropriate occasions arise for meaningful relations between persons, he stands ready for them.

Neither the abstractions of a depersonalized secular society nor the dehumanizing myths of a religious society are ultimately conducive to that community of persons which alone offers hope that the fragile human enterprise will not break asunder through its own inner failure. The tragic encounter between Christian and Jew has an importance which transcends itself. James Baldwin has commented that all that white men fear and distrust about themselves is reflected in their image of the Negro. The same can be said of the relation of Christian and Jew. If a human being is incapable of regarding the other as a genuine person, it is because of his incapacity so to regard himself. That is why both religion and contemporary psychoanalytic thought find ultimate agreement in asserting the primacy of love in human relations. In love the disguises and lies with which we hide ourselves from both the other and ourselves are of no avail, for in love all we have to give or withhold is ourselves. Every encounter in which we fail to meet the other as a person, in the openness of I and Thou, is to a degree psychotic. It is a turning away and a failure to be present to the most important reality we have—the reality of human existence. Nor can we fail to meet a single person in encounter without this failure's radically affecting all such meetings. So terrible a failure cannot be compensated for by an ability to handle lesser, safer, and more predictable realities.

Our greatest need is the need to know who we are. Only a person who has gained such knowledge, who has come to terms with himself, can meet the other in openness and fellowship. It is here that a demythologized Judaism and Christianity together hold the contemporary world's best hope. If we concentrate less on what our religious inheritances promise and threaten and more on the human existence which we share through these traditions, we will achieve the superlative yet simple knowledge of who we truly are.

Through our religious traditions we come to a knowledge deeper than words of our guilt, our alienation, and our pathetic finitude. Nothing so humbles and teaches us our true station as do our traditions. Here we see all human projects cast into their proper perspective. We intuit the insurmountable irony of existence. As we pass through life, each crisis of transition and each seasonal renewal is celebrated and marked within a meaningful community. We know where we are on life's road. When finally we return to the Holy Nothingness from which we have come forth, we do not leave our survivers so bereft of resources that our end denies them the openness of the life which yet remains to them.

When I hear the *Agnus Dei* of the Mass, I am separated from my brother in his belief that the Christ is in truth and in fact the Lamb of God who takes away the sins of the world. I cannot join him in his myth. I can, however, join him in common recognition that we are all guilty men, that we all yearn for that precious healing promised by Isaiah: "Though your sins be as scarlet, they shall be made as white as snow."[2] The myth separates me from my brother. What the myth points to unites me with him. This is even true of the person of the Christ. I cannot accept the historicity of the tradition. The historical Jesus remains for me just another Jew. I can, however, share with my brother the complex intersection of promethean self-assertion and pious submission which all men feel before the incarnational reality of the Divine.

No such knowledge is possible in a purely secular society, for it lacks a sense of the tragic. It has yet to know what even the most archaic religions comprehended: that all men are destined to falter and fail. For technical society, failure is an incident and an accident leading to the replacement of older units of manpower with newer units. For the human person, failure is of the very essence. Perhaps one of the most important functions of the religious community in the modern world is that within its domain the person is neither denied nor falsified, as he so frequently is in the corporation or the managerial hierarchy. Productivity can increase from year to year, technology can become ever more adequate, but human beings remain relatively constant. By its emphasis on technical competence and the pathetic illusion of success, secular society breeds the *mauvaise foi,* the "bad faith" which Sartre has so graphically described. Before I can be a person to the

[2] Isaiah 1:18

other, I must forsake the temptation to be a liar to myself, so assiduously bred by success-intoxicated contemporary culture. The whole weight of religious tradition, with its insistent and dramatic reiteration of God's holy majesty and the finitude and creatureliness of man, reminds me over and over again of what I am. Furthermore, it does more than teach us these lessons at the conscious, intellectual level. It allows us to share these truths in the many dimensions which religious ceremony at its highest can elicit. We can in religion share the reality toward which the myth points, but which it can never adequately attempt to express without incurring the sin of idolatry. We have been cast up absurdly and without reason into a world which knows no warmth, concern, care, fellowship, or love save that which we bestow upon one another. The child seeks the gift; the adult would bestow it. Our myths tell us of gifts which await us. We can be far more certain of the need which makes the promise alluring than we can be that the promise will be fulfilled. Since we cannot be brothers in promise, let us at least be brothers in need.

There are no innocent men. Freud's myth of the primal crime may tell us little concerning religious origins, but it can illumine our present predicament. Civilization begins, not with the recognition by brothers of their impeccable virtue, but with the first and awesome discovery of their ineradicable guilt. In the beginning was the deed—the guilty deed. The man who confesses his own potential for murder, and that of his religious tradition, is far more likely to master this potential than the one who refuses this terrible truth about himself. I do not love my sons the less because I am aware of the unconscious parricide dwelling in their psyches. When I see Christian *Heilsgeschichte* as leading potentially to murder, I do not forget its Jewish origin. I can sense the potential murderer in my brother only because I have intuited it in myself. As Christian and Jew we cannot be united in innocence. Let us at least each be united in guilt, leaving it for God alone to weigh each man's measure thereof. If we fail to learn the simple lesson that the community of men is possible only through the encounter of persons rather than of myths or abstractions, we will only doom future generations to repeat the horrible deeds of our times in ways which will arise out of their as yet unrevealed situations. But perhaps out of our tragic common past there can arise a deeper compassion, a deeper mutual involvement, and a deeper sense of the urgency and the perils of the human vocation.

I have been attracted to Reconstructionism for many years. It combines fidelity to Jewish tradition with a lack of institutional rigidity which is unusual in contemporary American Jewish life. It is the only authentically American philosophy of Jewish life, and, through its founder, Mordecai M. Kaplan, it has been shaped by pragmatism. In spite of the recent unparalleled tragedies of Jewish life, it has remained fundamentally optimistic about man and his future.

I have been unable, however, to accept its optimism. I believe that the tragic vision is both more realistic as an account of the human predicament and more consistent with human dignity and maturity. The fundamental truth of the tragic vision is that we pay for what we get. Reconstructionism's rejection of the tragic vision is typically American. It is shared by Harvey Cox in his vision of the secular city as the self-realizing Kingdom of God and by Thomas Altizer in his apocalyptic enthusiasm for the time of the death of God. It is very much the style in current American religious thinking.

I found Reconstructionism's optimism especially untenable in view of the experience of the West in the first half of the twentieth century. The human evil perpetrated in those years could not be dismissed as a sport of history. Man's image of himself and of God was permanently inpaired by what took place.

This essay first appeared in The Reconstructionist *for January 23, 1959. It is a tribute to the openness of that journal that its editors welcomed this criticism within its pages.*

4 / Reconstructionism and the Problem of Evil

SINCE THE 1940's there has been a growth of interest in Jewish theology in the United States. The war experiences, the renaissance of Protestant theology, the new insights of depth psychology, and above all the failure of Judaism to die on schedule in accordance with many of the sociologically oriented predictions of the 1920's, all contributed to the new interest in contemporary Jewish thought.

Much of the thrust of the Jewish existentialists, as with their Protestant counterparts, was directed against the Jewish religious liberalism of the 1930's. For a long time it was the fashion in both religion and politics to damn or recant the errors of the liberalism of the thirties. In Jewish thought, the attack was directed largely against Reconstructionism and the religious philosophy of Mordecai M. Kaplan.

Fortunately fashions change and what was thought to be without merit or outdated is discovered to be significant and contemporary. The thirties was in many ways one of the most creative, individualistic, and novel periods in American life. It was a period of social challenge and intellectual awakening. The experience of the depression and the anticipation of the soon-to-be-fought war gave American intellectual life a social and humanitarian concern which may have been partial but which certainly contained within it elements of continued relevance. Perhaps, if good can be plucked out of misfortune, the continuing pockets of urban poverty may remind a prosperous and suburban America that the problems of yesterday's urban and depression-ridden America were not entirely fictitious.

The Reconstructionist position has been under implicit or explicit attack by those Jewish theologians who assert that Jewish existence is validated by a special relationship to God rather than by Israel's natural historical existence as a people. In one way or another all of the newer theologies, such as those of Will Herberg, Abraham Heschel, Martin Buber, and Arthur Cohen, affirm the centrality of the message of "Praised be Thou, O Lord, our God, who has chosen us from among all peoples," though each would spell out the meaning of this choice and the character of the response differently. They see Reconstructionism's assertion of the primacy of the peoplehood of Israel above the religion as untrue to their understanding of both Scripture and tradition on the one hand and the special peculiarities of Jewish historical experience on the other. Without this supernatural validation, they claim, Jewish existence becomes an absurd concatenation of tragedy and irrational, external malice.

In two recent volumes, Rabbi Jack J. Cohen's *The Case for Religious Naturalism*,[1] and Mordecai M. Kaplan's *Judaism Without Supernaturalism*,[2] the centrality of the peoplehood of Israel as the basic affirmation of Reconstructionism is restated. Thus Rabbi Cohen rejects every attempt to seek a theological definition of Jewish life and experience, though he allows and welcomes theological speculation once it is seen as flowing from the life of the Jewish people instead of as justifying that life. For Rabbi Cohen as for Mordecai Kaplan, the Jewish religion does not arise out of some absolute encounter with the Divine. It has evolved out of the normal development of the community of Israel.

There are many reasons why this insistence upon the ethnic and nonprivileged character of Judaism must be welcomed. If Jewish existence is not self-validating, there is a real danger that what we take to be theological justifications of our existence may turn out to be extensions of thoroughly unhealthy and irrational non-Jewish myths about Jews and Judaism. For two thousand years the assertion that Jewish existence is specially related to

[1] New York: Reconstructionist Press, 1958.
[2] New York: Reconstructionist Press, 1958.

the Divine has been a commonplace of both Jewish and Christian theology. The difference between the two depended upon whether one accepted the belief of Jewish theologians that this relationship continued to be one of special love and concern on God's part for Israel, or whether one accepted the Christian version of the same myth, namely, that the Church had become the true Israel and that the Jews, for the crime of rejecting the Christ, had become the rejected of God. Unfortunately the only proof which the Church could offer was the historical facts of Jewish degradation and disaster. Too often the human psyche has attempted to make reality conform to its myths.

Perhaps the most significant contribution to Jewish self-respect made by Reconstructionism has been its insistence that it is not wrong, impious, or irreligious for Jews to insist that there is no special pre-eminence possessed by Judaism which justifies Jewish existence. A religious group with a strong sense of self-respect need not trouble itself with such justification. Nothing in the fertile and creative theological literature of the forties and fifties has improved on this fundamental insight of Reconstructionism. It continues to be valid today.

Much of Jewish religious naturalism is an attempt to harmonize Judaism with contemporary philosophical naturalism, especially the pragmatism of John Dewey. Like his teacher Mordecai M. Kaplan, Rabbi Cohen justifies his *God-idea* on the basis of the claim that science validates, if it does not prove, that the universe is amenable to human self-fulfillment. Taking account of natural disasters, which he admits offer a strong argument against the contention that nature is amenable to man, he pleads for the pragmatic argument, first suggested by William James, that when confronted with two hypotheses about the nature of reality, neither of which can be proven, we must act upon that hypothesis which is most likely to enhance life. Certainly of the two hypotheses, the one, that nature is antagonistic to human endeavor, and the other, that nature aids in human self-fulfillment, there are strong grounds for acting *as if* the second were true. It may very well be that by acting according to this hypothesis we will validate it.

Nevertheless, it becomes obvious in studying Rabbi Cohen's discussion of both God and naturalism that he is fundamentally concerned about the harmony of religion with the insights of modern physical science, *as if the real challenge to religion came from this quarter*. Undoubtedly it was from this quarter that Rabbi Cohen found his religion challenged; but to many European and American thinkers the real challenge to religion does not come from the order of nature. Rabbi Cohen contends that science has ruled out the possibility of God's conscious interference with an orderly nature. Thus, the reason for not believing in a personal God is taken to be the objections of modern physical science. Yet there is a paradox in this, if it were true, in view of the fact that most students who enter the modern physical sciences as orthodox Jews continue to be orthodox throughout their professional careers. Of course, this should not occasion surprise. The quest for order often leads to religious orthodoxy. The orthodox Jewish intellectual can see in the discipline of the *Halakha* a counterpart of God's wisdom as it is revealed through the insights of the physical sciences. The real challenge comes in the social sciences and in literature. It is here that the limitations, the conflicts, the ironies, and the inevitable tragedies of human existence are felt. Nature is far more sympathetic to human self-fulfillment than is man himself. Man is a problem to himself. Human evil has done far more harm throughout the ages than natural catastrophe. The real objections against a personal or theistic God come from the irreconcilability of the claim of God's perfection with the hideous human evil tolerated by such a God.

In *The Brothers Karamazov,* Dostoevsky puts into the mouth of the atheist Ivan the final, irrefutable, and unanswerable objection to a personal or theistic conception of God. In the chapter on Rebellion, Ivan first offers example after example of the cruelty of man to man and of *God's implication in that cruelty if He has the power to control it*. He then demonstrates that the only possible religious answer is that human suffering will be justified in the final Divine harmony at the end of history. He rejects this suggestion, saying: "I renounce the higher harmony altogether. It's not worth the tears of that one tortured child who beat itself on the breast with its little finger and prayed . . . with its unexpected tears to 'dear God.' "

A God who tolerates the suffering of even one innocent child is either infinitely cruel or hopelessly indifferent. Our ancestors attempted to solve this problem by projecting the existence of another world wherein this world's cruelties would be rectified. We cannot accept such a solution and we would do well to recognize the disguised yet nonetheless strong criticism of God's government of this world implied in their fantasy of another world in which He would ultimately do a better job. Rabbi Cohen is right in insisting that modern man cannot believe in a personal God. Nevertheless, I believe that the moral and psychological objections are more telling than the objections arising from the physical sciences.

Furthermore, there is the problem of God and human freedom. Paul Tillich discusses this problem at great length in his book *The Courage To Be.* It is a far stronger objection to a personal God than the one Rabbi Cohen has suggested. Tillich insists that the God of theism (that is, a personal God) is dead and deserved to die. He claims that a God who stands above all human activity and who controls the cosmos is ultimately the enemy of human self-fulfillment. As Job discovered, we must be in the wrong before such a God. Tillich praises the German philosopher Nietzsche who proclaimed that God is dead. Tillich claims the theistic God is dead and deserved to die because He opposes human freedom. When Tillich's contention that a personal God is the enemy of freedom is compared with Erich Fromm's analysis of the types of human personality which an authoritarian conception of deity either reflected or engendered, it becomes apparent that human moral autonomy is incompatible with the traditional conception of a personal God.

This leads to the question of whether a God-idea can or even should be "that upon which man relies to give meaning to his life," as Rabbi Cohen suggests. Because of his pragmatism, Rabbi Cohen is always concerned with what a thing or an idea *does*. If it does not do something assignable, it is either meaningless or nonexistent. But need the mature man rely upon anything beyond his ability to create his own meanings out of the matrix of responsibilities, destinies, affiliations, roles, and relationships in which he finds himself? From the strictly naturalistic point of

view, I find the suggestion that a God-idea does something toward the creation of meanings both extraneous and unnecessary.
From the psychological point of view it may very well be possible
to show that dependence upon a God-idea for meanings is to
some degree unhealthy. To seek to find life's meanings with the
support of a God-idea is to lean upon a crutch. Men can and ought
to learn to stand upon their own resources. Rabbi Cohen's naturalism is not naturalistic enough. This does not mean that every
man can or should come to an inherently private and subjective
understanding of what life's meanings are for him. Quite the
contrary, the real significance of ethnic religion is that it continually reminds us of the community of experience, wisdom, insight,
and common need which has linked the generations of Israel one
to another. Certain behavior patterns are Jewish and we freely
choose to live in a way in which our ancestors have done, not because we have to, or because we are commanded to, but because
our free understanding of our Jewish situation makes these choices
more rewarding and meaningful than others. There is no necessity
in this, but in a real sense there never was. This does not mean
that there is no God or that a God-conception is meaningless. It is
only meaningless if we accept Rabbi Cohen's implied logic that
only a functional definition—that is, a definition which tells us
what a thing does—is a significant definition. Without going further afield, I should like to suggest that the existence of God is not
bound up with the problem of our assigning identifiable functions
to His nature.

It is the vogue in some Jewish intellectual circles to dismiss
existentialism as essentially the product of Protestant theology and
only relevant within that context. This simply is not factual. Existentialism is in fact a disciplined critique of certain key problems
on the nature of reality. It is an attempt to rediscover the concrete,
the singular, and the particular in human experience.

In his book *The Challenge of Existentialism*[3] John Wild
has called existentialism a triumph of empiricism and rationalism. What he means is that existentialism gave philosophy a
host of new concerns which demanded rational analysis. Among
them were problems such as care, anxiety, guilt and conflict. In

[3] Bloomington, Ind.: 1955.

the twentieth century it is impossible to dismiss these problems, which existentialism has found so central, as irrelevant. Our experience of tragedy, guilt, conflict, and the inherent limitations of human decency have been far too profound to warrant rejecting existentialism's insights as irrelevant. The heavens have a way of going on with or without human contemplation. Man is his own greatest dilemma. The optimism of religious liberalism and of Reconstructionism was their weakest plank, and it has been this unwarranted optimism about man and human possibilities which has given both traditional religious forces and existentialists their greatest weapon against liberalism. Ironically both existentialism and traditional theology can turn Reconstructionism's demand that religion deal with the empirically validated and the provable against it when they attack Reconstructionism's optimistic philosophy of man. Man has proven capable of irredeemable evil.

Contemporary depth psychology has suggested that the growth of the restrictive demands of civilization upon the sparse ability of the human animal to discipline himself creates dilemmas which will never be solved. Guilt, ambivalence, human evil, and human aggressiveness are as inescapable as human love, affection, and self-sacrifice. They are inextricably bound together. Reconstructionism has demanded that religion face the challenge of modernism, yet it has consistently refused to meet this challenge in its doctrine of man. This century has never been called the century of John Dewey. It has frequently been called the century of Freud. One does not have to call forth the Protestant doctrine of original sin to sense the human desolation of our times. If anything, the Protestant doctrine has had a renewed vogue because it seemed so much closer to the real facts than the optimism of liberalism. Freud was deeply pessimistic about human potentialities, though few men ever lived who had less concern for validating theological doctrines than he. I do not want to suggest that the Protestant doctrine of original sin is entirely correct and that we Jews must find a way to incorporate it into contemporary Jewish theology. I am appealing for the same empiricism, naturalism, and fidelity to what the best in current science has said about this problem that Rabbi Cohen has insisted on in his discussion of what turns out to be not all of science but physical science. Were he to be as naturalistic in his doctrine of man as he has been elsewhere, he would see man as essentially a tragic, ironic figure of extremely limited possibilities. He would certainly reject the conception of this-worldly or other-worldly salvation as an illusion. In a real sense every human advance is also a retreat; salvation is unattainable. Only a modicum of ability on the part of the mature man to make the most of what he is and has and to learn to love his necessities can be expected in a universe which is *not* so constituted as to make for human satisfaction.

Behind the pragmatic arguments of some religious naturalists that we must act as if this world were capable of fulfilling human salvation is their fear that a radical pessimism about human possibilities will stultify all attempts to make the most of man's limited existence. I think this is both factually untrue and psychologically unsound. There is something morally and psychologically satisfying in making the very best one can of a limited and tragic existence. Nor is it the gloomy and humorless philosophy that it is often represented as being. Reality is infinitely more comforting than fiction, even the fictions with which we falsely attempt to deceive ourselves. Man can learn to live in a world without myth or fantasy about himself or his possibilities. Freud is a very good case in point. His pessimism did not prevent him from devoting his life to the task of liberating men from those unnecessary and unreal fears which enslaved them. The knowledge that life is bracketed between two oblivions does not cause life to stop nor does it make those joys which are attainable less joyful. Pragmatism and naturalism are not the only possible philosophic allies. It is quite possible to insist on a religion devoid of the miraculous, the arbitrary, and the unscientific without resting it upon the insights of John Dewey. If anything, this philosophic superstructure is outdated and a distinct handicap.

Finally, existentialism must acknowledge its debt to religious liberalism.

Religious liberalism was wrong on many issues, yet on those issues of freedom, choice, pluralism, and voluntarism which were at the heart of its message, it was and continues to be right. Many are the appellations men have given to God. Not the least of them is Truth.

Few aspects of contemporary Jewish theology offer as much promise as a reconsideration of the abiding relevance of the sacrificial elements of the liturgy. For the past century Jewish thinkers of all schools have tended to be acutely embarrassed by the sacrificial survivals in our tradition.

I have come to believe that the archaic elements in religion are often the most meaningful. We need not be enslaved to them because we recognize their abiding significance. I do not see man as capable of much improvement through homiletic exhortation, but rather, as a creature of inescapable conflicts which he but barely understands. He cannot abide the very disciplines and limitations he recognizes as absolutely necessary for his own preservation. He needs the drama and the consolation of religion as much to share his inevitable failings as to be encouraged to further striving.

Sacrifice is the drama of man's hatred of God and his ultimate submission to him. Men cannot come into the sanctuary and declare to God, "I hate You and would destroy Your order if I could." They can achieve catharsis by symbolically acting out that hatred through ritual violence against the sacrificial victim without even being consciously aware of what they are doing. I suspect that almost all sacrificial victims are ultimately surrogates for God, if not the symbolic presence of God Himself. In sacrifice, we overcome God and, at the very same moment, we submit and recognize His inevitable victory.

5/ *Atonement and Sacrifice in Contemporary Jewish Liturgy*

A<small>N AURA OF EMBARRASSMENT</small> hangs over the treatment of sacrifice in contemporary Jewish liturgy. This embarrassment undoubtedly reflects the very old tension between the priestly and the prophetic aspects of Judaism. In modern times, the movement to exclude the recitation of sacrificial readings from Reform Jewish liturgy has been one expression of a perennial problem. However, antipathy to the idea of ritual sacrifice has been by no means confined to Reform Judaism. Conservative Jews "remember" the offering of sacrifice in the Jerusalem sanctuary in their Sabbath and Holy Day *musaf* services, but they omit the traditional petitions for its restoration.[1] Orthodox Jews usually offer dogmatic appeals to Scriptural authority in their defense; seldom, if ever, do they offer a reasoned analysis of the relevance of the sacrificial prayers for contemporary Jewish life. There are, however, important reasons why the symbolic assertion of the primacy of sacrifice ought to be retained as a central element in Jewish religious life.

The modern embarrassment with sacrifice runs counter to the fact that sacrificial ritual, in real or symbolic expression, has been one of the most universally accepted activities in the majority of the religions of mankind. Though prayer, contemplation, and moral exhortation undoubtedly have played an important role in religion, they are late expressions of a tendency which has been

---

[1] Cf. *Sabbath and Festival Prayer Book* (New York: Rabbinical Assembly and United Synagogue of America, 1946), pp. 140, 150.

by no means universal. In the nineteenth century, under Protestant influence, there was a tendency in "enlightened" Jewish
circles dogmatically to regard the priestly tradition and its liturgical heritage as inferior to the prophetic. Sacrificial ritual was regarded as "primitive" and was contrasted with the superior
"spiritual" qualities of prophetic religion and morality.[2] Above
all, the ethical and moral fruits of the religious life were stressed
as central and decisive. Prophetic religion alone was regarded as
true religion. It was thought to be the culmination of mankind's

[2] The idea of the sacrificial order of the Day of Atonement as an
impediment to genuine spiritual growth is clearly expressed by Leo
Baeck, a representative thinker on the subject: "So long as Judaism
recognized the validity of the sacrificial service, the clear distinctiveness
of the idea of atonement was subject to a certain limitation. . . . It [the
sacrificial system] was a valuable means for education of the people. But
once the idea of atonement was understood *in its true significance* . . . the
sin-offering, and with it the entire sacrificial system, became obsolete. . . .
By the *substitution of the good deed* which is the worship of God in actual
life for an offering on the altar, the *idea* and the *ethical significance* of
the sacrificial service were retained intact. Sacrifice steps out of the Temple, the forecourt of life, into real life; atonement and repentance enter
into their innermost sanctuary, the human heart." Leo Baeck, *The Essence
of Judaism* (New York: Schocken Books, 1948), pp. 167–69 (italics
mine).

Geiger, perhaps the best nineteenth-century Reform thinker,
expressed a similar disdain for sacrifice: "But animal sacrifice is no less
the expression of a low religious sentiment. . . . Nor did animal sacrifice
spring from the soil of Judaism; it was tolerated, and only tolerated; it
was continually inveighed against by Israel's best and noblest men, the
prophets, who point out its low degrees in the most emphatic terms."
Abraham Geiger, *Judaism and Its History,* tr. Charles Neuburgh (New
York: Bloch Publishing Co., 1911), pp. 64 ff.

In nineteenth-century Protestant thought, Wellhausen's conceptions are deeply influential. He regarded the prophetic criticism of ritual
as the real climax of Israel's religious development. The cultus of the
Priestly code was, in his opinion, the beginning of the degeneration of
Israel's religion, from which it was only saved by Jesus. Cf. Herbert H.
Hahn, *The Old Testament in Modern Research* (London: SCM Press,
1956) pp. 12–27.

development toward ever more significant religious and moral attainments. A negative judgment was pronounced upon those forms of religion which continued to stress the sacrificial and the cultic. The Mass in Roman Catholicism was, for example, regarded as a retrograde concession to the ineradicable paganism of the gentile world.

The problem of the sacrificial recitations is perhaps most insistent in connection with the great liturgy of the Day of Atonement. Traditionally the Scriptural reading for the morning service on that day is a verbal re-enactment of the archaic sacrificial rite of atonement in which the High Priest cast lots between two animal victims, choosing one as the offering within the Sanctuary and utilizing the other as the scapegoat, upon which were placed symbolically the sins of the congregation of Israel.[3] Through the death of the scapegoat, atonement was said to have been effectuated for the entire congregation of Israel. The animal laden with the sins of the people went forth to its rocky destruction as an atonement for and in place of the people. *At the heart of Yom Kippur is the conception of vicarious ritual atonement.*

Although this doctrine lies at the heart of both the Yom Kippur ritual and Christianity, few Jews can feel altogether comfortable with it. Too frequently, the Jewish community has itself been the vicarious victim used by the sick and the psychotic as a magic sacrifice for their own guilts and misfortunes. The tragedies of Jewish life have lent a very real measure of repugnance to the scapegoat theme. The recitation of the Scriptural account of the archaic atonement rite has been completely eliminated from the Reform Jewish liturgy for the Day of Atonement. Instead, a reading from Deuteronomy (29:9–14; 30:11–20) has been substituted in which Moses exhorts the people to choose the way of life, blessing, and goodness rather than death, evil, and the curse.

This substitution of moral exhortation for sacerdotal atonement is typical of modern Judaism. Contemporary Jewish religious sentiment has tended to stress the element of moral decision and the capacity to meet and fulfill this exhortation while

[3] Lev. 16:1–34.

underplaying the element of ritual atonement.[4] This stress presumes that the religiously inspired choice of virtue is in fact a real option for most people. Although Conservative Judaism has not gone so far as Reform Judaism in eliminating the Scriptural reference to atonement and sacrifice, the Silverman High Holiday Prayer Book, which is almost universally used by Conservative congregations, precedes the English translation of this central reading from Scripture with an explanatory note, not lacking in apologetic tones, suggesting that the Scriptural reading has a historical interest but that we have "advanced" to a "higher" conception of religion than that implicit in the sacrificial recitations.[5]

It remains, however, strange that an institution of such universality, which even today has by no means lost its significance for the majority of mankind, should contain so little import for contemporary Jewish religion. Few terms are in any event as deceptive as "higher" or "advanced." They presuppose an implicit standard of reference which often reveals more about the person making the judgment than it does concerning the true nature of the subject matter at hand. It is doubtful that the matter will withstand disciplined scrutiny. A very good point of departure would seem to be the Day of Atonement liturgy.

It would seem that in both Biblical and rabbinic Judaism the object of seeking atonement on Yom Kippur was *to come to terms with one's failure to fulfill the religious and moral standards* accepted by the congregation as valid and binding on one and all. The participant sought through confession, repentance, and the shared knowledge that he was by no means alone in his failings,

[4] Again Geiger is instructive: "Judaism establishes itself as a religion that adores God as the Holy One, as the ideal of moral purity, by the fact that it invariably emphasizes moral worth also in its human relations. . . . Justice, the pure, moral relation between man and man, is its highest consideration. . . ." Geiger, *op. cit.*, pp. 61 ff; Cf. Baeck, *op. cit.*, p. 130: "To the Jew the unity of God finds its essential expression in the unity of the ethical. . . . As monotheism means the one God, so it also means the one command and the one righteousness."

[5] *High Holiday Prayer Book,* ed. Morris Silverman (Hartford: Prayer Book Press, 1939), p. 310.

to achieve religious and ethical renewal and purgation. No one came to the atonement rites as an innocent. The very basis for participation was that members of a guilty community confessed, acknowledged, and sought atonement for their sins. One of the most important needs which the Day served was that of catharsis. In addition to making confession for conscious religious and moral failure, the requirement that the participant make confession in the *al het* prayer for such sins as theft, violence, murder, and sexual misdeed suggests that on Yom Kippur one confessed not only actual sins but also sins committed in fantasy as well. No one comes to the celebration of this day with a feeling of moral success and attainment;[6] in some measure every Jew comes with a sense of moral and religious failure. Furthermore, enough is now known about the way people feel about themselves for us to say that, though they may publicly assert their indifference to moral and religious failure, the vast majority are nevertheless deeply troubled by their own sense of guilt. While the great atonement ritual is in one sense only a palliative and does not necessarily guarantee moral or religious renewal, the history of Calvinism offers ample evidence of the anguish to which men have been driven once the institutionalized modes of atonement and confession are no longer available.[7]

The central reality of Yom Kippur is the sharing of moral failure rather than the celebration of moral success. Few guilts are as difficult to bear as the feeling that the individual in his transgression is entirely isolated from his peers. One of the most

[6] Apart from the judgment of common sense that no man is ever entirely blameless, the rabbinic doctrine of the *yetzer ha-ra,* the evil inclination, postulated an ineradicable tendency toward behavioral deviance in all men. Cf. *Tanhuma,* Noah, 4, ed. S. Buber; J. Ta'anit 66c; Sukkah 52b (where the evil inclination is seen as the special affliction of scholars); and George Foote Moore, *Judaism* (Cambridge: Harvard University Press, 1927), I, 474–96.

[7] Weber is of course the *locus classicus* of this type of sociological analysis. Cf. Max Weber, *The Protestant Ethic and the Spirit of Capitalism* (New York: Charles Scribner's Sons, 1958), pp. 99–118; Ernst Troeltsch, *The Social Teachings of the Christian Churches,* tr. Olive Wyon (London: Allen and Unwin, 1931), II, 581–629; and Erich Fromm, *Escape from Freedom* (New York: Rhinehart and Co., 1941),pp. 84–98.

terrible aspects of the sense of guilt is that it tends to isolate the deviant, cutting him adrift from the community and fellowship of his peers. Since all human beings are in some measure guilty, we would be a "lonely crowd" indeed were it not for the knowledge that our guilt is no dark peculiarity which isolates each of us from our fellows. One of the most important functions of the atonement ritual is that, through communal confession and acknowledgment of guilt, the penitent is assured that his is the shared predicament of mankind. While this does not solve the problem of guilt, it makes it a common concern rather than the hidden secret of the private individual. Guilt, which threatens to fragment the community into individuals who must hide their deepest selves from one another and dishonestly pretend to an impossible show of virtue, becomes through the Day of Atonement an abiding mode of uniting the community and giving it a sense of common need and common program.

A discouraging aspect of the Day of Atonement can be the memory of past purgations and past resolutions to lead a life in the year to come significantly better than in the old year. Few such resolutions are kept and the hoped-for improvement hardly ever comes. After a while, the memory of so dreary an incapacity to effectuate real improvement can lead to a sense of the utter futility of the whole ritual. Yet this seldom if ever occurs. Something in the ritual draws us back to it in spite of the futility of years of resolutions made and broken. Were the ritual merely one of repentance and new resolve, it would quickly end in a debilitating sense of its own futility. There is, as we know, in the traditional celebration of the Day another element which transforms the Day and gives it its perennial character. That element is sacrifice, which, whether expressed symbolically or in reality, focuses our attention dramatically on the fact that we have assembled to share our failure as well as our resolutions for future virtue.

In sacrifice, there is a tragic intersection of contradictory motives. It is a very potent though altogether nonverbal teacher of the limits of human moral possibilities. Those who object to the retention of the sacrificial mode of religious life are quite correct in pointing out that the sacrificial act, when actually committed, is a violent and bloody deed. Even when it is committed only verbally, the emotional overtones of violence are not entirely lost. Those who reject sacrifice would remove mankind from occasions for violence, especially within the domain of the sacred. The sacrificial act is one in which a life is taken away in all innocence. That it is an animal life does not make the deed less distressing, as anyone knows who has witnessed the death of an animal. Another element that makes the death of the victim so distressing is the historical knowledge that the animal is a surrogate and that the real intended victim was originally a human being of pre-eminent importance to the community. In the very act of seeking an end to guilt, the community commits a violent act which is but a thinly disguised surrogate for its real desire, which is both to end crime and to continue its commission. Promethean self-assertion and penitent submission awesomely interact. With dramatic force which no conceptualization can match, the terrible lesson is borne in on the community that it has only the choice of controlled, regulated violence or irrational and uncontrolled violence. In sacrifice, guilt is partially overcome by its dramatic limitation. It is never done away with entirely.

In this connection, it is important to remember how deeply the laws of *kashruth* are rooted in and are the result of the sacramental aspects of Jewish religious existence. When all of the bad apologies and misrepresentations of *kashruth* have been offered, the fact remains that the whole system of *kashruth* was an extension of Israel's sacrificial system and that it was a response to the very obvious fact that eating is one of the most difficult, problematic, and indispensable acts of the human person. It is not and never can be a simple secular act with no emotional overtones beyond those of balanced nutrition and the satisfaction of hunger. Many of the deepest dilemmas of personality center about the problem of eating. It is emotionally overdetermined.[8] *Kashruth* dramatically emphasizes the fact that eating is a matter of high

[8] Cf. Bertram Lewin's elaboration of the dynamics of the "oral triad," the three related wishes to eat, be eaten, and sleep, in his *The Psychoanalysis of Elation* (New York: W. W. Norton, 1950), pp. 102 ff. Cf. Erik H. Erikson, *Childhood and Society* (New York: W. W. Norton, 1950), pp. 67–75; and Otto Fenichel, *The Psychoanalytic Theory of Neurosis* (New York: W. W. Norton, 1945), pp. 62–66, 389 ff, 488 ff.

and utter seriousness and that it is worthy of a place among the ultimate concerns of mankind.

Long before the dilemmas of orality were made conceptually explicit in psychoanalytic research, these dilemmas were intuited and dramatically regulated within Judaism. No one would pretend that *kashruth* solves all oral dilemmas; its extraordinary importance lies precisely in the fact that it represents an intuitive recognition and a dramatic focusing of attention upon them. Life exists only through the destruction and the incorporation of other life. All human beings are unconsciously tempted to some cannibalism[9] and this manifests itself in the psychic posture of every personality. The problems of orality cannot be solved by pretending they do not exist. Here, as well as in every other significant human striving, normative Judaism has always been as responsive to the covert and the unconscious as it has to the conscious and the rational. The key to understanding Judaism's basic method of dealing with such problems is that Judaism never sought to abolish what could in any event not be abolished. Instead it sought to limit and channelize emotions and strivings which become hopelessly destructive without such limitation. This is true of *kashruth,* which makes of every meal a sacramental act; it is also true of the sacrificial order in tradition. It is not surprising that those who sought to abolish the one also sought to abolish the other.

Sacrifice, even when expressed only verbally, is an infinitely more disturbing mode of religious life than either prayer or moral exhortation. *It is utterly impossible for the participant in the sacrificial act to have the same picture of himself as the person whose religious life is limited to prayer and the affirmation of certain propositions of conscious belief concerning the nature of God and concerning man's ultimate place in the cosmos.* A religion which stresses the latter realities can usually never do more than reach the level of rational, conscious decision in the worshipper. The worshipper is given a series of alternatives concerning what he may believe and do. He is asked freely to make a conscious decision in favor of one pattern of behavior and belief over another. At no point is there a hint of the irony, the am-

[9] Cf. Lewin, *op. cit.,* pp. 129–34.

biguity, and the hidden complexities of affirmation and denial which are involved in all human decision-making. Such religious activity is largely addressed to the conscious *ego* and has nothing to say to the unconscious elements in the makeup of the participant.

It is of course no accident that prophetic religion has always tended to a certain aesthetic barrenness. The contrast between the embellishments of the Gothic cathedral of the twelfth century and the New England church is very much to the point; the same contrast can be seen between the relative freedom of emotional expression in the traditional Jewish service and the insistence on "decorousness" which characterized the rise of modern Judaism. A religion which stresses free rational decision and which distinguishes itself by well-defined propositions concerning the nature of the cosmos and man's place within it is bound to be aesthetically and emotionally impoverished. The worshipper is exhorted to moral uprightness and charged to affirm certain highly dubious propositions concerning man's relation to God as the essence of his religion. Nothing is suggested concerning the failure to perform and the failure to believe which are so frequent among those who nevertheless feel themselves drawn to the consolation of the religious community. Religious failure is simply regarded as undeserving of a place within the Holy Community.[10] All that the guilty man can hear is the exhortation to cease being guilty.

[10] Both Troeltsch and Weber make use of the sociological distinction between the *church* type and *sect* type of religious organization. Troeltsch stresses the importance of the sect in Protestantism as does Weber. Weber says: "Affiliation with the *church* is, in principle, obligatory and hence proves nothing with regard to the member's qualities. A *sect,* however, is a voluntary association of only those who, according to the principle, are religiously and morally qualified." Max Weber, "The Protestant Sects and the Spirit of Capitalism," in H. H. Gerth and C. Wright Mills, *From Max Weber: Essays in Sociology* (New York: Oxford University Press, 1946), p. 306. Religious groups which stress moral decision and the church as the community of the righteous, saved, or elect are usually sect types. Since the member is presumably among the blessed, little is done by way of providing for rites of confession or atonement, and *public* moral failure usually leads to expulsion from the sect. The

But is this not cruelly to rub salt on pathetically open wounds? No one knows as deeply as does the guilty man that he cannot meet such expectations. He is not a participant in the religious community in order to be told to be a better human being but because of his recognition that he is incapable of being better. Telling him to improve does nothing but emphasize his sense of isolation and heighten the inner fragmentation of an already fragmented community. Such exhortation may create a society of rugged individuals in which each man is in the deepest sense for himself, but it cannot end the sense of hopeless alienation which so frequently attends guilt.[11] All that such a religious community can share is virtue and success. In sacrifice, whether real or symbolic, failure is shared in the act itself. It is this which takes the futility out of Yom Kippur. In the religion of moral exhortation, there is no real place for such sharing.

There is usually a direct relationship between one's religious posture and one's social standing. Since Weber, sociologists of religion have been aware that religious practice is very likely to influence economic and social standing. The naïve belief that the richest members of the community tend to be Reform Jews because the Reform synagogue is a kind of comfortable social club presents a very partial and oversimplified view of the

---

result is a separation of the conscious levels of conforming and public behavior from the more hidden private levels of inner moral struggle and failure. There is obviously an increase in hypocrisy. In the church-type group, both the saved and the doubtful are regarded as members. Moral failure does not lead to expulsion. Rites of reparation, confession, and atonement are available. A "scarlet woman" could never openly practice her "profession" and retain membership in a small-town, sect-type Protestant church. There would be no impediment to her membership in a Catholic church, where the fact of her "profession" might lead her to greater use of its resources for confession and atonement than more morally conventional members. Cf. Troeltsch, *op. cit.,* II, 461 ff.

[11] An element in the feeling of guilt is the anxiety over the *loss of love* which originates in the child's earliest relations with the mother and is the core of later feelings of isolation and estrangement which attend guilt. Cf. Fenichel, *op. cit.,* pp. 44, 123, 136. For a theological description of the same phenomenon, cf. Paul Tillich, *Systematic Theology* (London: James Nesbet, 1957), II, 77–84.

actual relationships. There is a readily observable relationship between the social and economic standing of members of a community and the type of religious life current in that community. As a rule, the religious life of the upper and managerial classes, outside of Roman Catholicism, tends to be decorous and controlled. The wilder vagaries of religious emotion seem to be definitely prevalent among the lower classes. Furthermore, Protestantism, with its rejection of Roman Catholic ceremonialism, provided an earlier and more fruitful soil for the growth of capitalism than did Catholicism. Religions which stress rational decision tend to be hostile to the emotional side of faith. This is as true of "classical" Reform Judaism as it is of Calvinism. They encourage and/or reflect tendencies among their members to regard the world as a place to be mastered rationally rather than enjoyed with any degree of emotion. The lonely rugged individualist passing as a stranger through a world which has given him far more of its bounty than he can possibly enjoy, if indeed there is much beyond mere acquisition which he can enjoy, is typical of such traditions. By way of contrast, an important aspect of the sacrificial act is its corporate character. Those who participate are aware of their unity in both common consumption and common guilt. Robertson Smith has pointed out that one of the oldest functions of sacrifice among the early Semites was to provide a concrete mode of expressing the corporate unity of all participant members of the sacrificial community.[12] By consuming a common offering, the participants became one body in a real as well as a symbolic sense. There can be no such thing as a world of isolated rugged individuals in the sacrificial traditions.

Futhermore, the customary dichotomy between the sacrificial and the moral types of religion cannot withstand examination. Shalom Spiegel has suggested that the Ten Commandments may have originally been a "torah of entry" prescribing the proper religious and moral requirements which were encumbent upon the participant before he might partake of the sacrificial offering. He has also contended that Psalm 24:3–4 ought to be read as a ritualized question and answer in which the prescriptions for

[12] W. Robertson Smith, *The Religion of the Semite* (Edinburgh, 1888), pp. 239 ff., 254 ff.

participation in the sacrificial offering are prescribed. Thus, "Who shall ascend the mountain of the Lord? and Who shall stand in His holy place?" asks the question as to who may in fact participate. The answer is given in the following verse: "He that hath clean hands and a pure heart; who hath not lifted up his soul in falsehood, and hath not sworn deceitfully."[13]

In Roman Catholicism, the Mass is an extraordinarily important source of moral control. One cannot participate in the sacrifice of the Mass while in a state of sin. To do so would be to make a fool of God rather than face the suspicion and hostility of one's fellow men. Graham Greene has illustrated this very well in his novel, *The Heart of the Matter*. An adulterous police inspector knows that if he refrains from taking Holy Communion, he will betray himself to his already suspicious wife. He is faced with the choice of alleviating his wife's suspicions by illicitly taking the wafer in a state of unpardoned sin at the cost of alienation from God, or of making peace with God but betraying his adultery. He very humanly chooses to deceive his wife and in this act finds his downfall as a human being.[14] The sacrifice, both in ancient Israel and in modern Catholicism, was far more an instrument of social and moral control than its opponents understood. Only those who had adequately purged themselves of both hidden and revealed sins could properly enter the full domain of the sacred. Few sins were more terrible than participation in the sacrifice while unfit. No comparable mode of purification exists where religion consists of moral exhortation and ethical preachment. There is no objective act which is the center and the focus of the demand for inner purification as there is in the domain of the sacred.

Of course, the real objection to sacrificial worship is that it is a thinly disguised surrogate for an original human sacrifice. Sacrificial ritual has its roots in murder. One of the most consistently praised tokens of the "superiority" of Judaism over the ancient

[13] Cf. Shalom Spiegel, "Prophetic Attestation of the Decalogue: Hosea 6:5, With Some Observations on Psalms 15 and 34," *Harvard Theological Review*, April 1934.

[14] Graham Greene, *The Heart of the Matter* (New York: Viking Press, 1948).

pagan cults was that Judaism, especially prophetic Judaism, had eliminated such inhuman barbarities. Yet there is a bit more of a puzzle here than some are perhaps prepared to allow. Some of the greatest and even most humane civilizations the world has ever known, civilizations to which our own owes many a debt, were not above the practice of human sacrifice. The contrast between the Eden-like character of the South Sea Islands and the barbarity of their religious cults has struck more than one American writer.[15] Ritual murder and ritual cannibalism have been extremely widespread among the religions of mankind, and in Christianity the Mass or Holy Communion is a symbolic return to one mode of ritual cannibalism.

Implicit in all ritual murder is the hope or conviction that the death of the victim will forestall or prevent the death of the whole community. In many ancient religions the king had to be sacrificed as soon as he manifested any sign of decay or weakness. Since the king was the bearer of the blessings of the community, the health and well-being of the group was regarded as in some sense dependent upon him. Lingering failure had to be avoided at all costs. Thus one of the king's most important functions was to die for his community. In other rituals a criminal or a person of significant evil was done away with in order that his impurity or guilt not affect adversely the community.[16] One wonders whether the public beheadings and hangings which were until recently so popular in Europe were not in some measure secularized versions of the same ritual magic act. Even today's "humane" capital punishment undoubtedly has overtones of ritual murder. Certainly nothing else of value is thereby accomplished.

The rational and enlightened man of the twentieth century will immediately protest: "All such ritual murders are the product of magic thinking and superstition; no human being or even animal can possibly accomplish any alleviation of another's

[15] Cf. James Baird, *Ishmael: A Study in the Symbolic Mode of Primitivism* (New York: Harper Torchbooks, 1960), pp. 83–121.

[16] This subject is well covered in James George Frazier, *The New Golden Bough,* ed. Theodore Gaster (New York: Criterion Books, 1959), pp. 223–78. Gaster's notes bring Frazier's epoch-making study up to date.

guilt by its own suffering or death. Nothing could be a more pointless or gratuitous destruction. It is important that mankind
achieve sufficient rationality to realize the futility of such magic."

It is at this point that we encounter the crux of the difference between the prophetic moralist, who seeks ethical improvement by rational and exhortatory means, and the cultic participant. *At the heart of the sacrificial system lies the unspoken conviction that human beings are more likely to repeat their failings
and their characteristic modes of behavior from one generation
to the next than they are to improve upon them.* Where the
prophet is constantly dissatisfied with the moral state of the community as he finds it, the priest is very doubtful that much can be
done to change human nature; his effort is directed primarily at
making the best of a not entirely perfect creation.

If one could invent a sophisticated priestly answer to our
rationalist's call for the elimination of magic and superstition in
religion, it might conceivably sound something like this:

"I know as well as you do that the sacrificial cults were
magic palliatives which did not in actuality cleanse the community
of either guilt or evil, but I am also convinced that any attempt to
take *controlled* magic out of religion will not result in greater
rationality or insightful behavior but in periodic outbursts of devastatingly *uncontrolled* irrationality. Only a few men, at the very
most, have the capacity to attain the kind of rational behavior and
insight which you demand of the entire community. They have
attained this insight after years of the greatest possible inner struggle. If you take magic away from the generality of mankind, you
will not make them more rational but more dangerously superstitious. Oh, I know that some of my colleagues have perpetrated
bloody horrors in the name of religion. Thousands of human
beings have had their lives cut off before their proper time so that
by their deaths they might serve as the vicarious atonement and
purgative for others far more guilty. We who countenanced these
terrible deeds bear a terrible guilt, but we are not so guilty as those
who altogether abolished them.

"I have no quarrel with those who changed human sacrifices into animal sacrifices. The magic thinking of the multitude
and its quest for a cleansing blood remained satisfied. I stand in
especial horror of those who abolished sacrifice altogether. The net

result can only be an enormous increase of seemingly gratuitous criminality in times of stress when the thin pose of rationality disappears from the generality of mankind. Ritual murder is the magic attempt to avoid guilt and danger by the death of another. Do you regard the death of six million Jews as anything but a colossal ritual murder carried out on the vastest possible scale? Do you think that all of the barbarities of ancient paganism could ever equal the enormity of this modern barbarity? What difference is there between Auschwitz where the death of millions of Jews was a ghastly scapegoat offering of the Germans and the scapegoat offering of the ancient pagans save that the ancient pagans, *recognizing human nature for what it was*, never let it get entirely out of hand.

"I would not want to suggest that there is a danger of mass murder on a day-to-day basis in modern society, but I am aware of how thin is the veneer of civilization, rationality, and morality in any society. Normally this delicately textured fabric will maintain itself, but in times of great communal stress, such as war, depression, or national frustration, people become very different from what they seem when things are going well. Your modern psychoanalysts use the term regression to describe what happens in these times; our ancient priests knew that people came to us in greatest need at just these times.

"Nor did we disappoint them. We did not exhort them to a goodness which the stress of events precluded, but neither did we permit things to get entirely out of hand. Never did the community disintegrate into a cannibal horde in which the order of the day was that of *bellum omnes contra omnes*. We satisfied their magic hunger for a victim and scapegoat, at times with innocent human beings and later, happily, with animals, but *we always limited the destructivness of these periods of stress*. This we were able to do because we understood clearly how little human nature could be changed. Today we have largely lost the field, at least among Jews and Protestants. The rationalists have gained control and people seem to have lost their thirst for victims. Were they asked to restore the practice of animal sacrifice, people would protest vehemently against this limited, controlled destructiveness as inhumane and barbaric. Yet never in history has the thirst for the violent and the inhumane been as great as it is today among the 'civilized.' A veritable pornography of violence floods forth in literature, in the cinema, and in television. Insensitivity to human suffering is greater than ever, and the carnivals of death have reached proportions which the ancients never knew.''

Of course, this sophisticated priest lives in the no-land of Erewhon. What is important is that our cultural perspectives not be limited by the very special prejudices of the nineteenth century when we confront the problem of sacrifice in Judaism. There is another reason why the matter cannot be avoided. Attempts to alter or seriously change the text of the prayerbook and the forms of Jewish liturgy are matters of high seriousness. It is not enough to say that liturgical forms which have been established by men can freely be altered by men. Obviously modern Jews can do as they please with the prayerbook without fear of sanction, but it is important that, if they make any changes, they do so for reasons which are very good indeed. Simply to remove the sacrificial readings because of a conception of "higher" and "lower" religion, which will not stand the test of scrutiny, is an injustice not only to one generation but to the generations which are heir to the fruits of this misconception. A misapplication of the gift-theory of sacrifice to the problem of the liturgy—arguing that God wants the gifts of the inner determination of the heart rather than the bloody offering—can do equally great harm. The sacrificial offering was in all probability seldom meant to be a gift and hence the proposal to substitute a better gift (prayer, etc.) can hardly have any relevance.

Our attitude in approaching the liturgy ought to be one of extreme conservatism, not for the sake of conservatism, but rather because the harm we can do by making the wrong decision affects the continuity of Jewish history and of Jewish religious sentiment itself. There is nothing necessarily sacred about any given liturgical form. What is impressive, however, is the extent to which both conscious and unconscious themes tend to intersect creatively in any liturgical mode. This contrasts with the call to obliterate the sacrificial modes which comes from a false theory of sacrifice and an attempt to suppress important aspects of human personality.

One of the greatest achievements of historic Judaism has been its ability to retain a meaningful aspect of every layer of Jewish religious experience in its contemporary expressions. Nothing which has ever been meaningful in the Jewish past has been entirely suppressed. It may have been sublimated, subdued, partially altered, but, until modern times, nothing was ever suppressed without trace. Thus the student of religious history can find in the religious experience of the Jew residues of the pagan and Canaanitic traditions which form a substratum of Jewish religious history. Psalm 29 is now known to have had its origins in Canaanite religious poetry,[17] yet as a hymn to God, whose voice is over the waters and is mighty in strength, it is sung on the Sabbath day in connection with the reading of the Torah, the literary residue of that same Divine voice. Parents long ago gave up the slaughter of the first-born, yet the transition from this expression of the hostility of the generations has been formed through a ceremony in which the hostility is acknowledged but deflected by a surrogate offering of coin in the "redemption of the first-born" ceremony. Canaanite agrarian holidays are no longer celebrated as orgiastic occasions for magically increasing the fertility of the land, but they continue to form one substratum of the Passover-Shavuoth-Succoth festival cycle. Neither prophet nor priest has won the day in traditional Jewish practice. Each has found his place in a tradition which was wise enough to endure the tension between them, rather than falsely choose one in preference to the other.

Even the sacrificial cult was never done away with. It served many purposes. It was a means by which a community was dramatically made one substance in holy communion. It was an enormously efficacious instrument of moral and social control. It brought the ever-pressing problems of orality, aggression, and sadism into the domain of the sacred, where they could be regulated and dealt with effectively rather than ignored. And, if Freud is correct, it offered a dramatic catharsis wherein mankind's oldest and darkest crime was continually confessed through symbolic re-enactment and, in the process, again abjured. This analysis does not depend upon the validity of Freud's primal-crime hypothesis, though the author does accept it to a degree.[18] What is significant

[17] Cf. Theodore Gaster, *Thespis: Ritual, Myth and Drama in the Ancient Near East* (New York: Anchor Books, 1961), pp. 443 ff.

[18] Cf. my "Psychoanalysis and the Origins of Judaism," *The Reconstructionist,* December 2, 1962.

in Freud's hypothesis is that it hints at the many dimensions of conscious and unconscious concern which are dramatized in the sacrificial act. It is the multidimensional character of human strivings highlighted by sacrifice which Judaism can ill afford to ignore.

Yet, when all has been said in defense of the sacrificial mode of religious life, two facts stand out: sacrifice does dramatize many of mankind's most significant but least revealed dilemmas and strivings, yet sacrifice remains at best only a magic palliative. If men had more insight, they would by no means need the gratuitous ritual of harming even an animal. On this fact rests the strongest argument in favor of the abolition of the sacrificial mode. The argument, however, cannot stand, because it is based upon a very questionable premise, "if men had more insight . . ." The twentieth century has taught us how utterly tenuous is the grasp of the generality of mankind on those forces in their own makeup which make for rationality and civilization. World War II was not a fortuitous accident but a deep revelation of the night side of human existence. The more we know of what took place, the greater does the stigma of guilt seem to be and the more far-reaching does its extension become. Men do not have more insight. We are caught between the realization of the gratuity of the magic and the concomitant realization of the inability of mankind to rise above magic. Ultimately the choice may be only between the compelling magic symbols of death, such as the swastika, and the compelling magic symbols of life, such as were represented in religious tradition. One thing is certain. If the symbol-makers and magicians of life refuse their task because of its ultimate gratuity and fictitiousness, they will by no means be joined by the symbol-makers of death, who stand ready to give modern man what he thirsts for most, an integrated psyche in which his personal goals, both conscious and unconscious, are at one with the goals of the larger community. That such a community might very well be a community of human lemmings, led by a demonic Pied Piper to its collective death, will hardly stop the power and the fascination of the masters of irrationality. In the *Götterdämmerung* ending of Hitler's Third Reich, we have seen one instance of the power of such symbols.

It would seem that the rabbinic compromise represented

the very best response to this dilemma. Judaism never did away with sacrifice entirely until modern times, but Judaism progressively limited the gratuitous harm which the system could do. At first the animal was surrogate for the human; later, after the destruction of the Jerusalem sanctuary, the verbal was surrogate for the concrete, and sacramental existence was united with nutritive necessity in *kashruth*. It is to the wisdom of the Rabbis rather than to the blood of the pagan or the idealism of the rationalist that we ought to turn. A verbal re-enactment elicits much of the emotional association which was present in the concrete deed, while completely avoiding the gratuitous harm of the concrete. In both liturgical form and homiletic embellishment, the verbal provided Judaism with a very apt compromise. The psychoanalytic interview is a testament to the power of the verbal to alter personality through a properly controlled rehearsal of personal dilemmas. One does not, one ought not, "act out" the psychic dilemmas which are discussed in the psychotherapeutic encounter. A verbal relationship to these areas of emotional life, especially when accompanied by the emotions of the real encounter, offers much profit for the constructive alteration of the psyche. As long as the relation is verbal, nothing is harmed. Similarly the human problems in depth to which sacrifice points cannot be done away with, but the Rabbis were intuitively wise enough to place the problem of sacrifice where it belonged—in the domain of the verbal which was nevertheless sufficiently potent to elicit from the community many of the same responses which had formerly been forthcoming only as a result of actual sacrifice.

Many of the most creative aspects of religious literature dwell on the mysteries and profundities of sacrifice. The mystics did not need more than liturgical formulations and the vivid presentations of the old order which they found in rabbinic literature to create a vast and significant body of literature. Our own time bespeaks its religious and emotional impoverishment in its failure to find a place for the totality of the human psyche within its religious life. At the very least, those who are concerned with a meaningful religious life ought not to remain insensitive to the enormously fruitful potentialities which this aspect of our liturgical inheritance has to offer.

This paper was first delivered in German at the Fifteenth Annual Conference on Church and Judaism at Recklinghausen, Germany, in February 1963. It is an attempt to answer the question: "What can the modern Jew retain of the Torah as the authoritative source of Jewish religious inspiration?" My turning away from prophetic religion and the God of History to priestly religion and the God of Nature is evident in this effort.

6/The Meaning of Torah in Contemporary Jewish Theology

An Existentialist Philosophy of Judaism

I<small>N THE</small> nineteenth and twentieth centuries, the scholarly disciplines have achieved an ever greater measure of precision in determining the history of Judaism. This heightened sophistication has added an important element of religious difficulty to the cataclysmic social and political changes which occurred within the Jewish world between the French Revolution and the Israeli War of Independence. In a period of such vast social instability, it is hardly surprising that the theological foundations of Judaism have exhibited a concomitant instability.

Biblical scholarship has had an especially important impact on modern Jewish thought. At least one result of this scholarship seems beyond refutation: The Torah is not, as normative Jewish tradition had claimed, a unitary work communicated by God directly to Moses, save for a few verses at the end of Deuteronomy. As long as this view had been convincingly maintained, it had enormous consequences in the life of the individual Jew. If the Torah was the perfect revelation of God's will, when properly interpreted, then none of its injunctions, no matter how opaque to the lucidities of common sense, could be ignored. To have ignored them would have been to rebel against the will of the Creator. The modern Jew lacks the security of knowing that his religious acts are meaningfully related to God's will. Whether he fulfills all of the Torah's commandments or none of them, he enters a spiritual wager not unlike that made by the believing Christian when he makes a decision concerning the centrality of the Christ in his personal life. As Kierkegaard has suggested, religious life hovers over a sea of doubt seventy thousand fathoms deep.[1]

When doubts have lain fallow for many centuries, as they have in normative Judaism, and are quite suddenly the object of concerted attention, one must look beyond mere thought to understand the full scope of the crisis. The theological foundations of normative Judaism were most keenly disrupted in a period when Jews were entering the secular society of contract and commerce which developed in the Western world following the French Revolution. Full participation in this new society demanded a radical curtailment of the sacramental aspects of Jewish life. These had included distinctive modes of dress, religious behavior, eating, and the measurement of sacred and profane time, which had been ordained by or derived from the Torah. The decision to "reform" Judaism was as rooted in economic and social reality as it was in any purely religious need for change. In a highly competitive bourgeois society the Jewish middle classes were hardly concerned with the strict maintenance of those aspects of religious life which were rooted in the priestly or the sacrificial. The well-known tendency of all branches of nineteenth-century Judaism, but especially of Reform, to emphasize the moral and the rational aspects of the Torah at the expense of the sacerdotal served a dual need: it addressed the Jew most practically in his economic activities and it sought to guide him against their misuse at a time when Jews were stressing the minimal differences separating them from their neighbors. In addition, the new stress on the moral aspects of the Torah provided an unconsciously formulated defense against the Judas-image of the Jew which an increasingly secular society not only failed to repress but actually magnified.

Psychological and economic pressures alike forced a new

[1] Sören Aabye Kierkegaard, *Concluding Unscientific Postscript,* tr. David F. Swenson (Princeton: Princeton University Press, 1941), p. 188.

attitude toward the Torah by Western Jews in the nineteenth century. Just as the continuing differences between Jew and gentile were glossed over by surface similarities of dress and appearance, so too the rational and the conscious in religion were emphasized over the unconscious and the mythic. It is no accident that those Jews who tended toward greatest success in economic enterprise were those who were least impeded by the priestly and sacerdotal aspects of their religion. By and large, adherence to Deuteronomy made for better and more successful capitalists than diligent attention to Leviticus, which has, in any event, been the most embarrassing book of the Torah for "enlightened," "modern" Jews. A similar shift from the sacramental to the moral, from the ritual to the barrenly creedal, in Christianity had analogous results in the rise of capitalism, as Troeltsch, Weber, and other Protestant sociologists of religion have demonstrated.[2]

The new freedom to question and reformulate Judaism, which figured so prominently in the nineteenth century, was not expended by Jews solely in economic activities. The time was one of the most exciting in all areas of intellectual and artistic creativity. It was usually easier to retain a measure of loyalty to the reformulated Judaism for the acquisitive than for the creative and intellectual classes. With an intuitive feeling for authenticity in all domains of the human spirit, the creative artist could hardly regard bourgeois, moralistic Judaism as an "advance" over the older and more traditional forms. Though the great themes of religion—sacrifice, atonement, confession, and human brokenness, —which had nourished so much of the art and music of the Western world were largely of Jewish inspiration, the newer Judaism was as barren of artistic creativity as it was of emotional depth and excitement. This contrasts with the continuing vitality of Hasidic themes in the art of Marc Chagall and the thought of Martin Buber. The estrangement of the creative spirit from the Torah and the life of the synagogue has remained a problem throughout modern times.

[2] Cf. Ernst Troeltsch, *The Social Teachings of the Christian Churches,* tr. Olive Wyon (London: Allen and Unwin, 1931), pp. 640 ff; and Max Weber, *The Protestant Ethic and the Spirit of Capitalism* (New York: Charles Scribner's Sons, 1958), pp. 98 ff.

In military strategy, when faced by a seemingly successful attack, the good general withdraws and regroups. Nineteenth-century Jewish thinkers, leading their ill-starred community in the land of Clausewitz and Von Moltke, employed a similar tactic. In the face of a many-pronged intellectual, economic, and social attack against normative Judaism, they employed a withdrawing and a regrouping strategy. They sought to assert the priority of those elements of the Torah which they believed remained relevant and defensible in their own times. One of the strategies they employed was at least as old as St. Paul. They tended to distinguish between the spirit of Torah and its frequently embarrassing letter. They stressed the abiding relevance of the moral elements of the Torah. The intent of the Torah, they contended, was to call men to a life of holiness, which they usually equated with the moral relations between man and fellow man. *Imitatio dei* was reduced to fulfillment of the ethical deed. This is explicit in such representative German Jewish thinkers of another day as Abraham Geiger and Leo Baeck.[3] Little was said of religious and moral failure or of the tragic inevitability which so frequently destines men to incur guilt in the very act of existing.

As in the economic domain, so too in the religious domain, the keynote was personal success. Judaism, whose power had ever been enhanced by intimate contact with the tragic and the ironic, turned its back on the destined fatalities of men. Those aspects of the Torah which were irreducible to the moral demand were discarded. The old sacrificial order and *kashruth* (the dietary laws), its continuing embodiment in the everyday life of the Jew, were rejected. The opaque, the irrational, and the mystical were equated with the "primitive," and a pseudo-evolutionary mythology was employed to obscure their frequently continuing relevance. Whatever in the Torah dealt with the dilemmas of bodily existence and sought to root Jews in the vicissitudes of earth and human biology became an acute embarrassment. The ancient longing of Judaism for an existence in its own earthly

[3] Abraham Geiger, *Judaism and Its History,* tr. Charles Neuburgh (New York: Bloch Publishing Co., 1911), pp. 61 ff.; Leo Baeck, *The Essence of Judaism,* tr. Irving Howe (New York: Schocken Books, 1948), p. 130.

sphere was rejected as inconsistent with the "higher," "spiritual" forms toward which Judaism had "evolved." What remained was a desiccated, unimaginative moralism with little symbolic or mythic power.

Paradoxically, in spite of all attempts to divide the Torah into "higher" and "lower" spheres, the liturgical pre-eminence of the Torah has remained unchanged in Jewish life. In all three branches of Judaism, the Torah has continued to be read on an annual or on a triennial basis. No distinction has been made in its recitation or in preaching betweeen the sacrificial and the moral portions of Scripture. All alike have the same pre-eminent status. In spite of the theological, social, and critical objections, the Torah remains the decisive center of Jewish religious life, though there is no longer any assurance that all, or even an identifiable part, expresses God's will explicitly and unambiguously. At the heart of Jewish life today, there is an ineradicable tension between fixed form (the Torah) and personal subjectivity which all must endure.

Long ago the rabbis asserted the primacy of the religious act over its interpretation in normative Judaism.[4] Their insight has a perennial relevance. What Jews do is often a greater indication of what they truly think than what they sometimes verbalize. One of the tasks of contemporary Jewish theology is to understand the meaning of the religious act whereby, in spite of all theological objection, the Torah remains the decisive center of Jewish life.

In order to understand the religious centrality of the Torah for contemporary Judaism it is necessary to comprehend why the secular alternatives are unacceptable. The most radical Jewish alternatives are extreme atheism and/or secular humanism. These are respectable intellectual positions and have the virtue of unambiguous clarity. For those who accept secular humanism, the problem of Judaism ceases to exist. We reject secular humanism, not because we have a less tragic view of ultimate human destiny, but because secular humanism is unmindful

---

[4] *Mishnah Aboth* 1: 14: "Simeon [the Son of Rabban Gamaliel] said . . . not learning but doing is the chief thing." The "doing" is of course pre-eminently the religious deed.

of the full determinants of the person, which root each individual
irrevocably in a definite situation involving the shared vicissitudes
of history, culture, and psychological perspective. Affirmation of
secular humanism involves a dilution of the facticities of each
man's specific human situation. The secular humanist is most
cognizant of what he shares with all men. The grandeur and the
degradation of twentieth-century Jewish life are too much a
part of the fiber of our beings for contemporary religious Jews
to regard as meaningful any philosophy which ignores the actualities of present-day Jewish fate and destiny. One must be a
particular kind of man with a limited, concrete life-situation to be
a man at all. The conception of humanity in general is a meaningless and tragic abstraction. As Hannah Arendt has illustrated,
the process whereby Jews were turned into men in general, lacking
all concrete legal, political, and national status, was the final
preparatory step to turning them into superfluous men whose
extermination was of no consequence to any existing political
group.[5] Those Jews who achieved the longed-for goal of the
secular humanists, that of being merely human rather than rooted
in the actualities and limitations of a historically determined
community, found that this was no messianic blessing but the
final preparation for annihilation.

Another spiritual possibility for contemporary Jews is an
atheism which is combined with Jewish nationalism in some
form. In actual fact, this alternative has been elected by many
Jews in contemporary Israel. The Jewish atheist recognizes and
shares with other Jews the essential particularity and "thrownness" *(Geworfenheit)* of the Jewish situation. This is the special
strength of Jewish, nonreligious nationalism. The limitation of
Jewish atheism is that it offers no way of actively sharing or participating with other Jews in the wisdom, the aspirations, the re-
membrances, and the insights of earlier generations. In the severity of its honesty, Jewish atheism knows the surface manifestations
of the living Jewish present but little more than the surface manifestations of the Jewish past. Only he who can also experience or
empathize with the agonies and the yearnings of past Jewish gen-

[5] Hannah Arendt, *The Origins of Totalitarianism* (New York:
Harcourt Brace, 1951), pp. 277 ff.

erations in their awesome confrontation with the God of Israel can truly partake of the fullness of Jewish experience.

The Jewish atheist frequently forgets that process is as important as result in life. Even the most pious Jew, in his innermost self, knows that human existence is a tragic and gratuitous absurdity, entirely without meaning save for the meanings and the projects we ourselves actualize and, above all, bracketed in its "thrownness" between two oblivions. The religiously compliant Jew can expect neither future boon nor salvation. We live in the present and know no future hope. The Jewish atheist may, however, fail to see that it is precisely the ultimate hopelessness and gratuity of our human situation which calls forth our strongest need for religious community. If all we have is one another, then assuredly we need one another more than ever. Even the old religious assurances of redemption and resurrection have decisive meaning for those who are nevertheless undeceived concerning man's fate. They are a most significant index of the extent to which only the religious community in modern society constitutes a domain in which the aspirations, the hopes, the tragedies, and the guilts of the human condition can be continuously and meaningfully shared. If we cannot unite with previous generations in a community of faith, we are the more strongly united with them in a community of shared predicament and ultimate concern. Nor could we, at this late date, invent a better medium in and through which we could remain so united with our own and past generations.

The situation of the contemporary Jew is absurd, tragic, and free. Paradoxically, the recognition of this situation allows us to recapture for the first time in the modern period the entire Torah as our decisive religious text. Jewish religion is inseparable from Jewish identity. In turn, identity is inseparable from the facticity of the Jewish situation.[6] This facticity is, in part, historically determined, and time is, as we know, irreversible. Jews are not simply abstract men devoid of the defining limitations of a very special history, psychology, and culture. They are what they are as a result of the entire range of Jewish history. Part of

[6] By "facticity," I mean the irreducible givenness of the Jewish situation.

that history involves the fact that the Jewish community is what it is because it has accepted the Torah as its decisive religious text. This is the community's concrete mode of being-in-the-world. It has had awesome, and occasionally terrifying, consequences in the lives and deaths of millions of Jews over thousands of years. In its dialogue with Christianity, the Synagogue insisted that its religious life needed neither additions nor subtractions from the form in which the Torah had been received. The canonicity of the Torah made Christianity's way impossible for Judaism. At every level of their beings, Jews are heirs both to that text and to the historical conflicts it has engendered. Nor is it likely that any amount of critical skepticism would diminish the fervor with which we take our stand with it. If we are no longer entirely convinced that God has commanded the Torah, we are nevertheless grateful that it remains the inheritance of the house of Jacob. It has became a part of the very fabric of what we are. To deny it would be to deny an important element in ourselves.[7]

The discovery of the Torah as our decisive religious text, rooted at the very least in the facticities of Jewish identity, has in no sense diminished the religious insecurity in which we find ourselves. There is no way in which we can ever again avoid our freedom. At times we experience it, as does Sartre, as a condemnation. We hold the Torah to be holy, yet we cannot and will not eliminate the subjectivism, the voluntarism, and the consequent anxiety which in fact, if not in theory, have triumphed in all contemporary Jewish groups. There can be no retreat from freedom. No two decisions concerning religious involvement will exactly resemble each other. No division of the Torah into "essential" and "inessential" elements will offer an altogether convincing rationale for a new security in religious life. There is, and there will continue to be, a recognizable anarchic element in contemporary Jewish life. This anarchy coexists with the affirmation that the Torah is supreme in Israel. The anarchy can be ended only by bringing an end to freedom. We will not pay that price.

[7] In this analysis I am indebted to Jean Paul Sartre, *Réflexions sur la question juive,* known in English as *Anti-Semite and Jew,* tr. George J. Becker (New York: Schocken Books, 1948).

Some of the contents of the Torah will be an embarrassment to every age, though what puzzles or embarrasses the Jews of one period will not necessarily embarrass their successors. For the Reform Jews of nineteenth-century Germany and America, imbued with a fervor for moral perfection and rationality in human affairs, the sacrificial aspects of the Torah were an acute embarrassment. We have sought to learn from their mistakes. We would use our freedom to ignore or reject what we find embarrassing for ourselves alone in the Torah and not, in our arrogance, to decide that our embarrassments will be shared by those who follow us. In this sense we reject the path of liberal Judaism, though our alternative is by no means Orthodox. The old religious dichotomies have become as theologically meaningless in Judaism as they have in Christianity.

In another place I have suggested the meaningful character of the atonement and sacrificial aspects of the Torah for contemporary Judaism.[8] At the heart of the sacrificial system lay the unspoken conviction that human beings are more likely to repeat their characteristic failings from one generation to the next than they are to improve upon them, as the nineteenth-century religious moralists had hoped. The sacrificial system carried implicit within it the archaic, tragic verity that men frequently, if not invariably, have the choice only of mastering their violence and aggression by limiting and channeling it, as was done in sacrifice, or of facing continually the terrible possibility of its unmeasured, irrational explosion, as we have seen in our times. The liberal Jews of the nineteenth century were so convinced that their embarrassment with the Jewish sacrificial order would be shared by their successors that they expunged all reference to it from the Scripture reading of our holiest of days, Yom Kippur. True to their own preferences, they substituted a Deuteronomic exhortation to moral choice.[9] Whether ultimately they were correct in their embarrassment with the sacramental aspects of the Jewish religion, or we in our renewed appreciation of the cultic and the sacramental, is less

[8] Cf. Chapter 5 of this volume.

[9] The traditional reading from the Torah on Yom Kippur is Lev. 16:1–34; the Reform substitution is Deut. 29:9–14; 30:11–20.

important than that we understand that freedom is a subjective matter. He who claims it must forego the privilege of speaking for anyone but himself. Jews are free to accept or reject all or part of the Torah as individuals. Freedom carries with it the responsibility that each generation make its own commitments in the light of its insights, while leaving the inherited corpus of tradition intact for subsequent generations. Here again we have the perennial tension between form and subjectivity in Judaism.

Many today would regard some aspects of the Torah as cruel, if not bordering on the barbaric. We have radically different ways of handling sexual malfeasance today, for example, than the violent ones suggested in the Torah, even allowing for their humane limitation in rabbinic interpretation. Yet here again a measure of restraint is advisable before turning a personal standard into a community evaluation. Much misunderstanding has been heaped upon the *lex talionis* in the Torah, often with no small measure of malice. Yet we know that the law of an "eye for an eye" introduced an element of equity where previously retaliatory violence knew few limits. Few seeming cruelties found in the Torah have the measure of barbarity we find utterly rampant in modern life. While we would undoubtedly turn away from the Torah's harsher injunctions, as Jewish tradition has done for centuries, there is little in the Torah which could embarrass us after the exhibitions we have witnessed in the twentieth century. We will never contrast the "primitive" character of even a single verse of the Torah with the "advanced" character of contemporary civilization. We assert the unity of the Torah because only thus can the essential continuity of Jewish religious and historical identity be maintained. It is an irrevocable part of our facticity as Jews. We can rid ourselves of it only by being quit of our Jewishness.

Tradition and history alike have emphasized the pagan character of the religion of our earliest ancestors. Having learned at far too great a cost the difference between nihilism and paganism, we look today with increasing respect for and sense of community with our pagan origins. It was inevitable that, with the return of the Jewish people to their ancestral earth, there would be a renewed interest in, if not contact with, the old gods of that land. While Judaism has wisely asserted the ultimate unity of the

God of nature and the God of history, our times are peculiarly suited for a rediscovery and a reaffirmation of the primordial powers of earth and fatality that have on occasion bedecked themselves in the guise of the God of history. The reformers of the nineteenth century were quick to note the underlying paganism of much of the priestly tradition in Leviticus; they were embarrassed and they sought to expunge this phoenix.[10] For some, it was enough to identify a source as containing pagan relics in order to dismiss it. It is no accident that those who most bitterly opposed the continuing viability of the priestly traditions were those who were most vociferous in their opposition to the never-suppressed longing of the children of Israel for the earth of Israel. Both the earth of Israel and its gods were part of the same reality, as the liberals understood all too well.

We who have rediscovered the earth of Israel are not nearly so disturbed by the gods of earth as were the nineteenth-century reformers. Whereas their evolutionary mythology cast the primal and the archaic into disrepute and gave to modernity a specious respectability which rested on no greater credential than temporal sequence, we have acquired a renewed respect for the primal and the archaic.

While yet a student at Tübingen, Hegel bitterly complained that the Teutons, in accepting Christianity, had alienated themselves, not merely from their own past and history, but from their innermost beings.[11] According to the young Hegel, the acceptance of Christianity created a radical split in the German soul which had yet to be healed in his time.[12] More than one hundred years ago, Heine warned that the rejected gods of the Teutons slumbered but had not died. When Thor awoke with his

[10] Abraham Geiger, *op. cit.*, pp. 76 ff.

[11] G. W. F. Hegel, *Early Theological Writings,* tr. T. M. Knox and Richard Kroner (Chicago: University of Chicago Press, 1948), pp. 145 ff.

[12] *Ibid.,* p. 147: "Thus we are without any religious imagery which is homegrown or linked with our history, and we are without any political imagery whatever; all that we have is the remains of an imagery of our own, lurking amid the common people under the name of superstition."

mighty hammer, there would be played out on the European scene a catastrophe which would make the French Revolution seem like child's play.[13] We have lived through that drama. The grandeur of the Torah is that it never permitted a comparable split to occur within the Jewish psyche. The priests of ancient Israel wisely never suffered Jahweh entirely to win his war with Baal, Astarte, and Anath. That is why Jews were never puritans, cut off from their inner life and the powers of earth which engendered it. Paganism was transformed but never entirely done away with in Judaism. In the ceremony of the redemption of the first-born son *(pidyon ha-ben),* for example, the murderous quality of paganism was deflected, but its essential insight into the hostility between the generations was retained.[14] Canaanite agrarian festivals were transformed into celebrations of Israel's sacred time, but their inner connection with nature's fertility was never lost. Even Jewish folkways enjoyed this wisdom. Whenever possible, no Jew made his inevitable journey of return to the earth in entirely strange soil. A token of the sacred earth of the land of Israel accompanied him. No element, pagan or monotheistic, in the formation of the Jewish religious consciousness was ever entirely repressed in the Torah. In the twentieth century we have learned much concerning the futility of repression in personal matters. The Torah instinctively and intuitively understood this futility long ago in religious matters. Nothing within the domain of human experience escaped its attention. It understood the paradoxical truth that one can best overcome atavisms and primitivisms, in so far as they are destructive, by acknowledging their full potency and attractiveness and channeling their expression to eliminate their harm.

The Torah is also the record of Israel's continuing confrontation with the holiness of God. Jewish religious liberalism and rationalism fail before this primordial and ultimate reality.

[13] Heinrich Heine, *Religion and Philosophy in Germany,* tr. John Snodgrass (Boston: Beacon Press, 1951), pp. 158 ff. This is a paperback reprint of the edition of 1882.

[14] For the text of the ceremony, cf. J. H. Hertz, *The Authorized Daily Prayer Book* (New York: Bloch Publishing Co., 1957), pp. 1034 ff.

Liberal Judaism wants a good and moral God because it lacks the courage of the absurd; it cannot abide the limitations of the tragic and demonic cosmos in which we are enclosed without hope of exit. It envisages a world in which men, like corporation returns, can get better and better in every way. It knows nothing of the fated destiny which so frequently turns human encounter into tragic conflict. One does not have to join Sartre in his reiteration of Hegel's dictum, that conscience desires the death of the other, to know how deeply tragic human encounter can be.[15] Where the holiness of God is real, the tragic element inherent in existence can never be ignored. One has only to read the many accounts in Scripture concerning the fatal consequences of an improper or an unprepared approach before the Holy to understand that God in His holiness is more than a moral force. He who makes alive is also He who slays by His very presence. This teaching of Scripture embarrassed the liberals. Had they paid attention to it, rather than relegated it to the domain of outlived antiquities, they would have had a fuller appreciation of man's existence before God. Incidentally I believe few men knew the truth about God in His holiness as did Martin Luther.

Earth is a Mother, but Earth is a cannibal Mother. Sooner or later it consumes what it gives birth to. Before the opaque facticity of Earth we can ask with Schelling, but never answer, the question: "Why is there something rather than nothing?" Out of this unanswerable question comes our sense of the mystery and the absurdity of existence. Before this Abyss, we come to intuit something of the holiness of God. When we speak of it, we dimly point to the realm of His utter singularity, uniqueness, and incommensurability with all categories of measurement, logic, or relation. He who intuits, no matter how dimly, the holiness of God, need construct no "God above the God of theism," as does Paul Tillich, to provide a hint of the mental image of that which dwells in its own groundlessness.[16] God in His holiness is beyond both the masculinity of the Judaeo-Christian tradition and the femininity

[15] Jean Paul Sartre, *Being and Nothingness,* tr. Hazel Barnes (New York: Philosophical Library, 1956), p. 237.

[16] Paul Tillich, *The Courage To Be* (New Haven: Yale University Press, 1952), pp. 186–190.

of the pagan goddesses. The old problem of patriarchal and matri-
archal religions evaporates in this final reality. Rabbinic mythology loved to dwell on kingly metaphors for God's relation to
Israel. This too was a limitation and an anaesthetizing of the awe
and mystery men felt before the cannibal powers of Earth. Both
the Jews and the Greeks attributed masculine traits to God in
order to dull the sense of terror and wonder men feel before
Earth's demonic facticity. Sky and thunder gods were invented to
be superior to Earth, but to no avail. In its awesome awareness of
the holiness of God, Biblical monotheism is at one with the old
Earth paganisms from which it had been engendered. The com-
manding Father God, the King who lovingly guided His regal
son, and the thunder-god dwelling in his heavenly abode, are all
manifold aspects for the same faceless Abyss.

The tragic truth of earthly existence was never lost in the
Torah. It came out of disguise when least expected. In sacrificial
offerings of the temple service as well as in *kashruth,* Jews were
enjoined to return the blood of the slaughtered animal to the
Earth before consumption of the rest of the animal was permitted.
Is this not one of the oldest offerings made by men to thank and
appease their cannibal Earth-Mother? By offering Earth the blood,
in which the soul was found, it was hoped that the rest of the
animal would be permitted. To this day, this symbolic recognition
of the power of Earth continues in *kashruth* to play an important
role in Jewish religious life.

Psychoanalysts have tended to see the Scriptural demand
that the first-born of men, cattle, and field be devoted to, or redeemed from, God's grasp, as an example of the acting out of the
Oedipal conflict.[17] This perspective has the virtue of recognizing
how deeply rooted the Torah is in the actual dilemmas of personal
existence. Nevertheless, in formulating its insights in terms of the
Oedipal metaphor, the psychoanalytic school seems to have lost
sight of a deeper reality. It is not merely the first-born of men
which must be redeemed or devoted; the first-born of all fruitful-

---

[17] Theodore Reik, *Ritual* (London: Hogarth Press, 1931),
p. 71. Cf. Erich Wellisch, *Isaac and Oedipus* (London: Routledge and
Kegan Paul, 1954).

ness stands in a special relation to the Holy Abyss.[18] Is this not another attempt to appease the Earth-Mother with the first portion in the hope that men will be allowed safely to retain the remainder? The holiness of God knows neither masculinity nor femininity; it knows only life, fecundity, death, mystery, and wonder.

We do not know whether Moses received any or all of the Torah on Sinai. It hardly matters. The Torah is for us the record of Israel's encounter with God in His terrible holiness. We have stressed some strange and atavistic elements rather deliberately, not because destructiveness is all that Earth offers, but because this aspect of divinity has hardly received the attention in recent Jewish thought which recent Jewish experience suggests it deserves. We have had a further reason for this stress. We want to emphasize the extent to which no element in Torah, no matter how seemingly cruel, primitive, or atavistic, is without a potentiality of relevance and significance in our own times.

The tension between the historically determined form of the Torah and our own free subjectivities cannot be ended cheaply. In our freedom we can reject any or all of the Torah. We are our acts. We actualize ourselves by accepting full responsibility for our freedom. Nevertheless, all of the Torah is holy; all of it confronts us, as it has confronted Israel and the world for millennia, with the holiness of God. As God's holiness can never be contained in fixed immutable form, our response will be what we in our freedom choose to make it. No two responses will ever be the same. We may be unable to endure more than a measure of the confrontation; we may find elements which are so endurable as to be trite and commonplace. But we know that there is an inner connection between our modern absurd freedom before the facticity of existence in the world and the mysterious awe with which our ancestors experienced His presence.

The final paradox is that the Torah, which is a book of words, points to a reality before which words are utterly helpless. He who confronts the holiness of God touches a domain in which art and music safely carry man a little further into the Being's

[18] Exod. 13:11–16.

Holy Abyss than words. Art and music communicate much that
is hidden beneath the surface in man. In the *Kedushah* of the
Jewish liturgy, as well as in the *gloria,* the *sanctus* and the *rex
tremendae* of the Mass, musicians of all ages have expressed, better than words can utter, their sense of wonder and mystery before
the Source of all existence. In the chant of the Hasidic Rebbe, in
the songs of the ascending Levites in Jerusalem's temple, and in
the soaring elevations of the great cantorial masters of eastern
Europe, Jews have confronted the holiness of God in the fullness
of their beings. Perhaps the most terrible thing that could be said
of the liberal Judaism of the nineteenth century is that it was
incapable of art and song before God's absurd and mysterious
holiness.

Death and rebirth are the great moments of religious
experience. In the twentieth century the Jewish phoenix has
known both: in Germany and eastern Europe, we Jews have
tasted the bitterest and the most degrading of deaths. Yet death
was not the last word. We do not pity ourselves. Death in Europe
was followed by resurrection in our ancestral home. We are free
as no men before us have ever been. Having lost everything, we
have nothing further to lose and no further fear of loss. Our
existence has in truth been a being-unto-death. We have passed
beyond all illusion and hope. We have learned in the crisis that
we were totally and nakedly alone, that we could expect neither
support nor succor from God or from our fellow creatures. No
men have known as we have how truly God in His holiness slays
those to whom He gives life. This has been a liberating knowledge, at least for the survivors, and all Jews everywhere regard
themselves as having escaped by the skin of their teeth, whether
they were born in Europe or elsewhere. We have lost all hope and
faith. We have also lost all possibility of disappointment. Expect-
ing absolutely nothing from God or man, we rejoice in whatever
we receive. We have learned the nakedness of every human pre-
tense. No people has come to know as we have how deeply man
is an insubstantial nothingness before the awesome and terrible
majesty of the Lord. We accept our nothingness—nay, we even
rejoice in it—for in finding our nothingness we have found both
ourselves and the God who alone is true substance. We did not

ask to be born; we did not ask for our absurd existence in the world; nor have we asked for the fated destiny which has hung about us as Jews. Yet we would not exchange it, nor would we deny it, for when nothing is asked for, nothing is hoped for, nothing is expected; all that we receive is truly grace.

The two most significant events in Jewish history in the twentieth century have been the European catastrophe and the rebirth of Israel. Both events have decisive significance for contemporary Jewish theology. The European catastrophe marks the death of the God of History; the re-establishment of Israel marks the rebirth of the long-forgotten gods of Earth within Jewish experience.

Today I would be somewhat less enthusiastic about the messianic aspects of the rebirth of Israel. When I wrote this paper, I saw Israel's rebirth as "the beginning of redemption." I no longer so regard it. I see existence as co-terminous with exile and the grave as the real place of redemption. What I retain of this paper's perspectives is my fundamental belief that an insightful paganism, utilizing the forms of traditional Jewish religion, is the only meaningful religious option remaining to Jews after Auschwitz and the rebirth of Israel.

7/ The Rebirth of Israel in Contemporary Jewish Theology

THE MEANING OF GOD in human experience is a variable which is inevitably altered by radical changes in that experience. Scientific arguments for or against the existence of God are far less significant than the existential matrix out of which such affirmations or denials flow. The possibilities of renewal which the Zionist movement has made available to the Jewish people are evident in the life and culture of modern Israel, and its derivative by-products visible in the lives of diaspora Jews. Less evident but none the less real is the influence which Zionism is destined to have on the religion and theology of the Jewish people as well. It is not likely that the Jewish life-situation will change so decisively without a concomitant change in Jewish religious sentiment. We see the negative side of the change in the almost violent rejection of traditional Jewish forms by most Israelis; the full significance of the positive side has yet to come to full expression.

One of the most important but little noticed aspects of Zionism is the extent to which it represents a Jewish expression of the twentieth century's urge to return to primal origins. This is evident in many cultural endeavors of our times. In philosophy, Martin Heidegger has characterized his thought as an attempt to get behind more than two thousand years of European philosophy's estrangement from "being." In psychoanalysis there are similar indications. The concept of genitality as a key to the mature functioning of an adult personality casts a negative evaluation on all of the roles, status attainments, and cultural substitutions which men so frequently use as self-measures. The simple functioning of human sexuality—an act unaffected by both cultural and historical variation—achieves an importance possessed by no product of "civilized" strivings. In addition, the attempt to get at the hidden and the decisive in the early life of the individual has been paralleled by an attempt to restore, at least to consciousness, the hidden and decisive in the early life of mankind. The Freudians have pursued this theme in the myth of the primal crime; the Jungians have sought to restore to mankind a life lived in harmony with primal archetypes which our urbanization has almost destroyed. Zionism has pursued its return by making of ghetto Judaism an episode, and writing a Jewish ending to a struggle which Hadrian had seemed to terminate in a vastly different way almost two thousand years ago.

Perhaps nowhere does the Zionist return to the pagan, the primitive and the earthly exhibit itself more decisively than in folk music. Israeli folk music, with its explosive use of percussion instruments and drums, with its frankly dionysian aspect, and with its affirmation of the senses and sensuousness, goes further than any other medium in expressing the new Jewish reality. One has only to compare the best of the traditional liturgical music with the simplest of Israeli tunes to realize what a profound change has taken place. Perhaps there is no greater indication of the special difficulties of American Jewish life than the knowledge that no middle-class American suburb could produce such music. Yet, though it cannot be produced by Jewish suburbia, this music has an immense capacity to move American Jews, who recognize its truth and its reality even when they are incapable of expressing it out of their own beings.

Zionism is part and parcel of the twentieth century's recognition that much of the progress of mankind has been objectified self-falsification rather than the progressive distillation of the best in the human spirit. Any movement which possesses spiritual greatness has the power to engender the deepest human emotions. Words communicate primarily ideas; music communicates emotions. Whereas the ghetto proliferated words, Israel proliferates both words and music. The significance of Zionism does not lie in the fact that a pathetic human refuse has at last found a haven. Zionism's real significance lies in the fact that twenty centuries of self-distortion, self-estrangement, and self-blame have ended for a people which is now free to live its own life at every level of emotional and cultural experience.

Such a renewal cannot but affect every aspect of Jewish experience. For those who believe that theology is the quintessential expression of man's ultimate meanings, Zionism must result in a great renewal of Jewish religious sentiment rather than in its ending. Perhaps, just as it took forty years for the Jewish people to lose its slave-mentality and enter the earth-reality of the promised land at the first redemption, so the new redemption will require time before the old-new divinities can be freely and frankly spoken about. Israeli music may exhibit a prophetic function by expressing a truth about the Jewish people which has yet to find verbal or conceptual expression.

Zionism has frequently been referred to disparagingly as a messianic movement. There is much truth in this identification but little justification for the attendant disparagement. In the more obvious sense, without messianism as an integral component of traditional religious sentiment, it is unlikely that Herzl's call would have had the enormous impact on the Jewish psyche which it did. Unfortunately the hideous character of the German and Russian experiments in political messianism has led to a negative evaluation of all messianic movements in our time.

Properly understood, messianism is essentially an attitude toward time and history rather than a type of political movement. Its most characteristic feature is its fervid desire to bring time and history to an ending. Thus the study of messianism is called eschatology—"the word concerning the end." *The goal of messianism is neither the end of man nor of civilization; its real goal is the end of historical man.* In a very real sense, all of the twentieth century's attempts to return to primal origins, including Zionism, are attempts to make a circle out of a process which previous generations had regarded as linear and progressively developmental. The goal of much of the twentieth century's cataclysmic strivings has been to put an end to the development of historical man.

In the deepest spiritual sense, Zionism is and must be antihistorical. Zionism, the Jewish people's yearning to return to its ancient homeland, and to find a creative union with earth and earth's powers, begins with the alienation of that people from its soil. Jewish history has been for two thousand years the history of Jewish alienation. Hegel, perhaps the world's most sensitive critic of the ontological foundations of culture, intuited in the Jewish people the elements of estrangement and negativity.[1] Understandably he assumed that the slave loved his own chains. In actual fact, the yearning of the Jewish people for an end to the very negativities of existence, which Hegel so tellingly described, constituted their deepest eschatological hope. With the destruction of Jerusalem and Judea two forces converged to create guilt and self-blame as the dominant psychological motifs throughout two thousand years of dispersion. The stronger element was Jewish self-blame which saw in every misfortune the hand of an angry and punitive God; the lesser element was the Christian theological tradition, already explicit in Justin Martyr that the Jewish people's alienation from their soil and homeland was God's retaliation against a deicidal community.

In both traditions, the history of Jewish dispersion is equated with the history of Jewish guilt and punishment. An end to Jewish guilt would bring about an end to Jewish alienation. For the Christian this could come about only through submission to the Christ; for the traditional Jew this could be the result only of a Jewish piety of such perfection that its realization still lay in the very distant future. For Zionism the ending came neither through the Christ nor through Jewish piety; it came through action which was able to break the chain of sin and punishment simply by demonstrating that we are prisoners to our past only as long as we permit ourselves to be. By breaking the chain—a self-imposed chain in large measure—Zionism was able to bring to fruition that *telos* which was the goal of Jewish history by any reading, traditional or secular, the end of the alienation of the Jewish people from its ancestral homeland.

One of the reasons that Zionism is frequently misunderstood is that an end to history is taken to mean the necessary end

[1] Cf. G. W. F. Hegel, *Early Theological Writings*, tr. T. M. Knox and Richard Kroner (Chicago: University of Chicago Press, 1948).

to suffering or tragedy. Frequently messianism has been dismissed with the empirical argument that an end to tears, suffering, and death is not visibly at hand. Similarly Zionism is often thought to be discredited when one discovers the same human vulgarities and weaknesses alive in Israel as elsewhere. This completely misses the real point. Messianism's real meaning is the proclamation of the end of history and the return to nature and nature's cyclical repetitiveness. The end of history is characterized by the return to nature and its vicissitudes rather than the abolition of nature's tragic and inevitable necessities. History does not conclude with the abolition but with the restoration of *ananke* (necessity). Now nature's inevitabilities are seen as part of the tragic course of existence itself rather than as God's retaliation against human sinfulness.

Historical man, with his Lord of history and in his self-estrangement from nature, saw all suffering as the payment of a debt exacted by an angry Master. Even nature itself was interpreted as punishment, born not of necessity but of wrath. Earth's joys disappeared with earth's sorrows. Only supramundane terror and guilt were real. To the necessary and ineradicable anxieties of existence were added the unnecessary fears, anxieties, and estrangements which characterize contemporary culture. The couch is culture's necessity, man's last resort after the violation of nature's necessity. The tallest skyscraper is small consolation for failure to achieve the permissible and essential joys of the body. Art is a deep satisfaction to the extent that it celebrates and affirms life rather than substitutes for it. The dehumanization of the human spirit is the final term in historical man's self-estrangement. The death camps of the twentieth century may yet prove to be no aberrant accident representing a soon-to-be-forgotten fortuity. They may prove to be the terminal expression of man's historical existence. Unless mankind overcomes its history, these may truly prove to be the foretaste and substance of things to come.

The people who, in their estrangement, gave historical religion to mankind and who have suffered most bitterly from it are today the first to put an end to history and begin post-historical existence. The return to Israel's earth is more than a mere real-estate transaction or some American's act of charity toward a relative he would rather pay for than see. The result of the attainment of the goal of Jewish history must inevitably be that the people of Israel will cease to see gratification as a future hope and will learn to live their lives so that each generation takes its fair share of life's joys and sorrows, knowing that it will be succeeded by other generations who will repeat the cycle rather than improve upon it. Nor does Zionism mean an end to life's inevitable insecurities. It merely means an end to the interpretation of insecurity as guilt, with its psychic impediments to those joys which are realistically available. Sooner or later Israel's Jews will come to understand that they have no need of distant utopias or far-off lands, that their task is to enjoy the fullness of being in the present. This is, in principle, a decisive turning of world-historical significance. The deliberate turning of the people of the religion of history to the religion of nature is a moment of *kairos* fully in keeping with the twentieth century's return to primal origins and primal circularities.

Increasingly, Israel's return to the earth elicits a return to the archaic earth-religion of Israel. This does not mean that tomorrow the worship of Baal and Astarte will supplant the worship of Yahweh; it does mean that earth's fruitfulness, its vicissitudes, and its engendering power will once again become the central spiritual realities of Jewish life, at least in Israel.

In the religion of history, only man and God are alive. Nature is dead and serves only as the material of tool-making man's obsessive projects. Nature does not exist to be enjoyed and communed with; it exists to be changed and subordinated to man's wants—the fulfillment of which brings neither happiness nor satisfaction. In the religion of nature, a historical, cyclical religion, man is once more at home with nature and its divinities, sharing their life, their limits, and their joys. The devitalization of nature, no matter how imposing, has as its inevitable concomitant the dehumanization of man with its total loss of *eros*. Herbert Marcuse states the issue extremely well when he speaks of the subordination of the logic of gratification to the logic of domination.[2] Only in man at one with nature is *eros* rather than eroticism pos-

[2] Herbert Marcuse, *Eros and Civilization* (Boston: Beacon Press, 1948) pp. 112 ff.

sible. Historical man knows guilt, inhibition, acquisition, and synthetic fantasy, but no *eros*. The return to the soil of Israel promises a people bereft of art, nature, and expansive passion a return to *eros* and the ethos of *eros*. In place of the Lord of history, punishing man for attempting to be what he was created to be, the divinities of nature will celebrate with mankind their "bacchanalian revel of spirits in whom no member is drunk."

In the religion of history every generation is different from previous generations. In addition to its own burden of guilt, it must bear the guilts of all who have preceded. The effect is darkly cumulative. In the religion of nature, all generations are essentially the same; they grow, they unfold in ecstatic creativity, they ripen, and finally they return, becoming the substance of other individuations which will repeat the cycle. Nature and man are one; nature is man's true being and strength; man is nature's self-reflective expression. Fertility, fecundity, and joy are nature's piety rather than God's sins. Only *hubris* is man's real sin and *hubris*, man's sin against his limits, characterizes his refusal of the ecstasy and passion of existence as well as his insistence on too great an aggrandizement of it. *Hubris* characterizes his refusal of his limits. When all sins have been reduced to their final term, man's greatest sin will be understood to be his sin against his own being, his pathetic refusal to recognize and be himself.

Enthusiasm for nature must, however, be tempered by an understanding of the necessity of the historical period. The return to earth inevitably reveals the dialectic qualty of reality in which existent entities are fulcra, balancing life and death, individuality and universality, love and hate, growth and decay. Only the dead are without contradictory tensions. The return to earth does not cancel out the gains made by and in the historical period. It simply assures that the fruits of that period will be enjoyed for the first time. The paradox of unending acquisition and joyless repression are key motifs of the historical period. Only the rich can afford the couch, yet their pathetic need for its restructuring of the psyche points to the vast distance between possession and inner enjoyment. The historical period has provided the fruits which call for its own abolition.

Nowhere is the ironic character of possession, the fruit

of history, as visible as in diaspora Jewry. The problem is not to do away with possession but to acquire the capacity to enjoy it. Only an end to alienating guilts and their history can create the ground of enjoyment. Hegel saw the end of history as producing, as one of its fruits, the healing of the wounds of history and the spirit so that they reveal no scar. It is too early, and Jewry's wounding too deep, for that moment entirely to have come to Israel, yet a beginning has been made. A break with history means a break with history's hurts. Others may want to perpetuate the memory of Israel's injuries and a relation of resentment to those responsible for it; but Nietzsche taught us that resentment is the slave's aggression. Free men living in the awareness of the present deal realistically with it in terms of its promise and its necessities. This does not mean that the past need be ignored. One can learn from the past; one must never be enslaved to it.

The return to Israel has been characterized by a major break with bourgeois existence as the characteristic form of Jewish social organization. Bourgeois existence was the externally imposed lot of an essentially unemployable people rather than a token of elevation of status. Here again the ironies of possession and enjoyment are relevant. A religion which proclaimed its relevance and universality for all men was, in fact, the restricted possession of a very limited segment of the middle class. That there is a real inner connection between traditional Jewish values and the needs of a bourgeois acquisitive class has frequently been understood and commented upon. One of the great weaknesses of diaspora Judaism has been its total inability to transcend middle-class forms and sentiments. In the West this has been achieved only by the Catholic Church.

In Israel the growth of the *kibbutz,* the compulsory military service of women, and the simple national need of a laboring class represent a decisive break with the predominance of middle-class forms as the root expression of Jewish existence. This does not mean that middle-class life is deserving of its frequent caricatures, or that any other form of social existence is necessarily better or more humanly satisfying. It does mean that now the life and experience available to Jews who wish to continue to be religiously identified include a range of possibilities which does not automatically estrange every creative and emotionally fecund Jew. Too frequently these have left the Jewish community because they have identified Jewish life with bourgeois existence and have rejected the one with the other.

Above all, an old-new understanding of God is almost inevitable in our times. With the end of man's self-estrangement from nature, it is very likely that there will come an end to God's estrangement from nature as well. No more will God be seen as the transcendent Lord of nature, controlling it as if it were a marionette at the end of a string. God will be seen as the source and life of nature, the being of the beings which ephemerally and epiphenomenally are nature's self-expression.

There are parallel developments elsewhere. For over four hundred years Protestantism was enemy to both art and nature in a manner even more thoroughgoing than Judaism. Even in its religious hearth, the abstract beauty of icy symmetry replaced the effusion of forms, colors, and smells which characterized the medieval cathedral. Plainness, Puritanism, and Protestantism expressed the drabness of a people driven by their guilty and unalleviated fear of a wrathful Lord to deny nature even more severely than did the Jewish community. In our times Paul Tillich has proclaimed the death of the God of theism (the Lord of history), called for the expression of religion and life's meanings in the idiom of art, and has seen God as the ground of being of which all identifiable individualities are but partial and epiphenomenal expressions. Tillich saw an end to man's estrangement implicit in the Christ; we see an end to estrangement implicit in the return to Israel's earth and to the divinities at the source of that earth.

The dark wisdom of Heraclitus proclaimed that all things are alive with gods. In the return to Palestinian earth we become aware of the fact that we too are alive with and are the expressions of the powers and divinities of that earth. Only historical man in his alienation sees nature as inanimate and dead. Mankind at home with itself sees the cosmos as alive with the very same life which infuses its own being. That is why the ancients depicted their gods as suffering, mating, dying, and being resurrected. Mankind in its at-one-ness with the gods did not deny or annul passion or tragedy; it celebrated them as divinity's very life. No return, however, can deny the intermediate negativities. As Hegel understood, they are taken up *(aufgehoben)*, sublimated, in the final reconciliation. For Israel the return to nature will not mean a return to polytheism, though such a step has its real attractiveness. The unity of God will continue to be maintained, for the Lord of history has given us insight into the partial and tentative character of all polytheistic representations of the life and source of the cosmos. God will be seen as one, but He will be understood to participate in nature's vicissitudes and necessities rather than to create them outside of His solitary perfection.

A new understanding of God arising out of the return to earth and nature must inevitably confront the issue of the dark of divinity. The archaic ancients knew that the word holy-*kadosh-sacer* contained a hidden awesomeness which transcended all categories of goodness, virtue, and morality. For the Lord of history there can be no such issue, for all guilt and darkness rests on man's side. This is not so in the religion of nature. Insofar as there is a sense of mankind's unity with nature and nature's source, a demonic aspect to reality and divinity must be accepted as an inescapable concomitant of life and existence. *To say that God and nature are at one with each other, that they are alive and life-engendering, is to affirm the demonic side not alone in us but in divinity as well.* The tragedies, ironies, and ambiguities of existence cease to reflect historical man's willful rebellion; they become internalized in the self-unfolding of divinity. Virtue ceases to be a choice of separable alternatives; it becomes an overcoming. The contradictory character of existence, in contrast to the logical symmetry of essence, makes goodness and virtue an overcoming in us as well as in divinity. The very character of life makes the divine source a ceaseless self-striving in which the unending negativities and affirmations of existence follow one another and in which individual forms of life are expressions of the self-construction and self-separation of divinity. Life on life is thrust forward in divinity's ceaseless project to enjoy its hour and then to become the consumed substance of other life. Such a view of divinity makes tragedy and destruction inescapable and ineradicable. Paradoxically, though it ascribes an ontic quality to evil, it possesses far more compassion than the terrible view which makes of evil an entirely free act of will. In place of a moral philistinism which draws small comfort from the knowledge that others are more guilty, it affirms, but also endows with proportion and measure, both the loving and the demonic in man.

History comes to a stop religiously as it does politically. Religiously it achieves an ending in the recognition that there is absolutely no way out of the incessant self-strife of *eros* and *thanatos,* of individuation and separation, of affirmation and negation which is the very life of the cosmos and its divine source. The circle can be ended only by the self-identity of cosmic death; however, the Greeks enjoyed a wisdom that taught that even the return was infinitely repeatable. The existence of the present universe hints at the possibility that nothingness cannot tolerate its own solitude and that, were the present cosmic era to end, there would be other cosmic ecstasies of nothingness.

In place of a world ceaselessly and uselessly hoping for the unattainable and the unreal, there will, perhaps, come into being a world content to accept the joyful sorrow of what-is. Far more tragic than the denial of unrealistic possibilities is the impotent refusal of realities which lie at hand. Instead of the moralistic conception of good and evil, there will be restored the more meaningful conceptions of limit and excess. The real tragedy of historical man is neither his sinfulness nor his arrogance; these are but reaction-formations to his debted submissiveness. His real tragedy is that even when he goes through the motions of seeming to find pleasure, his guilt-ridden, wrath-begotten universe makes even the taste of permissible joys a sin. Having failed of the permissible, he is driven to the impermissible, never truly finding satisfaction or rest, until only aggression, acquisition, and self-destruction are for him the way of the world.

We therefore conclude that Zionism can be far more than the provincial strivings of an insignificant people. In Israel the Jewish people has finished what it and fate had long ago begun. Spirit has in principle returned from its estrangement; and history, man's inescapable negativity, has returned to the nature which gave it birth. Some will maintain that a theological interpretation of Zionism is irrelevant, that it is a movement lacking either old or new gods. Yet long ago the Romans argued that the Jews, worshipping an invisible God, were atheists. The past two thousand years have demonstrated that the contention reflected Roman insensitivity to a power they could neither understand nor cope with. Today the world's largest shrine to that invisible God stands, as visible proof of Rome's turning, in the city of Rome itself. It may be that the resurrection of the divinities of Israel's earth again looks like atheism to those who only know or deny the Lord of history. For Him the gods of earth are a blasphemy; they may, however, be the very real and very potent expressions of the inner vitality of contemporary Israel. Atheism is at best a term of limited utility. One man's denials are frequently pregnant with the affirmations of many.

With the closing of the circle the Jew needs no longer be, as Jew, a stranger to art, life, creative passion, or his own body. Hopefully old guilts and resentments will dissolve in the fullness of a life devoid of "unlived lives," for the first time in many millennia. Perhaps in the place of unmanly and self-apologetic literature elaborating upon Jewish "contributions" to civilization and morality, a dubious gift at best by any reflective standard, there may arise, not in books but in life, a new Jewish contribution, the example of self-liberation and self-discovery, of mankind returned and restored to its only true hearth—the bosom of mother-earth whence we came and to which we must inevitably return.

In the spring of 1966, Norman Podhoretz invited me to participate in a symposium on Jewish belief which was published in Commentary, *August 1966. I welcomed the opportunity to address myself to the following significant questions. My answers speak for themselves. They represent my current thinking on the issues raised by* Commentary.

> *1. In what sense do you believe the Torah to be Divine Revelation? Are all 613 commandments equally binding on the believing Jew? If not, how is he to decide which to observe? What status would you accord to ritual commandments lacking in ethical or doctrinal content (e.g., the prohibition against clothing made of linen and wool)?*

> *2. In what sense do you believe that the Jews are the Chosen People of God? How do you answer the charge that this doctrine is the model from which various theories of national and racial superiority have been derived?*

> *3. Is Judaism the one true religion, or is it one of several true religions? Does Judaism still have something distinctive—as it once had monotheism—to contribute to the world? Is the ethical sphere, the sphere of* ben adam la-chavero, *what distinguishes the believing Jew from the believing Christian, Moslem, or Buddhist—or, for that matter, from the unbelieving Jew and the secular humanist?*

> *4. Does Judaism as a religion entail any particular political viewpoint? Can a man be a good Jew and yet, say, support racial segregation? Can a man be a good Jew and be a Communist? A Fascist?*

> *5. Does the so-called "God is dead" question which has been agitating Christian theologians have any relevance to Judaism? What aspects of modern thought do you think pose the most serious challenge to Jewish belief?*

8 / Symposium on Jewish Belief

I BELIEVE the entire Torah to be sacred but not Divinely revealed. It is the authoritative document out of which the inherited corpus of Jewish religious myth and ritual is ultimately derived. I find it impossible to accept any literal conception of Divine revelation. I do not believe that a Divine-human encounter took place at Sinai nor do I believe that the norms of Jewish religious life possess any superordinate validation.

Nevertheless, I do not regard the tradition of Divine revelation as meaningless. It has psychological truth rather than literal historical truth. Something happened at Sinai and in the experience of the Jewish people. Somehow the Jewish people structured their personal and group norms by objectifying the parental image, projecting it into the cosmic sphere, and interpreting these norms as deriving from the objectified group-parent. I believe religion to be the way we share the decisive times and crises of life through the inherited experiences and norms of our community. The Torah is the repository of those norms. Because of its origins in the psychological strivings of the Jewish people, it is largely appropriate to its function.

All 613 commandments are equally binding, but our existential situation is one of total freedom to accept or reject any or all of them. There is no agency, human or divine, which can compel our response. I suspect that, in our times, the re-

sponse to a large proportion of the commandments will be negative. I am, however, opposed to any contemporary Jewish group's
legislating its historically circumscribed reaction to the 613 commandments for generations to come. I hope it will be possible
for subsequent generations to confront all 613 commandments
in the light of the insights of their time in order to decide what
sector is meaningful for them. I seriously doubt that they will
respond as we have. They may very well be ritually more compliant. Since we are totally free before the commandments, no
two people will respond in the same way. I suspect that all attempts to construct a set of guiding principles to determine
what type of commandments remain meaningful are doomed
to failure. I think it is wisest, both theologically and practically,
to recognize *both* the binding character of all the commandments
and our total freedom before them.

I believe some of the commandments lacking ethical or
doctrinal content are among the most meaningful. We must distinguish between the *latent* and *manifest* content of the commandments. By proclaiming the continuing relevance of only
those rituals which have an explicit ethical content, we tend to
ignore rituals which dramatize our feelings concerning enormously important areas of life. At the manifest level, a ceremony
such as Bar Mitzvah has little ethical significance. Nevertheless,
something very important takes place. The young man passes
through a puberty rite. He is confirmed as a male and a Jew
at a crucial moment in the timetable of his life. The real question we must ask about ritual is how it *functions* in the life of
the individual and the group. Vast areas of Jewish ritual are
deeply rooted in our psychological needs. Religion's primary
function is priestly rather than prophetic, insofar as we can
separate the two categories. It is excessively difficult to effect
ethical improvement through religious instrumentalities. Most
rabbis function largely as priests. Their role is to help the individual pass through the crises of life with appropriate rituals
which have the power to alleviate the conflicts inherent in the
worst moments and heighten the joys of the best. People aren't
going to change much. Moralizing rituals have a severely limited
potency. Rituals which help us pass through such crises as birth,

puberty, marriage, sickness, the changing seasons, and death are indispensable.

I believe that my Jewish identity is an absurd given. It is the way I have been thrust into the world. This identity involves my having been born into a community which has an inherited mythic tradition. That *mythos* includes the doctrine of the election of Israel.

I find it impossible to believe in the doctrine of the Chosen People, yet I know of no way in which Jews can be entirely quit of this myth. The Jewish people made a fantastic claim for themselves, that their traditions and destiny were peculiarly the object of God's concern. Ironically, the gentile world took them seriously, so seriously that the Christian Church to this day asserts the election has passed from the "Old" Israel to the Church, the "New" Israel. Too frequently Judaism is criticized for its "chauvinistic" Chosen People doctrine, as if Jews were the only ones who had such a doctrine. In actual fact, Christianity cannot be understood apart from its Chosen People doctrine, the claim that the Church has replaced the Synagogue as the New Israel. The real problem implicit in the Chosen People doctrine is not Jewish ethnocentricism but the two-thousand-year-old sibling rivalry of Jew and Christian over who is the Father's beloved child.

When I recite the prayer, "Praised be Thou O Lord our God . . . who has chosen us from among all peoples and given us the Torah," I assert the appropriateness and sufficiency of the Torah as the authoritative document of the Jewish religion in the face of the continuing claim of the Church that my religion remains an imperfect anticipation of and preparation for Christianity. I do not see how a believing Christian can avoid claiming that he is a member of the New Israel, the truly elect of God. Even Jewish and Christian "death of God" theologians cannot avoid this Law-Gospel conflict. It has an Antigone-like quality. There is no way out, save moral and psychological modesty, from recognizing that the Christian has been thrust into his religious identity as absurdly as the Jew into his.

I see no inner resemblance between the Chosen People

doctrine and modern doctrines of racial superiority. The Chosen People doctrine has been the source of millennia of pathetic and unrealistic self-criticism by Jews. Because Jews felt under a special obligation to fulfill God's covenant, they have been convinced since the prophets that their religious performance was never good enough. They have interpreted every Jewish disaster, from the destruction of Jerusalem in 586 B.C.E. to the hideous disasters of the twentieth century, as God's attempt to punish His errant children in the hope that they would be restored to perfect fidelity to Him. This contrasts with modern ideologies of racial superiority. The racial doctrines are totally devoid of any shred of self-criticism or the feeling of unworthiness before God. On the contrary, these ideologies lend respectability to the most vicious kinds of aggrandizement by the nations involved at the expense of their neighbors. The bitter irony of the Jewish doctrine was that its effect was to magnify beyond all realism Jewish guilt feelings before God.

I believe that all of the major religions are psychologically true for their believers. As such, they are deeply congruent with the needs and identities of their participants. In terms of psychological function, Judaism is no "truer" than any other religion.

I believe that Judaism continues to make a unique contribution to the world, more in terms of the quality of its men and women than in terms of any special insight absent from other religions. Judaism will continue to make a distinctive contribution as long as it develops men and women who function as an element of creative discontent before the regnant idolatries of any given time or community. I also believe that Judaism possesses a peculiar sanity which ought never to be overlooked. Judaism is largely a this-worldly religion. It focuses attention upon the requirements of I and Thou in the here and now. In this context the old Law-Gospel controversy retains enormous contemporary relevance. Two thousand years ago the Christian Church claimed that some of the tragic inevitabilities of the human condition had been overcome through the career of Jesus. Before this claim the rabbis preferred their sad wisdom that the human condition had not been altered. They focused

Jewish attention on those norms which could make life's limitations more viable rather than on a saviour who promised to overcome those limitations. The fundamental Jewish posture is one of realism before existence rather than of seeking an escape from the world's necessities.

There is a sense in which I am forced to assert that Judaism is "truer" than Christianity. The Christian Church makes certain claims about the way the career of Jesus changed the meaning of the Synagogue and its traditions. The Church does not assert that it is an entirely different religion from Judaism. It claims that the full meaning of Israel is finally revealed through the Christ. That is why Vatican II could only go so far in mollifying the Church-Synagogue conflict. I regard the claim of the Church vis-à-vis Judaism as inherently mistaken. Insofar as Christianity is compelled to define the ultimate meaning of my religious community in its own special perspectives, I must be a dissenting partisan. I find myself in the paradoxical position of asserting that Christianity is as true psychologically for Christians as Judaism is for Jews, while maintaining that the manifest claims of the Church concerning Israel and Israel's Messiah are without foundation.

I find your question concerning whether the ethical sphere distinguishes the believing Jew from the believing Christian the most difficult to answer. I honestly don't know. As a this-worldly religion, Judaism stresses the ethical more insistently than does Christianity, the only realistic alternative in our culture. I might almost be caught saying that a truly believing Jew would be more fully committed within the sphere of I–Thou than others. I find that I have to pull back. I wish it were so. Certainly Jewish ethical standards are no worse than others. I doubt very much that one could demonstrate that unbelievers have a lower standard in behavioral matters than believers. I am convinced that any attempt to establish the current uniqueness of Judaism on the basis of the special virtues of its believers is doomed to failure.

Finally, I would caution against the tendency in contemporary Judaism to overstress the moral and the ethical. Admittedly Judaism seeks to inculcate high ethical standards, but one of the most important functions of a religious community is the *sharing of failure,* especially moral failure. We turn to the sanctuary less to be admonished to pursue virtue than out of the need to express and share our inevitable shortcomings in that pursuit.

In the absence of a Biblically ordained theocracy, which few contemporary Jews desire, Judaism has much to say about justice but very little about politics. From a purely religious perspective, it would normally make very little difference whether a practicing Jew were a Republican or a Democrat, provided the area of disagreement concerned the political means whereby an equitable society could be achieved. However, the problem of Judaism and politics cannot be divorced from the historic experience of the Jewish people. I do not see how Jews can possibly feel at home in right-wing groups or parties. The underlying appeal of these groups is for the supremacy of a particular racial or ethnic community. Inevitably, such groups must turn anti-Semitic or at the very least yearn to "put the Jews in their place." That is why Jewish opposition to the Goldwater campaign was so overwhelming. Jews understood instinctively that the half-Jew Goldwater was seeking to harness the irrational forces in American political life which were striving to assure white supremacy. They knew instinctively that the Goldwater campaign, if successful, would ultimately become anti-Semitic. Jews have fared best in multi-ethnic communities in which the ties between citizens were rational and contractual rather than emotional ties based on real or imagined membership in a primary group. For that reason Jews will usually favor that party which fosters a rational, contractual conception of citizenship and is neutral in religious and ethnic matters.

I do not believe a religious Jew can support racial injustice or enforced segregation. Nevertheless, Jews do believe in a measure of religious separateness. We do not favor intermarriage. Hence we tend to be cautious about a host of social arrangements which can lead to it. I am convinced that the Jewish community will continue to be an ally of the Negro community in its quest for political justice. There are, however, important areas of conflict between the two communities. The Negro community's goal seems to be the ultimate obliteration of the voluntary as well as the involuntary kinds of segregation in America. The Jewish community is not prepared to heed that call. To do so would be to destroy the religious and communal basis of Jewish uniqueness.

I see no impediment to a believing Jew's being a Marxist but I do not believe he could be a Communist. As a Communist, a believing Jew would have to endure an insupportable conflict between party discipline and loyalty to his religious community. I can never forget the way in which Communists of Jewish origin insisted that Hitler's war was of no concern to them until the Nazi attack on the Soviet Union on June 22, 1941. These people were indifferent as long as Hitler was murdering Jews but not when he attacked the Soviet Union. After the Hitler experience, I fail to see how any believing Jew could be a Fascist.

I am convinced that the problems implicit in "death of God" theology concern Judaism as much as Christianity. Technically death-of-God theology reflects the Christian tradition of the passion of the Christ. As such, the terminology of the movement creates some very obvious problems for Jewish theologians. Nevertheless, I have, almost against my will, come to the conclusion that the terminology is unavoidable. The death-of-God theologians have brought into the open a conviction which has led a very potent underground existence for decades. Death-of-God theology is no fad. It is a contemporary expression of issues which have, in one way or another, appeared in embryo in scholastic philosophy, medieval mysticism, nineteenth-century German philosophy, and in the religious existentialism of Martin Buber and Paul Tillich.

No man can really say that God is dead. How can we know that? Nevertheless, I am compelled to say that we live in the time of the "death of God." This is more a statement about man and his culture than about God. The death of God is a cultural fact. Buber felt this. He spoke of the eclipse of God. I can understand his reluctance to use the more explicitly Chris-

tian terminology. I am compelled to utilize it because of my conviction that the time which Nietzsche's madman said was too
far off has come upon us. There is no way around Nietzsche. Had
I lived in another time or another culture, I might have found
some other vocabulary to express my meanings. I am, however,
a religious existentialist after Nietzsche and after Auschwitz.
When I say we live in the time of the death of God, I mean
that the thread uniting God and man, heaven and earth, has been
broken. We stand in a cold, silent, unfeeling cosmos, unaided
by any purposeful power beyond our own resources. After Auschwitz, what else can a Jew say about God?

When Professor William Hamilton associated my theological writings with the death-of-God movement in his article
on radical theology in *The Christian Scholar*,[1] I was somewhat
dubious about his designation. After reflection, I concluded that
Professor Hamilton was correct. There is a definite style in religious thought which can be designated death-of-God theology.
I have struggled to escape the term. I have been embarrassed by it.
I realize its inadequacy and its Christian origin. I have, nevertheless, concluded that it is inescapable. I see no other way of expressing the void which confronts man where once God stood.

I am acutely aware of the fact that Christian death-of-
God theologians remain fully committed Christians as I remain
a committed Jew. As Professor Hamilton has suggested, Christian death-of-God theologians have no God, but they do have a
Messiah. Christian death-of-God theology remains Christocentric. I affirm the final authority of Torah and reject the Christian
Messiah, as Jews have for two thousand years. Professor Thomas
J. J. Altizer welcomes the death of God. He sees it as an apocalyptic event in which the freedom of the Gospels is finally realized
and the true Christian is liberated from every restraint of the
Law. I do not see that awful event as a cosmic liberation. I am
saddened by it. I believe that in a world devoid of God we need
Torah, tradition, and the religious community far more than in

[1] William Hamilton, "The Death of God Theology," *The Christian Scholar*, XLVIII (Spring 1965).

a world where God's presence was meaningfully experienced. The death of God leads Altizer to a sense of apocalyptic liberation; it leads me to a sad determination to enhance the religious norms and the community without which the slender fabric of human decency might well disappear. In the time of the death of God, Christian theologians still proclaim the Gospel of the Christ; Jewish theologians proclaim the indispensability of Torah.

I believe the greatest single challenge to modern Judaism arises out of the question of God and the death camps. I am amazed at the silence of contemporary Jewish theologians on this most crucial and agonizing of all Jewish issues. How can Jews believe in an omnipotent, beneficent God after Auschwitz? Traditional Jewish theology maintains that God is the ultimate, omnipotent actor in the historical drama. It has interpreted every major catastrophe in Jewish history as God's punishment of a sinful Israel. I fail to see how this position can be maintained without regarding Hitler and the SS as instruments of God's will. The agony of European Jewry cannot be likened to the testing of Job. To see any purpose in the death camps, the traditional believer is forced to regard the most demonic, antihuman explosion in all history as a meaningful expression of God's purposes. The idea is simply too obscene for me to accept. I do not think that the full impact of Auschwitz has yet been felt in Jewish theology or Jewish life. Great religious revolutions have their own period of gestation. No man knows the hour when the full impact of Auschwitz will be felt, but no religious community can endure so hideous a wounding without undergoing vast inner disorders.

Though I believe that a void stands where once we experienced God's presence, I do not think Judaism has lost its meaning or its power. I do not believe that a theistic God is necessary for Jewish religious life. Dietrich Bonhoeffer has written that our problem is how to speak of God in an age of no religion. I believe that our problem is how to speak of religion in an age of no God. I have suggested that Judaism is the way in which we share the decisive times and crises of life through the traditions of our inherited community. The need for that sharing is not diminished in the time of the death of God. We no longer believe in the God who has the power to annul the tragic necessities of existence; the need religiously to share that existence remains.

Finally, the time of the death of God does not mean the end of all gods. It means the demise of the God who was the ultimate actor in history. I believe in God, the Holy Nothingness known to mystics of all ages, out of which we have come and to which we shall ultimately return. I concur with atheistic existentialists such as Sartre and Camus in much of their analysis of the broken condition of human finitude. We must endure that condition without illusion or hope. I do not part company with them on their analysis of the human predicament. I part company on the issue of the necessity of religion as the way in which we share that predicament. Their analysis of human hopelessness leads me to look to the religious community as the institution in which that condition can be shared in depth. The limitations of finitude can be overcome only when we return to the Nothingness out of which we have been thrust. In the final analysis, omnipotent Nothingness is Lord of all creation.

The relations between Jews and Protestants in America pervade every aspect of Jewish life. Protestant power spells out the limits of Jewish entry in American life. When Digby Baltzell's The Protestant Establishment—Aristocracy and Caste in America *appeared in 1965, Steven Schwarzschild asked me to review it for* Judaism.

I disagreed most strongly with Baltzell in his optimism concerning the academic community. He is convinced that the universities have led the way in the utilization of talent on the basis of ability. I was convinced that they have followed exactly the same policies as the corporations: the hiring of Jewish talent in non-decision-making *capacities. While faculty and research positions are relatively open, Jews are conspicuously absent from decision-making positions in administration.*

My observations were based on personal experience. I did not have the resources to document them, although I had visited a sufficiently large number of campuses to feel that Baltzell was probably in error. On May 14, 1966, at the annual meeting of the American Jewish Committee in Washington, D.C., Morris B. Abram asserted, in his President's report, that no Jew had been appointed to the presidency of a publicly supported university or senior college since 1949. There have been approximately a thousand vacancies. Of 1,720 deans in 775 American colleges and universities, 2.6 per cent or forty-five are Jews. Twenty-nine of these are in six institutions. In the remaining 769 institutions, there are only sixteen Jewish deans, less than 1 per cent. The relations between religious communities in America cannot be understood apart from the power relations which underlie them.

9/The Protestant Establishment and the Jews

T HE 1964 REPUBLICAN ELECTION FIASCO highlighted a continuing problem in American life: the estrangement of a large sector of the old-stock white Protestant elite from a dominant role in the intellectual and political leadership of the United States. Since the days of the New Deal, the Democratic party has been the majority party, resting its power largely upon an odd alliance of religious, racial, ethnic, and sectional minority groups. Support for the Republican party has been greatest among old-stock white Protestants. In the last election, led by the "half-Jew" Goldwater, the Republicans based their appeal primarily on a single underlying issue—Protestant nativist racism. In spite of much talk about the economy and free enterprise, the fundamental platform of the Goldwater Republicans was that of a racist America dominated by white Anglo-Saxon Protestants (or WASPs, as they are known in the popular acronymous formulation). Goldwater spelled this out toward the end of the campaign. Speaking at a shopping center in upper-class, prosperous mainline Philadelphia, the Republican candidate complained to his predominantly WASP audience that the government had been in the hands of "minority groups" for the past thirty-two years. He expressed concern for the plight of the disinherited majority and promised, if elected, to restore it to political power.

Goldwater, situated precariously close to the social acceptance he purchased as the exception-Jew of American extremism, understood the yearnings of an important segment of the

WASP community. His supporters have been described as seeking the lost simplicities of the 1890's as an escape from the complexities of mid-twentieth-century America. The description is
accurate up to a point. It neglects an important aspect of WASP
nostalgia. The 1890's were not only a time of simple issues and
simple moral perspectives; they were also a time when, intellectually, social, and commercially, the Protestant elite was not seriously challenged by any of the newer minority groups, especially
the Jews. Goldwater's promise reduced itself to the restoration of
an America in which Jews, Negroes, and perhaps Catholics,
would accept an inferior place and in which Protestant supremacy would again be unchallenged. Goldwater understood the
issue as only a half-breed could.

        The election revealed an America still searching for self-
definition. The Goldwater-led Republican party rejected pluralism as a legitimate expression of American civilization. By its campaign, it implied that pluralism was at best an interim device, that
minority groups which retained their specific identity could not
fully participate in American political and cultural life. In the
case of the Negro, the alienation from the American mainstream
could never be entirely overcome. In the instance of the Jew, Goldwater's diluted identity and nominal Christianity were symbolic
of how the Jew could find his eventual place in America: Jews
were to be given the option of retention of Jewish identity coupled with pariah status, or gradual disappearance through intermarriage and conversion. Under no circumstance was whole-
hearted acceptance of Jewish identity to be regarded as a legitimate
way of living as an American. Furthermore, this unspoken but
very real program could be called the moderate position of the
Goldwater conservatives. There are men behind Goldwater, the
extremists he praised and cultivated, who genuinely admire the
efficiency of Hitler's "final solution" of the Jewish problem.

        All other election issues paled before the issue of WASP
supremacy. A leading member of the Republican National Committee stated to a Negro reporter on the Huntley-Brinkley TV
team during the campaign that the country would be better off
were it able to rid itself of its "rats and the vermin." The incident
was reported to this writer by the reporter, a former editor of the

highly respected *Pittsburgh Courier,* who added that there was no doubt that the reference was to Jews and Negroes. Since the fundamental issue could hardly be resolved in a single campaign, the Goldwater forces were far more concerned with securing an effective political base through control of a national party than they were in winning the election. In terms of the real aims of the Goldwater people, their election campaign was won at the Cow Palace. They understand the underlying irrational power of their program and are prepared to pursue it over a long period. In spite of their defeat at the polls and the resignation of Dean Burch as chairman of the Republican National Committee, Jewish experience is such that the program's ultimate failure cannot be anticipated with certainty. Throughout history the call to purify a country of its Jews has sooner or later met with a real measure of success. One hundred and one years separate the anti-Jewish excesses in Seville in 1391 from the final expulsion from Spain in 1492, but, once initiated, the process had an almost inexorable necessity. The Pan-German outbursts of the 1880's were followed with even greater dispatch by the Hitler movement and the end of Jewish life in Europe. If Hitler demonstrated anything to politicians, it is the effectiveness of anti-Semitism as a political weapon. It would be naïve to assume that this lesson has been understood only by Jews and not by their adversaries. Unless the moderate Republicans succeed in definitely wresting control from the Goldwater wing in the near future, it will be only a matter of time before an eventual shift in national sentiment brings the right-wing Republicans to full national power. If ever installed, they will not easily be displaced.

The Goldwater candidacy brought to fruition a crisis in American life which was implicit in the first introduction of Negro slaves to Jamestown and which became explicit with the tidal wave of immigrants from Europe who came as laborers in the period from the end of the Civil War until the beginning of World War I. The Constitution had assured Americans of equal rights at a time when America was fundamentally a homogeneous Protestant community. Although Negro slaves were specifically excluded from the rights guaranteed to other Americans, the American Constitution represented an enormous achievement.

The question has always existed whether its provisions could effectively be extended to all Americans regardless of background. This problem has been better solved in the political than in the social sphere. A number of *ad hoc* arrangements have been worked out in which a sharp distinction has been drawn between state and society. The direction of government policy at the national level has been toward the implementation of the Constitutional assurances of equality for all citizens. This implementation has tended to be more straightforward under the Democrats than under the Republicans. On the other hand, the dominant Protestant community has sought to withhold effective equality from non-WASPs, especially Jew and Negroes, in the private sector of American life. Since the public and private sectors cannot entirely be separated, *de facto* discrimination continues to be effective in some departments of the national government, such as the State Department and the armed forces, where these sectors tend to coincide. In addition, vast areas of private discrimination prevent full participation by Jews in American life. One of the ironies of this discrimination is that it tends to create far more problems for the group which practices it than may be apparent at the outset.

Occasionally a book is written which is especially appropriate for its time. Digby Baltzell's *The Protestant Establishment—Aristocracy and Caste in America*[1] may prove to be such a book. Published immediately following the Republican defeat, Baltzell's work adds insight into the inevitability of that defeat and the dangers implicit in it for the future. Baltzell, a University of Pennsylvania sociologist of WASP background, has focused attention on the crisis in current Protestant leadership in a work which summarizes most of the contemporary sociological knowledge on the problem of caste and class in America. It adds little that was not previously understood, but it is of enormous value as a summary work which puts things into a meaningful context.

Baltzell's central thesis is that no nation can endure without both liberal democratic and aristocratic processes. He defines

[1] New York: Random House, 1964.

democracy as the process which assures that men of ability and ambition, regardless of background, are allowed to rise into the elite. He defines the elite as those individuals who have succeeded in rising to top positions in any society. The democratic process, according to Baltzell, means that the elite is open and based on the ideal of equality of opportunity.

Baltzell defines aristocracy as a community of upper-class families whose members are born into positions of high prestige and assured dignity because their ancestors have been leaders for one or more generations. These families are said to be carriers of a set of traditional values which command authority because they represent the aspirations of both the elite and the rest of the population. In America, aristocracy has been Protestant and largely Anglo-Saxon. According to Baltzell, the Protestant elite can continue to justify its special position and authority only if it contributes its share of contemporary leaders and if it assimilates new members in each generation. In Baltzell's estimation, it has failed to an increasing extent on both counts.

According to Baltzell, when conditions of aristocracy and democracy are met, upper-class values will carry authority within the elite and within society as a whole. Upper-class leaders then form an *establishment* which is essentially traditional and authoritative rather than coercive and authoritarian. It is always dominated by upper-class members, but it is constantly in the process of rejuvenation through new members who are in the process of acquiring upper-class status. Baltzell indicates that the English system comes closest to filling this description.

A society is endangered, according to Baltzell, when its upper class becomes closed. The principal thrust of the book is that the American Protestant upper class has become or is becoming a rigid caste. The process of caste formation is at work whenever an upper class protects its privileges and prestige but does not continue to contribute leadership or to assimilate new members because of their racial or ethnic background. The caste process is the antithesis of the aristocratic process. It leads to a decline of authority and a crisis in national leadership. This is evident in the estrangement of the Republican party from both national leader-

ship and national authority. The failure of the party has largely
been the failure of the Protestant elite to remain an open aristocracy.

The rigid policies of the private clubs in excluding Jews
has been a decisive factor in turning the Protestant aristocracy into
a caste. As has long been recognized, American social and financial power is intimately related to membership in the clubs.
Without access to such facilities it is impossible to conduct high-
level business of more than local scope. The rules barring Jews
from these facilities are as stringent as Hitler's Nuremberg laws.
The parallel to the Nuremberg laws is particularly apt: even a
single Jewish grandparent is sufficient to warrant exclusion from
the most influential clubs of every important American city. Conversion to Christianity is of no help in entering the club world.
Racial background is the determining factor. The zeal with which
those who sit on the admissions committees pursue the pedigree
of applicants has often been phenomenal.

One result of the club system is that even large corporations founded by Jews have tended to be taken over by Protestants who thereafter practice the same anti-Semitic discrimination
in the formerly Jewish firms as is practiced in firms founded by
Protestants. Among the corporations which have followed this
pattern are the Radio Corporation of America and Sears Roebuck.
Baltzell cites the case of one Jewish executive of a large international firm founded by Jews who was passed over for the presidency because of his inability to qualify as a member of the leading city clubs. Although his ability and experience made him the
logical choice, it was felt by the trustees that the man could not
successfully function as head of the corporation without membership in the proper clubs. The executive quit the firm in disgust
and became an important member of John F. Kennedy's "New
Frontier" team in Washington.

The dangers implicit in a closed upper class were expressed by de Tocqueville over a century ago in his analysis of the
failure of the French *ancien régime*. Had the older nobility manifested greater flexibility in the face of the aspirations of the rising
bourgeoisie, the history of France might have been very different.
In addition to Baltzell, David Riesman, C. Wright Mills, Walter

Lippmann, and others have pointed to a crisis in national leadership which has arisen out of the lack of any coherent upper-class authority in contemporary America. A similar point is made by John Wheeler-Bennett in his book, *The Nemesis of Power,*[2] the classic analysis of the history of the German General Staff during the period betweeen 1918 and 1945. The refusal of the German upper class to give the Weimar Republic its allegiance and loyalty was a principal ingredient in fostering Hitler's contention that treason to the German state was patriotism to the German nation. The current insistence by the American extreme right wing that Washington is as much the enemy as Moscow and that it is controlled by Jews and Negroes offers the seeds of the same sort of radical treason on these shores.

At first glance, one of the bright spots on the horizon of intergroup relations in the United States would seem to be the academic community. Today's educational institutions tend to train the most talented students and to hire the ablest professors, regardless of background, in contrast to the discriminatory policies of the caste-ridden clubs and corporations. According to Baltzell, the relative liberalism of the better universities will ultimately have a beneficial effect on the policies of the business community. He believes that friendships arising from school contacts, which cross ethnic and religious lines, are bound to affect club membership policies. This hope may prove without substance. It is true that men of talent mix freely in the faculty clubs. It does not follow that the universities are pace-setters for the larger community. The blackball system requires only a single dissent.

I must confess that I am continually surprised by the overoptimism of liberals such as Baltzell concerning the American university system. There is no doubt that American universities have made enormous strides since 1940. Departments such as English, chemistry, sociology, and engineering, which were formerly notorious in their refusal to appoint Jews to positions of tenure, have by and large reversed their discriminatory policies. Jews occupy chairs in every discipline at the major universities. Nevertheless, the Protestant caste system remains as rigidly opera-

[2] London: Macmillan, 1961.

tive in the universities as it does in most business corporations. It is almost impossible for a Jew to be appointed to an administrative position at any university not sponsored by Jews. This includes the vast majority of tax-supported state institutions. In spite of the fact that in many leading educational institutions fully a third of the students are Jewish, one can almost never find a single Jewish administrative officer at any level. The universities have exactly the same employment policies toward Jews as do most corporations. In the corporations a stringent distinction is made between management and research and, in a few instances, sales. Jews are hired for work in research; in some large corporations they may even become vice-presidents in charge of research. In the Pittsburgh headquarters of Westinghouse Electric, for example, Jews are employed in very fine positions in the company's research laboratories in suburban Churchill and Monroeville. There is even a Jewish vice-president in charge of research. However, no Jews are to be found in positions of any consequence in Westinghouse's administrative headquarters in downtown Gateway Center.

It is true that faculty clubs are democratic. The result is that top Protestant administrative personnel in some important universities refrain from using the faculty clubs. I know of at least one major university in which all upper-echelon administrators take their meals at the adjacent University Club. The University Club has a strict no-Jews, no-Negroes membership policy. Several years ago there was a local uproar when a Negro city councilman was refused service in the club's dining room to which he had been invited by a member. The administration of the university, which is somewhat dependent on public funds, immediately let it be known that there was no connection between the university and the University Club. The administration omitted to state that the university paid for the memberships of its administrators in the University Club. Furthermore, it pays for the membership of a number of academic stars of WASP background. In one instance a Jewish professor was urged to make use of a WASP administrator's card in the club. When the professor, one of the university's academic luminaries, discovered that a WASP professor of comparable status had been given a membership in his own name, he indignantly returned the proffered card.

University administration corresponds to corporate management as the university faculty corresponds to corporate research. As universities grow ever more complex, they tend in any event to be run as corporations. There are no indications that any progress has been made in changing the power structure of the American universities any more than significant indications can be found of alterations of the corporate power structure. This is most unfortunate for the university system as a whole. One of the most important problems facing American universities is the increasing failure of communication between the administration on the one hand and the faculty and students on the other. The difference between the mentality needed for administrative success and that required for faculty advancement is very great. The tasks performed by each group make for difficulty in communication in any event. These difficulties are further heightened by the growing social and intellectual isolation of the WASP administrators from the increasingly non-WASP faculty and students. This failure was much in evidence in the recent student disturbances at Berkeley. To anyone cognizant of the immense distance that separates the administration from the rest of the university in most institutions, it is indeed surprising that there have been so few such outbursts.

In many schools the faculty complains of the inaccessibility of the administrators. This is compounded in institutions in which the administration retires at lunch behind the barricades of racially and religiously segregated facilities of the University Club type, leaving the less exclusive faculty clubs for the religiously heterogeneous faculty. Decisions can be made easily and simply when faculty and administration share the same facilities. Informal conversations arising out of predictable chance meetings offer a far better setting for a host of academic decisions than the administrative red tape which must be employed when administration and faculty are in effect racially segregated. More than one university has lost a promising faculty member who was offered a post elsewhere because the department chairman could not easily communicate with the administration. The caste system is as instrumental in creating the increasing failure of communication between faculty and administration as is the growth in the size and responsibilities of the universities.

According to Baltzell, the American social system is becoming increasingly divisive as upper-class members of non-Protestant groups find positions barred to them by virtue of their background alone. A closed WASP upper class is increasingly an anachronism which commands little respect from the non-WASP intellectual elite. In a recent interview in *Newsweek,* Baltzell suggested that Americans were increasingly involved in three establishments, a Protestant business and social establishment, a Catholic political establishment, and a Jewish intellectual establishment. It is certainly true that the Protestant establishment carries little or no authority with the intellectual establishment. This is evident on any campus in which Protestant power has moved behind the barricades of the administrative offices and is regarded with hostility and occasional contempt by the more intellectually creative members of the faculty. It is also highly visible in the overwhelming estrangement of the intellectuals from the Republican party.

For the Protestant establishment to carry authority, its way of life would have to be one which is regarded as worthy of emulation. James Baldwin has commented, in *The Fire Next Time,*[3] that it is not likely that Negroes would want to marry the sisters of the whites they have served; they know the families too well. Many non-Protestants who come in contact with the WASP establishment are likely to come away with the feeling that it possesses enormous power but that it offers little else to be imitated. The novels of F. Scott Fitzgerald, John O'Hara, Mary McCarthy, Louis Auchincloss, and others have illustrated the dilemmas of WASP personal and social existence. The point made by all of the novelists is that social pre-eminence does not exempt a person from the problems of life. It is more likely that the non-Protestant will find a more viable personal existence by working through the manifold determinants of his own identity than by trying to copy the identity of others. This does not imply a negative judgment on Protestant identity for Protestants; it merely suggests its inappro-

[3] New York: Dial Press, 1963.

priateness for others. Baltzell seems to feel that the Protestant elite would have more success in disseminating its way of life as normative for all Americans were it an aristocracy rather than a caste. It apparently does not occur to him that there are other options which intellectually and culturally sensitive non-Protestants and even Protestants prefer to elect in our time.

The example of John F. Kennedy is crucial. Kennedy brought to the American presidency a flair and a grace which had been totally absent in recent years. He had, of course, come into close contact with the Protestant elite at Choate and Harvard and throughout his later life. Though he had assimilated elements of the eastern Protestant ethos, he remained identifiably non-Protestant. Through Jacqueline Kennedy he brought to the White House a certain patronage of the arts and intellectual pursuits which would have seemed odd at best had it been sponsored by Dwight and Mamie Eisenhower.

One of the results of an exposure to an upper-class Protestant environment can be a strengthening of the conviction that one is a stranger to that environment and could not without inner falsification conform to it. This is certainly true of both the religious Jew and the intellectual. Since alienation is the price paid by the intellectual in any event, he is not likely to regard even an open Protestant aristocracy as his model. The alienation of the Protestant upper class from the world of the intellectual has been a twofold movement: the non-Protestant intellectual has rejected the Protestant world as actively as the Protestant world has rejected him. This is in part due to the fact that the strongest components of anti-intellectualism on the American scene have been Protestant in origin. The Protestant ethos has tended to be rural and increasingly replete with subtle and not so subtle forms of ancestor worship; the intellectual ethos has tended to be urban, individualistic, and cosmopolitan. Frequently these worlds have talked past each other with almost no contact. Protestants have often been quite content to allow Jews to do the intellectual dirty work which they have never entirely respected. Protestant anti-intellectualism has deep roots. It is at least as old as Reformation theology and claims an even more ancient Christian lineage. Perhaps the most alienated educated Americans today are Protestant intellectuals. Their situation has become somewhat "Jewish." As a result, they find themselves outsiders to both the world of Protestant power and Jewish intellectualism.

As one reads the history of how the Protestant aristocracy has been turned into a racial elite, it becomes evident that the real reason for the change, which began with the exclusion of upper-class German Jews from resorts in the 1880's, was the inability of the Protestant upper class to assimilate large numbers of Jews into its ranks. Jews very quickly rose to a level of intellectual and financial equality with Protestant elite, but the very rapidity of the rise, coupled with the flood of East European Jewish immigrants, assured their pariah status in Protestant eyes. The history of the Protestant establishment can also be designated as the history of American mainstream anti-Semitism. Of course, Protestants have by no means been the only Americans persuaded of Jewish undesirability, but Protestant anti-Semitism has been combined with economic and social power to bar Jews from positions for which their abilities might otherwise have qualified them. The anti-Semitism of the non-Protestant groups has been muted by the common interest of minorities to form a political alliance. Jews and Irish have tended to be political allies even though overt anti-Semitic acts against Jews have more frequently derived from Irish-Catholic than Protestant sources. These attacks, though virulent in their immediacy, have had none of the effectiveness of the exclusions practiced by the Protestant community.

One of the limitations of sociological descriptions of Protestant-Jewish relations such as Baltzell's is that they tell us very little about what goes on beneath the surface in the individual or intergroup encounters. Baltzell, for example, understands that there is much irrationality in the exclusion of Jews from the clubs and positions of power. Like many liberals, he sometimes seems to believe that all that is required for its elimination is the realization that the system is socially dysfunctional. He never attempts an examination of the underlying motivations which have created such enormous barriers to normal relations between persons.

The violent rejection of Jews and Judaism which underlies the caste rules of the Protestant establishment is based upon needs and anxieties that are deeply rooted in the religion and the history of both groups. The durability of the attitudes involved suggests that those who nurture anti-Semitic prejudice are not likely to renounce it because it has proven socially costly, if indeed it really has for the Protestant group. It was interesting for this writer to read Jean Paul Sartre's attempted reconciliation of Marxism and existentialism in his *Critique de la raison dialetique*[4] immediately after completing Baltzell's work. Sartre pleads for a multidimensional understanding of human *praxis* in terms of its personal, cultural, economic, historical, and psychological context. He explicitly censures American sociology for its preference for journalistic descriptiveness over historical insight. Protestant rejection of Jews is a contemporary expression of a very old problem. It cannot be understood apart from the long history of the Judaeo-Christian conflict as well as the specifics of recent American history. The problem vastly predates the beginnings of American civilization, and we shall never understand it unless we pay more attention to its roots in Jewish and Christian history.

Uni-dimensional sociological description has other shortcomings. The Jewish executive who was passed over for the presidency of his corporation has already been alluded to. There must have been relevant facts about the executive's decision to quit which a sociologist could not know and which might have changed the meaning of what took place. One might ask whether the head of a large international corporation was so out of touch with reality that he was unaware of the system until its discriminatory aspect touched him personally. I would like to know more about the delicate balance of relationships between the executive and his colleagues, as well as about the executive's personal life, before I could accept the statement that the man resigned simply because he was passed over for the presidency. We have the beginnings of a drama, not a depth understanding of its complexities.

One extremely interesting footnote on Protestant-Jewish relations is Baltzell's revelation of the extent to which upper-class American Protestants were sympathetic to the Nazi treatment of the Jews before the war. Apparently it was quite fashionable to

[4] Paris: Gallimard, 1960.

travel to Europe first class on German ships, secure in the knowledge that these ships were as racially pure as the home-town clubs. Baltzell quotes a Protestant socialite who expressed a common sentiment during the Hitler years: "Thank God, since Hitler, there are no more Jews on the *Bremen* and the *Europa.*" In the light of Baltzell's remarks about the racial character of much of WASP prejudice, one wonders whether the tendencies currently visible, which would turn NATO into an American-German axis, are not rooted in a contemporary expression of the same northern European racialism.

The same ill-will toward Jews was also pathologically manifest in upper-class hatred of Franklin Delano Roosevelt. Anyone who expressed an approving word about Roosevelt during the early years of the New Deal at upper-class dinners was very likely to be called a "Jew-" or a "Nigger-lover." Hatred of Roosevelt was due less to his economic policies than to the social revolution he fostered which hastened the upward social mobility of American Jews. The real source of venom against Roosevelt was that he challenged the WASP feeling that they were superior people. The same violent hatred was to manifest itself again during the Kennedy years. The death of Kennedy fulfilled the wishes of disturbed people of far better background than Lee Harvey Oswald.

Perhaps the most depressing aspect of *The Protestant Establishment* is the fact that its author seems to have fallen prey to some of the very same prejudices he regards as harmful in others. Baltzell's elite remains Protestant and Anglo-Saxon. He seems far more concerned with *assimilating* dejudaized Jews to the Protestant elite than to foster an elite which is multi-religious and multi-ethnic. The multitude may be pluralistic, not the elite. He believes that members of the elite must be friends, join the same clubs, go to the same schools, and intermarry. It is hard to understand how one could retain a specific Jewish identity and at the same time be a member of the elite. When Baltzell cites examples of injustices done to qualified Jews who were unfairly excluded from clubs or business positions because of their background, his Jews inevitably turn out to be totally dejudaized Jews or "half-Jews." He cites the difficulties encountered by Sidney Weinberg, Fiorello LaGuardia, Bernard Baruch, John Schiff, the young man who was barred from the Scarsdale Country Club though baptized, and others. Baltzell complains that Jews who are no longer "pushy" or "grinds" still find acceptance difficult. As a university chaplain, I have had ample occasion to meet both the "grinds" and the imitation Anglo-Saxons. I found that I resented some of Baltzell's remarks as patronizing at this point. I question his insight. At least the "grinds" are devoted to intellectual values which are historically authentic within the framework of Jewish culture. I question whether the imitation Anglo-Saxons have much to recommend them, save their capacity to flatter the real Anglo-Saxons and convince them of their inherent superiority.

Most surprising, Baltzell regards Richard Amsterdam, the hero of Myron Kaufman's novel *Remember Me To God*,[5] as a pathetic but praiseworthy example of a young Jew in the process of turning his back on his Jewish heritage while a student at Harvard in order to qualify at least as an imitation Anglo-Saxon gentleman. Several years ago I reviewed this novel, while serving as Interim Director of the Hillel Foundation at Harvard. I called the review "A Harvard *What Makes Sammy Run.*" It seemed patently obvious that Richard was an immature pusher with no values and little dignity. I fail to see how in the name of a sociological process Richard can be transformed into a character admired by anyone. Richard is a self-hating young man whose greatest achievement is a notebook offering guidance on how to become an Anglo-Saxon gentleman. Is this to be the liberal's program for Jews? Must Jews look to WASPs, study them, and deliberately imitate their instinctively acquired life-styles? Wouldn't Richard Amsterdam have been better off had he paid less attention to the ways of the WASP and more to discovering himself? Isn't it perhaps better for Jews to discover themselves rather than self-consciously to attempt to become imitations of others? Mr. Baltzell may be a liberal, but there is more than a touch of unconscious patronizing in his preferences.

Baltzell's insights into the problem of Jewish authenticity and inner dignity might have been enhanced by a reading of

[5] New York: J. B. Lippincott, 1957.

another of Sartre's works, his *Réflexions sur la question juive*.[6]
Those Jews whom Baltzell seems to regard as most suitable for
membership in the elite are precisely those whom Sartre would
regard as inauthentic in that they seek to fulfill the impossible project of becoming other than what they are. When Baltzell discusses
the proliferation of post-war suburban synagogues, he seems to
regard this development as largely due to the rejection of Jews
by the elite. One is never quite sure whether Baltzell sees the development of Jewish institutions as wasteful impositions resulting
from gentile exclusion or as creative additions to a multiform
culture. Even where he allows the theory of the triple melting pot
at most levels, Baltzell argues that there is a single elite. At present
it is WASP. He argues, in effect, that it is too rigidly so and that
non-WASPs should be permitted to become WASPs. When the
white man's burden rested upon the Anglo-Saxon gentleman, this
choice was a likely one. For intellectuals, at least, the choice has
become increasingly untenable in our time. This is not because
there is a life-style of proven superiority to that of the WASPs.
It is simply that imitating other people's lives has gone out of
fashion in the twentieth century. It is improbable that today's intellectual of Jewish background will choose the suburban synagogue, though he could make far worse choices; it is, however,
less likely that he will find himself in the Episcopal Church.

The problem of the establishment is that it poses contradictory issues for Jews. All definition is by way of negation. To
be something means that one is not something else. The result is
always some form of *de facto* segregation. One cannot be a Jew
without paying some price. In America it has been exclusion
from the seats of national industrial and social power. Many Jews
readily accept the disabilities connected with their identities, as
they have since Biblical days. They realize that *any* human situation will be limited. There does not seem to be any way to retain
a specific identity without some sort of exclusiveness. The problem
is hardly a new one. It was old when Israel's prophets were young.

I would not want to defend *de facto* segregation, but it is
true that, in some respects, the average Jew has been better off
under the system than the average WASP, even apart from re-

[6] Paris: P. Morihien, 1947.

ligious values. The WASP situation is, if anything, more ironic than the predicament of most Jews. They are the lower- and middle-echelon personnel of the banks and large corporations of America. As bank tellers, branch managers, and corporation clerks they preserve a sense of doing dignified work for the "right" kind of firm but at salaries which allow only the most minimal of comforts and opportunities for personal growth. Many are hopelessly sunk in a vast sea of words and paper which constitute the actual context of their labor. No group of Americans, including factory workers, is so characterized by Marx's description of "alienated labor" as are the lower- and middle-level WASP clerks and managers. The computer revolution is bound to accelerate this process. Working in vast, overly symmetrical skyscrapers devoid of all human beauty, they spend their hours dealing with figures on paper. They are eligible for membership in the city or country club by reason of background, but not one in a thousand will ever see the inside of these institutions.

The Jew may be a pariah, as Max Weber has suggested; India is by no means the only land which has a problem of untouchables. Nevertheless, the work of the average Jew, by virtue of his exclusion from management, is usually carried on in a more human context. Although WASPs are most likely to talk about free enterprise and personal initiative, Jews are far more dependent upon these values for their advancement. The merchant, the salesman, the doctor, the lawyer, and the professor must deal with people rather than paper. The environment of Jewish *praxis* tends to be less dull than that of the Protestants. Most Jews simply refuse to accept a Protestant model of the desirable life-style, whether they are assimilated or Jewishly committed. Nevertheless, Baltzell's book suggests that many Jews make a virtue out of necessity and that they would leap at the opportunity to enter the elite Protestant world if given even a remote chance. There is certainly evidence that this sometimes takes place, as well as counter-evidence that the decision to remain committed to a Jewish identity is often the result of a free and meaningful choice. Sociological descriptions are not prescriptive norms of social processes. In any generation some will want out; some will elect to remain Jews. These decisions may often be rooted in early family experience rather than the inevitabilities of social process. What must be faced is that there is apparently no way to retain one's Jewish identity without excluding oneself from the business and social elite, though certainly not the artistic, intellectual, and even the political elite. Although Baltzell pleads for an open aristocracy, his primary concern for assimilated Jews on the periphery of Protestant society is evidence of how thoroughly closed that society actually is. Baltzell's work carries more conviction as a statement of the problem than as an indication that the problem will find a solution.

In his *Critique de la raison dialetique,* Sartre comments that every human being is defined by those possibilities which are impossible for him. Denial of opportunity is a dehumanizing process. Anyone who accepts less than full equality of opportunity within his society consents to his own partial dehumanization. It is for that reason that Jews, knowing the price of Jewish identity to be exclusion, must nevertheless fight every form of segregation with all the intelligence and insight they possess. To rest content with the present situation is to accept a system of social degradation which really does amount to pariah status. The present situation is eminently livable. Nevertheless, it is impossible for any American to accept second-class status and retain personal dignity. Second-class status will not disappear in the foreseeable future. One does not lose dignity because a power situation imposes social limitations which cannot be overcome. One most assuredly loses dignity when one consents to second-class status. The paradox of the American Jewish situation is that Jews must strive to overcome barriers to full participation in American life which, if removed, could conceivably dissolve Jewish life far more effectively than do the more limited opportunities of contemporary American life.

In a recent issue of *Newsweek,* Walter Lippman suggests that the Republican party has paid a very heavy price for its alienation from the intellectuals.[8] He notes the importance of intellectuals as formers of opinion and policy in contemporary America. As a dejudaized Jew, Lippman would never see the problem in

[8] *Newsweek,* November 23, 1964.

religio-cultural perspectives. Baltzell, however, is aware of the fact that, by becoming a caste, the Protestant elite has tended to lose ever more authority. This was certainly true of the 1964 national election. Part of the hatred of the eastern establishment by the Goldwater wing of the Republican party was rooted in the old Populist mistrust of the eastern seaboard. It also represented an inner struggle within Protestantism between those who had become so hopelessly isolated within their caste system that they had lost contact with domestic and foreign reality and those Protestants who sought some realistic accommodation with the non-WASP segments of the population. It is wrong to suggest that Goldwater was simply anti-eastern. He had many of his most vocal supporters in the East. By and large, they were the "Let's-put-the-Jews-and-Niggers-in-their-place" crowd. One of the most important issues facing America is whether it will become another India, hopelessly divided by castes who perform different tasks, live separate lives, and have only the barest of personal contact, or whether it can achieve a genuine pluralism. Historic experience suggests that America is more likely to follow the Indian example than it is to achieve a real community of diversity.

Every living organism has its tragic flaw. This land has yet to discover the full measure of the internal toxins which must inevitably stunt its growth and cripple its promise. Sooner or later, Americans will learn that they are within the ironies and the tragedies of the historical process. Yet, if the poisons must inevitably manifest themselves, they must be met by our resolve to overcome them insofar as we are able. Long ago Jews were instructed, "It is not for thee to complete the work, but neither art thou free to desist from it."

Arthur Cohen's The Natural and the Supernatural Jew *is probably the best and most comprehensive contemporary attempt to restate the Jewish belief in God as the ultimate author of the historical drama and the election of Israel as the people of God. The virtue of Cohen's effort is that he makes abundantly clear the entailments of the theology of election in the light of the contemporary Jewish situation. I know of no other work which does this so effectively.*

By the same token, I believe Cohen unwittingly does more to reveal the untenability of this theology than to establish it as a meaningful option. The reasons for this conviction are spelled out in some detail in this paper.

10/The "Supernatural" Jew

IN RECENT YEARS, Arthur Cohen has been one of the more articulate voices among the younger Jewish theologians. By the nature of the discipline, theologians remain young at least until their fiftieth year. There is simply too much to be learned, pondered and finally synthesized; hence early statements of the theological enterprise appear to be no more than prolegomena. Fortunately nature seems to be kind to theologians. It oft-times grants them more than the usual life span in which to formulate their understanding of the meaning of existence before the awesome presence of the Divine. This is evident in the careers of Paul Tillich, Mordecai M. Kaplan, Martin Buber, and Karl Barth. There is, however, no substitute for the agonizing crucible of life's experiences for meaningful theological statement. Verbal or intellectual competence may be necessary preconditions for theological maturity. They are not and cannot be sufficient conditions.

We are grateful to Mr. Cohen for risking so early an exposure of his theological perspectives to the hard scrutiny which inevitably follows publication.[1] Mr. Cohen, like every writer, exposes more than his point of view; in truth, he exposes himself. His statements concerning Israel's relation to the God who manifests Himself in history are deeply personal. I have a feeling that

[1] Arthur A. Cohen, *The Natural and the Supernatural Jew* (New York: Pantheon Books, 1963).

he is going to find a more appreciative audience among theologically conservative Christians than among Jews.

The crux of Cohen's concern is that the Jewish people has a supernatural vocation to be witness to the unredeemed, incomplete character of history, that the goal of history is redemption, and that the Jewish people has been elected by God to play a decisive and climactic role in bringing about redemption through its fidelity to its encounter with God in history.

As a corollary of his interpretation of the Jewish role in the *Heilsgeschichte* of mankind, Cohen goes further than any recent Jewish thinker in rejecting the *theological* significance of reborn Israel and emphasizing the centrality of Exile to the Jewish mission. In actuality, Cohen has only made explicit a fact which has been obvious to this writer for a long time. One cannot regard the rebirth of Israel as theologically significant without radically rethinking both the interpretation of Jewish history and the meaning, though not necessarily the content, of the Jewish religion. Since Cohen prefers to re-enunciate, in his own special idiom, the normative Biblical-rabbinic conviction that God is the Ultimate Actor in the historical drama, he must reject reborn Israel as religiously significant.

Cohen sees quite clearly that to participate in history is to be unredeemed. He understands redemption as the summation and fulfillment of history. Nothing, therefore, that happens *in* history can be finally redemptive. The secular state of Israel, predicated as it is upon the yearning of the Jewish people to possess a national existence devoid of superordinate frames of reference, is for Cohen a betrayal of Israel's supernatural vocation. Normalcy is for Cohen an act of betrayal. Hence he must combine his insistence on this superordinate frame of reference for Jewish life with a deliberate rejection of the significance of the birth of a normal Jewish state.

We would, on the other hand, start with the assumption that this event, which has so deeply penetrated the hearts and destinies of those ordinary Jews who are so frequently the butt of Cohen's censure, must be religiously decisive as well. Cohen can maintain his theology of the God of history only by a radical act of separation from the actual life and experience of the Jewish people in the twentieth century. We would insist that a Jewish theology cannot have any meaning for Jews, no matter who else appreciates it, if it is so fixated on a vision of the divine economy of events, on the redemptive end, that it ignores the moments of *kairos,* the decisive moments in the lived Jewish present. There can be no Jewish theology which is fundamentally out of contact with the actual life of the Jewish people.

After the death of six million Jews and the phoenix-like re-establishment of the Jewish state after almost two thousand years, I find Mr. Cohen's claim that "The rediscovery of the supernatural vocation of the Jew is the turning-point of modern Jewish history"[2] singularly incognizant of and indifferent to the actual life of the Jewish people in our times. I wonder just what Mr. Cohen's analysis would mean to a survivor of Auschwitz or to the young Israelis who stand guard in the *Galil* against the ever-present threat of Syrian incursion. I hardly dare mention the average American Jew, because I know in advance that Cohen would score and scorn his mediocrity.

There is a deeper issue than the genuine irrelevance to the actual situation of the Jew of Cohen's contentions. Since no other Jewish theologian has so insistently affirmed the supernatural vocation of the Jew as has Cohen, I do not see how his assertion can avoid being taken as a yardstick of the way he regards himself. This is explicit in the bulk of the book which reviews the issues and personalities of Jewish theology since Mendelssohn in such a way that they culminate in Arthur Cohen. There are men who in their own person reflect decisively culminating trends in a historical period. When they assert this fact, and it is true, we regard them as possessing a certain grandeur. In ancient philosophy Aristotle was such a person. In modern European affairs, Charles de Gaulle is perhaps entitled to this olympian pre-eminence. However, if one is wrong in one's daring assessment of oneself, a deserving grandeur is exchanged for a grating arrogance or a comic posture.

These are admittedly harsh words, but there is no other way to characterize the underlying tone of Cohen's work. I certainly do not share the theological perspectives of my teacher, Professor Abraham Joshua Heschel, but I believe that Mr. Cohen

[2] *Ibid.,* p. 282.

exceeds the domain of propriety when he reacts to Dr. Heschel's contention that our awareness of the ineffable Ground of existence is a "certainty without knowledge" by characterizing Dr. Heschel's difficult but important insight as "an example of *purposeful* obscurity" (italics mine).[3] Surely, there must be better ways in which a pupil can express his dissent from his teacher.

If this tendency to pronounce judgment, to denounce, and even wistfully to decry the fact that modern Judaism no longer has instrumentalities for excommunicating the heretic were extrinsic to Cohen's fundamental perspective, we could pass over it as a mere quirk of his personality. Unfortunately it is not. Mr. Cohen is convinced that the Jewish people has a supernatural vocation given to it by God. The refusal of this vocation is necessarily an evil failure to join with God in His plan for human redemption. If the disbeliever cannot be punished or banned, it is not because punishment is not warranted but because the current practical situation precludes it. Cohen's own words are instructive in informing us of the kind of world he hankers for and would create, if he had the power:

> We cannot afford in these days to deal with heretics, disbelievers, and malefactors with the same degree of authority and discipline with which they were treated by the Babylonian Exilarchate, the Spanish *Aljama*, or the Polish Council of Four Lands. In those days failure to accept the authority of the Jewish court, the flouting of its decisions, the bringing of dishonor to the community of Israel, religious heterodoxy, and, in such cases as those of Uriel Acosta or Spinoza, theological heresy, elicited the varying decrees of excommunication which the Jewish courts could impose. . . . This would not be to interpret the power of excommunication as a mere device of power. Beneath power lay belief; the power of the community was valid because the beliefs upon which it rested were acceptable.[4]

Walter Teller has reviewed Cohen's book in *The Saturday Review*.[5] I fail to see how it is possible to do other than concur in

[3] *Ibid.*, p. 240.
[4] *Ibid.*, pp. 192–93.
[5] January 26, 1963.

Mr. Teller's estimate that the book is "Jesuitic in language, it seems . . . to belong to the esoteric rather than the mainstream of Judaism."

Strangely enough, Mr. Cohen has almost nothing to say concerning the annihilation of the six million Jews. There are at most one or two phrases which refer to it, although the dominant note in Cohen's conception of God is that He is redemptively active in history. At second glance, this omission is not very strange at all. The same indifference to the facts of the twentieth century which leads him to ignore the theological significance of modern Zionism and the rebirth of Israel is also operative here. Cohen talks about the God of history and the Jew's supernatural vocation in turning history into a meaningful mirror of the Divine, while remaining almost completely silent concerning the theology of contemporary Jewish history. He totally avoids the decisive theological questions of contemporary Jewish thought: the problems of God and the death camps and God and the rebirth of Israel. In this, however, he is not alone among the "younger" theologians, most of whom write as if nothing had happened to Jews in the twentieth century.

Furthermore, after Jewish existence has been called into question so radically in our times, it borders on the cruel, with regard to others, and the masochistic, with regard to oneself, to refuse the blessing of life, lived in its own terms, in and for itself, with no need for superordinate validations or justifications. For Cohen a natural Jewish existence is a truncated Jewish existence. Only if the Jew justifies his existence in terms beyond its own frame of reference does existence have meaning. This is a savage denial of the meaningful character of genuine human encounter, which can only exist when human beings are present to one another, not as ideological marionettes acting out superordinate roles, but simply in the presentness, the spontaneity, the openness, and the risk of I and Thou. Were people to live Mr. Cohen's supernatural vocation, they would be role-playing in a mythic drama rather than existing as genuine persons in the fullest sense.

When we turn to examine Mr. Cohen's theology of history in overall conception, it turns out to be a meaningful and highly sophisticated statement of the mystical conception of God and the historical process. According to Cohen, "Time is the medium and history the substance of divine actualization." He identifies this view with Lurianic Kabbalism, Jacob Boehme, and Nicholas Berdyaev. He insists that "Process within God is providence for man; unceasing actualization in God is destiny for man . . . our age and our aeon are but moments in eternity; that what we know as history is but an epoch in God's 'history' . . ."[6]

Cohen is not so naïve as to identify *every* moment in history with the divine process. He will not be caught in the Deuteronomist's trap which is ultimately to regard every last event in history as derivative of God's will. Cohen therefore avoids the question of God's responsibility for the death camps which must plague every Deuteronomist.[7] He distinguishes the perfection of God, which is extra-historical, and the potency of God which is His living, historical passion to consummation. Although Cohen does not use the explicit imagery of the *Deus Revelatus,* the passionate God who seeks redemption and perfection, and the *Deus Absconditus,* God the perfect, unknowable Ground of Being who dwells in the womb of His own omnipotence, this honorable, and, I believe, unavoidable theological tradition lies behind his analysis.

For Cohen, the goal and meaning of history is and must be extra-historical. The reality of evil is the foundation of history. The special destiny of Israel is to witness the evil men do, both to their fellows and to providence. Israel's Exile is coterminous with the historical process. The Dispersal of the Jews may have partly ended with the reborn Israel, but the Exile cannot end until history is redeemed. So far, so good; but Cohen nowhere spells out or even hints at the nature of redemption. In rabbinic literature, the Rabbis were reluctant to spell out the meaning of redemption save in poetic images which were not meant to be pressed too vigorously. By and large they were Deuteronomists who saw the entire historical process as subject to the guiding action of God in History. Whatever dialectic of freedom and

---

[6] Cohen, p. 298.

[7] Cf. "The Dean and the Chosen People," pp. 47–58.

necessity they were driven to formulate, they never denied the omnipotence of God and His omnipresence in the historical process. Their messianic eschatologies tended to envisage a human existence devoid of tragedies and fatalities. Their *aharit ha-yamim* (the end of days) was a time of human existence, albeit a perfected human existence. Some of them would certainly have regarded the re-establishment of the State of Israel as *athalta d' geulah* (the Beginning of Redemption), if not *geulah* (Redemption). At any rate, they would not have been nearly as indifferent to it as Cohen.

From a technical philosophic or theological point of view, Cohen is absolutely correct when he insists that the Jew remain in Exile because history remains unredeemed. He refuses to buy cheaply a realized eschatology which will only release manic-depressive energies in the Jewish people; nevertheless, his concept of Exile has thus become so generalized that it means nothing more than the inescapable alienation of the real from the ideal in the historical process. One can have no quarrel with this, but I fail to see why the Jewish people is necessary to symbolize this unavoidable fact of reality.

Paul Tillich, for example, is able to make the same kind of analysis of human finitude without the kind of mythic or symbolic reference to Jewish destiny Cohen deems so important. The analysis of alienation in its ethical, ontological, psychological, and historical dimensions has been carried forth with a great deal of precision in contemporary thought. I fail to see how Cohen's conception of the centrality of the Exile of the Jewish people adds a category of significance. Jewish suffering must have more concretely explicit categories of meaning. For the Rabbis, such categories were to be found in the cycle of sin, punishment, repentance, atonement, and redemption. Exile was punishment for Jewish sin rather than a symbolic quintessence of the human condition. With or without Jews, the world is going to be in Exile as long as history lasts. All a person or a community has to do to understand this phenomenon is to look deeply into itself; one needs no Jews as teachers.

The inevitable alienation involved in the human predicament is the reality behind Mr. Cohen's mythic conception of the Exile. Redemption will end the historical process and its estrangements. Cohen interprets evil as the result of the incomplete nature of the divine consummation. The *eschaton* or redemptive consummation will be that time (metaphorically speaking, since the *eschaton* is extra-historical) when God's actualizing nature is perfected and there is no further separation between God as He is in Himself and God as He actualizes Himself in history.

This is, like Cohen's doctrine of the Exile, a very respectable doctrine. It has, however, only one possible content which Cohen has failed to specify: *Death is the Messiah*. Death is the perfection and completion of life. Life is a system of needs. A system of needs is a want of perfection, whether in God or man. One can perfect a system of needs only through ending need, but this would be tantamount to ending all motive for motion, passion, and change. Only in terms of the phenomenology of the psyche is death nothingness. Death abolishes the needs and instabilities of the organism. It unites the organism's constituent parts with its encompassing environment. In Cohen's language, it ends the Exile of the organism from the wider matrix out of which it has arisen. This is as true of the actualizing God, whom Cohen explicitly defines in terms of life,[8] as it is of men. The consummation of history can only be a return of all things to God's Nothingness.

Cohen's use of Lurianic Kabbalism is instructive, for in it the actualization of God in the world is a fall from perfection. This fall results from the self-division of the God who dwells in the ground of His own perfection. Redemption will come only when this self-division of the divine nature is healed. God will then be all in all, lacking nothing, having united Himself to Himself. By the same token, there will be absolutely no difference between the unity and simplicity of God's final perfection and Nothingness. Hegel's insight is especially relevant: pure Being, lacking all content and internal division, can in no sense be distinguished from Nothingness. The redemption toward which Cohen looks, the supernatural reality of the supernatural Jew, turns out to be almighty and omnipotent *Thanatos*. Death is the only master of redemption.

[8] Cohen, p. 29.

Those of us who have refused what Cohen calls the supernatural vocation of the Jew (the unbelievers and heretics he would ban if he could) do not part company with him on his analysis of finitude. Here Cohen reveals himself to be very much the contemporary theologian. We have also speculated on the domain of the redemptive and the supernatural, but we have not rested content with the sound of seemingly virtuous metaphors whose ancient religious associations have been rejected *ab initio*. Redemption and Exile had a content for the Rabbis. Exile is alienation from Israel. Redemption is return under conditions of restored virtue and fellowship with God. Cohen rejects the rabbinic conception, or maintains that they really meant what he is talking about. He fails, nevertheless, to demonstrate any meaningful content to supernatural redemption. Above all, I cannot see what possible meaning can be appended to the supernatural Jew that so separates him from Cohen's natural Jew as to make Cohen hanker for courts of ban and excommunication. Unless the supernatural Jew has a more specified vocation than the one Cohen has suggested with so little precision and real content, how can the rediscovery of the supernatural vocation of the Jew be the meaningful event Cohen has proclaimed?

If this content is the revelation of finitude in the human condition, it is Jewish megalomania to imagine that the world needs Jews for that lesson. If the vocation of the supernatural Jew is to bring about the redemptive end of history, one need only commit suicide to achieve it. Cohen had best reconcile himself to the fact that to be human is to be locked in a condition of alienating finitude from which death is the only exit. Whatever improvement the human condition affords will come about only through the compassionate joining together of finite, failing men. Of course, such human fellowship requires a sense of solidarity rather than the sense of the radical separation of one human being from another which is implied in Cohen's dichotomous abstraction of the natural and supernatural Jew.

Redemptive history makes sense only if certain events in history decisively and qualitatively affect the content of either the present or the end. Redemptive history made sense for the Rabbis for the reasons we have suggested. Cohen excludes their association of Israel with redemption from his scheme. Redemptive history also makes sense from the point of view of Christianity. Christ is the union of the essential and the existential, the historical and the trans-historical, the natural and the supernatural. Furthermore, the idea of the supernatural vocation of the Jew makes a great deal of sense for Christians. Unless Jews have a supernatural vocation, the Christ makes absolutely no theological difference. He is just a tragic figure born within a small Near Eastern community, but by no means the decisive personality around whom the whole drama of human destiny is played. Mr. Cohen complains that "the non-Jew conserves our supernatural vocation; while we—its legatees and bearers—would sacrifice dogma for fact, vocation for our natural condition."[9]

In more than one place, Cohen scolds Jews for the fact that Christians are more concerned with the superordinate interpretation of Jewish life and history than are Jews. He does not seem to understand that it is bad enough that we Jews have been condemned to the domain of the sacred by non-Jews, where we can alternately be praised as Jesus-like and murdered as Judas-like, without our confirmation of this radical distortion of the Jew as a person.

Human relations are possible only between persons in encounter. Where one of the persons in the relationship is playing a role, teaching a lesson, or acting as a symbol, something rather dreadful happens to the potentialities of encounter. The only possible supernatural role for the Jew that makes sense to the Christian is that of witness to or betrayer of the Christ. Cohen rejects the good news of the Christ as the content of the Jew's supernatural vocation, substitutes for it a redemptive end which can have no possible content, and then berates his fellow Jews for, by and large, failing to follow him.

I suspect that Cohen lets the cat out of the bag when he berates the Jewish community for not taking its vocation as seriously as do Christians. It tells us the real frame of reference in which he is operating and why he is doomed to have only the smallest esoteric following among Jews, whatever his popu-

[9] *Ibid.*, p. 281.

larity may be among gentiles. He cannot bring himself to approve
of or feel genuine empathy for Jews as they are. He scolds. He
passes sweeping condemnatory judgments. He is not beneath
some pretty vulgar rabbi-baiting with little or no feeling for the
extraordinary difficulties men endure in serving modern communities.[10] He tells us that he is less afraid of abnormalizing the
Jews than normalizing them (something anti-Semites have done
very well without Jewish assistance), that he is less afraid of
harshness than inauthenticity. Almost two million Israelis and
five million American Jews are wrong in their quest for normalcy
after the insanity and murder through which Jews have lived,
for they refuse Cohen's vocation of testifying to the evil of the unredeemed world more than they absolutely have to.

It never seems to occur to Cohen that people are the way
they are largely because of forces they can but little understand
and less control, that most people have an exceedingly difficult
time just living their normal lives. It is not bad enough that Christianity finds difficulty in taking an altogether sane view of Jews
and Judaism. Cohen has to compound that distortion by attempting to confirm it. If Mr. Cohen wants to be great, spectacular,
or saintly, that is his privilege. I fail to see why he must berate
his fellow Jews, albeit in the name of God, for the fact that most
of them simply want to live their lives as best and unspectacularly
as they can. Can Mr. Cohen only love Jews when they are a community of saints? Why must he complain that Jews want primarily to be normal or even just a bit vulgar and bourgeois? Why
does he agonize over the fact that Jews have wisely elected to
reject saintliness as a profession?

Cohen's *The Natural and The Supernatural Jew* is not even remotely the beginning of a meaningful statement of contemporary Jewish theology. There will undoubtedly be supernatural,
naturalist, and existentialist Jewish theologies in our times. They
will not necessarily agree. On the contrary, the area of meaningful debate will be exceedingly broad, but no theology will

[10] Cf. his "A Theology of Jewish Existence," *Christian Century*,
January 23, 1963.

have any meaning for the contemporary Jew if it is not distinguished by a certain modesty and compassionate tone which marks men who realize that the Truth is finally known, if at all, by God alone. A Jewish theology will be bound up with Jewish reality. It need not be encased in it; indeed it must transcend it, but it must do so compassionately and with a sense of the perils of the human vocation in our times. If any man feels that he has the key to a more meaningful life than others, let him quietly count his blessings rather than look upon the less fortunate in angry contempt.

Jewish theology will be *Jewish theology*. Its frame of reference will not be the way others see us. Its frame of reference will have to be the experiences and the destiny of the Jewish people as they have actually been lived. Jewish theology will in a very significant measure have to be a Zionist theology, for ours is a religious tradition living a disembodied existence not in the abstractions of intellectual debate, but in the experienced concreteness of the life of the people. There is room for many options in Jewish life, but an intellectualized or a theologized anti-Zionism is not likely to be one of them.

Finally, Jewish theology must be a theological anthropology more than a theology of history. It must meaningfully assess the risks of human existence in our times and seek to illumine and enlighten the human burden for ourselves and for others. It will turn its face to the light of the Lord that it may the better re-enter the darkened cave of human striving, there to help create neither Mr. Cohen's society of myth nor modernity's society of technical abstractions, but a true community of persons rooted in human solidarity and helpfulness. If the fruit of the supernatural vocation is arrogance, contempt, censure, and harshness, would not God Himself prefer that we forsake it and find ways of truly making every man our brother?

Harvey Cox has addressed himself to some of the most important theological problems of the sixties in his The Secular City. *The issues he raises are of as much concern for Judaism as for Christianity, although the Jewish response will be largely different from the one suggested by Cox.*

In the fall of 1965, Daniel Callahan of Commonweal *invited me to contribute an essay to his book* The Secular City Debate. *This invitation afforded me the opportunity to confront some of the issues raised by Cox in terms of my own theological perspectives. The fruits of that encounter are summarized in this paper.*

II / Judaism and "The Secular City"

Harvey Cox is a disciple of Dietrich Bonhoeffer. Like his spiritual master he is preoccupied by the problem of how we speak of God without religion. This question haunts *The Secular City*. I would like to suggest that the real question is not how we speak of God without religion, but how we speak of religion in the time of the "death of God."

Religious intellectuals are profoundly indebted to Professor Cox for his forthright attempt to explore the theological significance of the modern metropolis. One need not agree with Cox's method or his conclusions to recognize the enormous importance of his work. To the best of my knowledge, no other theologian has focused attention so forcefully or so originally on the theological interpretation of contemporary secular society. Cox poses questions which no theologian concerned with our culture can readily ignore.

According to Cox, the rise of urban civilization and the collapse of traditional religion are the main hallmarks of our times. Cox contends that "The secular metropolis stands as both the pattern of our life together and the symbol of our view of the world."[1] It has been made possible by the related processes of urbanization and secularization. Cox quotes approvingly Cornelius van Peursen's definition of secularization as: "the deliver-

[1] Harvey Cox, *The Secular City* (New York: Macmillan Co., 1965), p. 1.

ance of man first from religious and then from metaphysical control over his reason and his language. . . ."[2] Secularization involves
humanity's "turning away from worlds beyond and towards this
world."[3] For Cox the age of the secular city is the age of "no
religion at all."[4] Increasingly men look neither to religious rules
nor to ritual for their morality or for their understanding of the
meaning of life. The fruit of secularization and urbanization is
"technopolis," the evolving form of contemporary urban civilization. According to Cox, the relations between men in technopolis
tend to be functional and contractual in contrast to the emotionally overdetermined relations which characterized the earlier and more primitive forms of social order he designates as the
tribe and the town.

Few theologians have celebrated the anonymity and mobility of the secular city as enthusiastically as Cox. While he is
aware of the rootlessness, the loneliness, the alienation, and the
loss of identity which contemporary writers and social theorists
have seen as the standard concomitants of metropolitan culture,
Cox sees urban anonymity and mobility primarily in terms of the
liberating opportunities they offer the individual to choose his
friendships, relationships, and values with the least impediment
from small-group social pressure. Cox makes the very telling
point that few of us would return to the culture of the small town
with its seething hostilities, envies, and built-in limitations to personal freedom in spite of the problems of technopolis.

Critics of life within urban society often regret the absence of what Martin Buber has described as the I–Thou relation
in its interpersonal encounters. Cox is very helpful in pointing
out that urban life need not necessarily be dehumanized because
of its absence. He suggests the possibility of what he calls the I–
You relation as typical within the anonymous metropolis. Such a
relation may involve far less spontaneity and intimacy than the I–
Thou relation. It does, however, offer the opportunity for the
dignified meeting of persons who must maintain their distance
because of the impersonal demands of city living. Cox's insight is

[2] *Ibid.*, p. 2.
[3] *Ibid.*
[4] *Ibid.*, p. 3.

a healthy antidote to those who bemoan the absence of genuine I–Thou relations but who fail to understand that there can be a decent alternative.

Perhaps the most theologically questionable aspect of Cox's enterprise is his enthusiastic embrace of the secular city and his identification of it with the Kingdom of God. Cox is too competent a theologian to be trapped into identifying the contemporary metropolis with the *realized* kingdom. There are obviously too many negative aspects to it. He is amply safeguarded with an arsenal of categories such as "immature" and "primitive survivals" which he can conveniently append to unpleasant and degrading aspects of the secular city. He relies heavily on the notion that the Kingdom is in the process of realizing itself in history. It is neither something that has already occurred nor something which will finally occur sometime in the future. It has been occurring at least since the Christ event.

I must confess that I fail to find any meaningful content in Cox's eschatology-in-process or his identification of elements within the secular city with the Kingdom. I get the feeling in reading Cox, as I do in reading Thomas J. J. Altizer, that I am thrown into the oldest of all Judaeo-Christian debates—the question of whether it can meaningfully be stated in any sense that the Messiah has come. Even in the world of the "death of God," the new Protestant theologians cannot forego the good news of some order of Messianic fulfillment. Like the Pharisees of old, I look in vain for any real evidence of God's redemptive work as continuously manifest in the world. Although Cox identifies Pharisaism with compulsive attachment to a dead Law, I think the real significance of Pharisaism rests in its openness to the question of man's relation to God and fellow-man in a world in which eschatological yearning is a vain and futile illusion.

Apart from the age-old Judaeo-Christian debate on Messianism, an eschatology-in-process such as Cox's threatens to become a specialized form of religious journalism in which the eschatological interpreter picks and chooses those events of which he approves as evidence of the Kingdom, while relegating events he regards negatively as evidence of "immaturity" or "tribalism." Thus Cox strongly approves of Saul Alinsky's Woodlawn experiment and interprets it as evidence of the Kingdom. I do not know enough about Alinsky to form a sound judgment, but I have heard some responsible men of good will bitterly denounce both Alinsky and Woodlawn while others have been equally unreserved in their praise. The prophet's role is a hazardous one. Are we to interpret the Kingdom in terms of today's newspaper reports or are we to await the more balanced assessment of the historian writing long after the fact? When and how do we really know that the Kingdom is breaking in upon us?

It may be that Cox's conception of eschatology involves the notion that everything that happens in history is part of the process of the Kingdom realizing itself. This would be somewhat similar to Hegel's view, but Hegel understood that the final return of *Geist* unto itself could only be accomplished through all the negativities, crimes, and tragedies of the historical process. I doubt that Cox would really be disposed to accept this. It would involve seeing evidence of the Kingdom in such expressions of contemporary technopolis as Auschwitz, which was a highly rational, technopolitan factory for the manufacture of corpses, and the Negro urban ghetto. Cox has things too easy when he can identify those social phenomena of which he approves with the Kingdom while dismissing those he rejects as primitive survivals.

There is a deeper reason for Cox's dilemma. It is doubtful that a meaningful theology of history can be formulated at all unless one believes that some moment of *kairos* which has happened or will happen has the power to transform the conditions under which men experience their world. It is possible for the Christian who believes that the coming of the Christ has made an actual, discernible difference, to have a theology of history. The Christian believer will, however, have to explain the apparent lack of empirical warrant for his assertions. It is equally possible for the traditional Jew to have a theology of history, viewing the story of humanity as a progression toward an as yet unrealized Messianic fulfillment. I doubt that Cox's indefinite, unspecified identification of the Kingdom with some aspects of technopolis will yield results. He wants the best of two somewhat incompatible worlds, those of the social scientist and the theologian. Cox must insist upon assigning superordinate meanings to empirical events which they themselves do not yield. The last thing social science can countenance would be the kind of pejorative evaluation of modes of social encounter to be found on almost every page of *The Secular City.*

It is entirely possible to regard the modern metropolis simply as one of the many possible arrangements men have devised for securing the conditions and commodities necessary for their survival. Such a view of technopolis is more in accord with contemporary anthropological and sociological insights than Cox's view, which uses theologically and emotionally loaded terms such as "Gospel" and "Law" to distinguish technopolis from societies which require a less rational technology but a more complex structure of myth and ritual. Other societies have employed alternative modes of social and cultural organization. None has succeeded entirely in meeting the biological and psychological needs of their members. Each has characteristic advantages and disadvantages. The Spanish peasant living in an authoritarian, impoverished, traditional milieu is not necessarily worse off than the rootless, anxious, prosperous junior executive working for a large technopolitan corporation and living in the pleasant, well-to-do Shadyside district of Pittsburgh. There are many things the Spanish peasant has which the Pittsburgh executive needs: a sense of inner dignity, a secure knowledge of the rules of the game of life, a tragic sense of his place in society and in the order of things, and, above all, a strong sense of personal and sexual identity. He may not live as long as the Pittsburgh executive. He certainly will have none of the American's comforts or his high mobility, but he will be far less likely to be beset with the emotional disturbances which are endemic among successful Americans.

Although Cox utilizes the language of psychoanalysis when it suits his purposes, he seems indifferent to an important analytic insight about the function of myth and ritual in religion, namely their capacity to objectify and dramatize the unconscious strivings of the individual in a significant social structure. Cox welcomes the advent of technopolis because of its use of a rational, pragmatic approach to the problems of life. He sees this structure as preferable to those societies which cope with the problems of life through the instrumentalities of myth, ritual, and folk tradition. He is anti-traditional in the extreme. The past is the trap from which men must extricate themselves; traditional societies are to technopolis as Law is to Gospel. According to Cox, most traditions are irrational reminders of the childhood of mankind. Only those men who are free from the restraints of tradition and myth and who are capable of dealing with life in the most functional terms can be regarded as truly mature and fit for full adult citizenship in technopolis.

I am somewhat surprised at Cox's excessive concentration on the rational and conscious aspects of life, although such an overemphasis is by no means uncommon in Protestantism as Paul Tillich has suggested.[5] Myth is more than prescientific explanation and ritual more than superstitious mumbo-jumbo. If the insights of depth psychology have any validity, myth must be seen as the attempt of a community to objectify and thus to deal with its deepest psychic and interpersonal dilemmas. Similarly, traditional ritual offers members of a community the opportunity to cope, both consciously and unconsciously, with the crises of life.

There are at least two overall styles of religious life, one of which is moralistic, didactic, anti-emotional, and anti-ritualistic, whereas the other stresses the importance of ritual, tradition, and emotional catharsis. I would like to call these two approaches Protestant and Catholic respectively. Cox's approach is severely Protestant. Were I a Christian, I would undoubtedly be Anglican or Roman Catholic. I believe that Protestantism's fundamental difficulty is that it has attempted to weaken or eliminate those elements in religion which permit us to deal with our emotions as we face the decisive crises of life. The chaste severity of the New England church reflects a certain icy chilliness; the florid expressiveness of Mediterranean baroque allows infinitely more emotion to enter religious experience. Is it really progress,

[5] Paul Tillich, *The Protestant Era,* Abridged Edition (Chicago: University of Chicago Press, 1957), p. xiv: "Protestants often are unaware of the numinous power inherent in genuine symbols. . . . They have replaced the great wealth of symbols appearing in the Christian tradition by rational concepts, moral laws and subjective emotions."

as Cox seems to suggest, to exchange a religious life with a plenitude of emotional expressiveness for a desiccated rationalism
which forces emotional response out of the sanctuary and into
the market place?

The Protestant rejection of Mary and the confessional are
two examples of the process of rationalization which Cox views so
positively. It is possible to see both rejections as containing psychological difficulties from which Protestantism has never extricated itself. By rejecting Mary, Protestantism lost any mythic way
of coming to terms with the awesome, though terrible, realities
of femininity and maternity. A myth was swept away, but an
opportunity was lost for providing men with a religio-cultural
context in which their most archaic conflicts could be expressed
and partly dealt with. The loss of the confessional left most Protestants, as Cox understands, without an effective instrumentality
for dealing with their feelings of guilt. Since so great a proportion of our feelings of guilt are irrational and unconscious,
the loss of mythic and ritual structures with which to manage
them could not be balanced by a gain in conscious rational insight. It seems to me, as an outsider, that Cox's understanding of
religion is provincially Protestant. I understand the inevitability
of his Protestantism. I question his attempt to deal with other,
equally valid religious options as if they were primitive, prescientific anticipations of his "mature," "free," "adult" approach.
Hegel saw the history of philosophy as culminating in his own
thought. He viewed every previous position as a *praeparatio evan-
gelium* of his own. There is more than a little of the same kind of
systematizing in Cox. Kierkegaard understood in opposition to
Hegel that the experiences of unique, irreplaceable men could not
be reduced to ontological categories. Neither can they be reduced
to Cox's socio-theological categories.

Every society has its characteristic advantages and disabilities. The social scientist can describe the ways in which
societies function. Nothing in his empirical or conceptual ap-
paratus allows him to interpret what he finds in such theological
categories as the realization of the Kingdom of God. When Cox
attempts to introduce theological categories into his interpretation
of historical or sociological phenomena, his assertions are either

meaningless or arbitrary. If he wishes to assert that whatever has happened in history is an exemplification of the coming of the Kingdom, he has so relativized the category as to make it meaningless. If he means that only certain events express the realization of the Kingdom, he reduces the theology of history to his own special collection of likes and dislikes concealed under the rubric of categories such as "mature," "immature," "tribal," "ritualistic," and the like.

I should like to suggest another eschatology in place of Cox's. Perhaps it is an anti-eschatology, for I believe that eschatology is a sickness with which man conceals from himself the tragic and ultimately hopeless character of his fate. There is only one Messiah who redeems us from the irony, the travail, and the limitations of human existence. Surely he will come. He is the Angel of Death. Death is the true Messiah and the land of the dead the place of God's true Kingdom. Only in death are we redeemed from the vicissitudes of human existence. We enter God's Kingdom only when we enter His holy Nothingness. Eschatology has absolutely no meaning in terms of earthly existence. I do not desire to enter God's Kingdom, because I prefer the problematics of finitude to their dissolution in the nothingness of eternity. No actual historical event can be identified with the coming of His Kingdom.

In a recent issue of *Commonweal,* Father Andrew Greeley of Chicago asked whether the secular city pictured by Cox exists at all.[6] He argued that the American metropolis offers little evidence of having evolved into the pragmatic, future-oriented community based upon function and contract which Cox describes. According to Father Greeley, religion and ethnicity seem to play ever larger roles in American cities. He cites the example of Chicago, which is divided into a host of religious and ethnic subgroups. These function as primary groups for many of the residents of technopolis. Most people enter the larger technopolitan world only to fulfill specialized contractual relations. What Father Greeley writes of Chicago is also true of Pittsburgh and, I suspect, every other large American city. What appears

[6] November 12, 1965.

to be a metropolitan community turns out to be a series of relatively small subcommunities separated by race, religion, national origin, and economic circumstance.

There is devastating anonymity in the modern metropolis. One can be murdered in the streets without causing a flicker of concern on the part of one's nearest neighbors. There is also a strong need for primary groups, the *Gemeinschaft* of which the German sociologist Ferdinand Tonnies wrote in the last century. The proliferation of new churches and synagogues in the suburbs of America since World War II has perhaps been a partial response to that very need. Although didactic religious belief seems to have declined among virtually all American religious groups, there has been an unparalleled increase in the number and institutional strength of churches and synagogues. It is not surprising that Cox exhibits more than a little hostility to the organizational aspects of religious life in America. The institutional strength is a response to many of the primary needs which Cox would regard as archaic survivals.

Cox admits that there is a great deal of tribalism in American religion. He hopes for its eventual disappearance. In several places he quotes Paul's remark in Galatians, "There is neither Jew nor Greek . . . " as a scriptural warrant for technopolis. However, he does not complete the verse: "for ye are all one in Christ Jesus. . . ." For a non-Christian this is hardly the emblem of a secular society. It is the call of men to dissolve their previous religious and ethnic ties in order to create a *new primary community*. Cox may argue that this community is the forerunner of a truly secular society, but it hardly seems that way to non-Christians. A truly secular society would not require the kind of superordinate religious justification Cox offers in *The Secular City*. Furthermore, nothing so divides Jew and Christian as does the Law/Gospel dichotomy. That is not because Jews are compulsively bound to a meticulous system of legalistic trivia, but because Jews cannot conceive of a religious community or life without some degree of structure and discipline. We are not prepared to accept Cox's simplistic definition of what Law means to us. We have learned how to liberate ourselves from legalism while finding Law and freedom essentially compatible and interdependent. This is not the place to debate the primitive, unhistorical view of Pharisaic Judaism which is implicit in Cox's categories. What must be stressed is the degree to which his categories are Protestant Christian. I fail to understand why one man's religious life must be regarded as tribal while Cox, Christian to his very core, insists that his theology has transcended the tribalisms and traditionalisms of the "earlier," "immature" religious postures. From the perspective of the non-Christian, Cox's theology of secularization is as deeply rooted in the Protestant past and even in Protestant tribalism as any other religious option. I can only ask that he refrain from making men of other religions over into primitive anticipations of what he has become.

If anyone has any doubt about the pervasiveness of Protestant tribalism, E. Digby Baltzell's *The Protestant Establishment—Aristocracy and Caste in America* makes excellent reading. Baltzell's major concern is the extent to which the Protestant aristocracy which controls the major areas of economic and social power in America has become a caste based upon birth and race rather than an open class which admits men of ability regardless of background. The very areas of American life which Cox praises as being the most secular and pragmatic, the corporation and the university, are precisely the institutions in which Protestant tribalism is strongest. There is a very simple rule concerning eligibility for entrance into the managerial elite of the larger American corporations: one must be a WASP, a white Anglo-Saxon Protestant. This rule is observed with equal stringency in the administration of almost all non-Catholic American universities. Jews and Roman Catholics may hold distinguished academic teaching posts. They are almost never to be found directing or helping to direct the destinies of the universities at the administrative level. Baltzell's research suggests that the tendency of the Protestant community to form a caste within a larger American society has grown rather than diminished in recent years. I find it extremely difficult to take seriously Cox's contention that there is an evolving secular city. I find it even more difficult to take seriously Cox's view that the organization or corporation is the future-oriented, flexible, secularized institution Cox claims it is or is becoming. It may be that for Protestants, but for many others it remains a closed tribal enclave.

I seriously question the way Cox demolishes his opponents. He does not argue against their positions. He dissolves them into sociological or theological categories which exemplify progressions toward or regressions from his secular city. Thus philosophic existentialism and Paul Tillich's philosophy are dismissed as "expressions of the mourning period which began with the death of the God of metaphysical theism . . ." The existentialists are "arcadian and anti-urban,"[8] and, of course, there is "something immature about existentialism."[9] Cox sees *Angst* as a category which seems "increasingly irrelevant to the ethos of the new epoch."[10]

There is something olympian in this approach. The existentialists were attempting to give an accurate picture of their world as they experienced it. The best of them understood that no two men experience the world in quite the same way. *Angst* is more than an increasingly irrelevant category. It is a terrifying mode of encountering the reality that all life hovers over a nothingness into which it will ultimately dissolve. As long as men are going to die, some will experience the terrors of *Angst.* Paul Tillich insightfully describes *Urangst* in *The Courage To Be* as a primordial mode of experiencing one's world rather than as a cultural phenomenon which will disappear in time.

Cox may not have experienced *Angst.* His may be a contemporary example of "the religion of healthy-mindedness" described by William James. There is no reason why Cox must experience *Angst*, but he might well take James's typology of "the sick soul" seriously. James did not dismiss "the sick soul" as an outmoded survival. He understood that there are a number of equally valid modes of religious experience. He described them insightfully and accurately. He never reduced a religious or psychological experience to a primitive expression of a particular era.

I wish Cox were right about *Angst.* Life would be a lot easier. Cox's inability to appreciate the reality of *Angst* is, I believe, symptomatic of a larger defect in his vision. Cox offers little evidence of possessing anything remotely like a tragic sense of life. There is something very success-oriented about his theology. He

[8] *Ibid.*, p. 252.
[9] *Ibid.*, p. 253.
[10] *Ibid.*, p. 80.

approves the mobility and anonymity of the city but says hardly enough about the hideous price the poor have had to pay in rootlessness, disorientation, and suffering as a result of these phenomena. Anonymity and mobility can be enormously helpful to successful, highly educated young men who are part of what *Life* magazine recently called the "take-over generation." They constitute an impossible burden for the millions of Americans who lack the personal, social, or psychological resources with which to take advantage of the new freedom. *Angst* may not be too great a problem for young men who have succeeded in their chosen vocations beyond their expectations. It is natural for such young men to view life optimistically and to derive great satisfaction from the knowledge of their own competence. Unfortunately, they are exceptional even in our age of prosperity and advanced technology. For every person who can look back upon his life and say, "I'd do it the same way if I could do it over again," there are a hundred who have experienced a large measure of inner conflict, turmoil, and defeat, no matter how outwardly successful they may appear. Few of them, few men of any condition, can look with equanimity upon old age or death. It is not likely that any society will reduce the level of realistic anxiety most men must endure.

Men do wonder where they come from, what is the meaning of life, and what shall be their ultimate destiny. From the time of the earliest attempts of archaic men to deal with the questions of origin and end through their simple but compelling images of the Great Mother to the present day, what Paul Tillich has called ultimate concern has been an awesome reality. Ultimate concern as a term may have been invented by Tillich, but the human reality to which it points is as old as religion itself. Paul Tillich has but barely departed from our midst. A new generation of theologians is arising, most of whom were his pupils. Let us not dismiss too readily or with undue haste those insights in his work which are of perennial significance and which may very well become a part of the classical inheritance of theology in the Western world.

Cox's inability to see the tragic dimension shows through in his interpretation of Albert Camus. According to Cox, Camus went far beyond the anguished existentialism of many of his contemporaries.[11] Camus did celebrate the joys of "the invincible summer" as Cox has suggested, but he wrote with great lucidity of the price we pay for those joys. Few modern writers have celebrated the satisfactions of the flesh and of this world as fully as Camus in his marvelous essay "Summer in Algiers," yet this very essay describes with uncompromising clarity how those who live by the flesh have nothing but the flesh in the end. Death in Algiers was devoid of all consolation. For Camus the invincible summer was inevitably followed by the cold of autumn and winter. Of all the evils let loose from Pandora's box, Camus tells us, the worst was hope. Camus was undeceived about life. His vision is ennobling but unreservedly tragic. Camus was not, as Cox suggests, an atheistic Christian. He was a Mediterranean pagan. He lived in the realm of the Great Goddess, and all of his work can be seen as a latter-day expression of her religion. In his essay "Helen's Exile" as well as in the concluding part of *The Rebel,* Camus rejects the very Messianism which permeates Cox's work. Camus had a sense of limit.

It is not true as Cox has suggested that Camus rejected God primarily because he contradicts human freedom. This is true of Sartre and Nietzsche but not Camus. The God whom Camus rejects is the very God whom Cox affirms, the Biblical God of history. In *The Plague,* Camus utilizes the character of Father Paneloux to illustrate the difficulty of believing in the God of history in the twentieth century. The bubonic plague which besets Oran in the novel is Camus's symbol for the irrational human and natural evils which have confronted men in our times. The varying responses of Camus's characters to the plague represent the ways in which men have reacted to the disasters of the twentieth century, especially World War II and the death camps. The most important reactions are those of Father Paneloux and Dr. Rieu. Camus utilizes a sermon by Father Paneloux to illustrate the classical Judaeo-Christian reaction to the terrible fact of disaster. Because Father Paneloux believes God to be the omnipotent Lord of history, he must see the plague as an expression of God's primitive retribution. He interprets the disaster, as the Prophets and teachers of Israel and the theologians of the Church have

[11] *Ibid.,* p. 70.

interpreted similar disasters for millennia, as God's chastisement of a sinful world. He must interpret the plague in this way or accept an element of absurdity and mystery in the order of things for which he is psychologically unprepared. He lacks the courage of the absurd. "Men have sinned, God has punished. Repent and God will heal!" is the essence of his message.

Father Paneloux's theology of history breaks down as he watches a small boy die horribly of the plague. According to his theology, the child must be a sinner, but every human instinct within the priest rejects this. In the presence of the real suffering and death of a child, Father Paneloux's whole attempt to construct a theological interpretation of history disintegrates. Paneloux dies shortly thereafter, not of the plague but of the loss of his world. What Camus demonstrates is that, if there is a God of history, the measure of punishment he metes out to men is totally incommensurate with their actual guilt. The God of history is incompatible with human dignity as well as with human freedom. Cox insists that "God does reveal His name in history, through the clash of historical forces and the faithful efforts of a people to respond to his call."[12] Were Cox to take Camus seriously, he would understand how profoundly untenable such a position is. If there is a God of history, He is the ultimate author of Auschwitz. I am willing to believe in God the Holy Nothingness who is our source and our final destiny, but never again in a God of history. Cox sees the action of the God of history in technopolis. If there is such a God, He has also manifested himself in Auschwitz. Few ideas in Jewish religious thought have been more decisively mistaken, in spite of their deep psychological roots, than the terrible belief that God acts meaningfully in history. When the existentialists claim that they fail to find meaning and purpose in the order of things, they do not mean, as Cox seems to suggest, that *everything* is meaningless and purposeless. No serious existentialist ever claimed this. Sartre, for example, insists that human existence is inseparable from the reality of *praxis,* by which he means any meaningful labor toward an end or a goal.[13] What the exis-

[12] *Ibid.,* p. 266.

[13] Jean Paul Sartre, *Critique de la raison dialetique* (Paris: Gallimard, 1960), pp. 165 ff.

tentialists do mean is that there is no *ultimate* meaning to existence. They call upon men to create with lucidity their own private
meanings and purposes in the knowledge that no power in the
cosmos will ultimately sustain or validate them.

Those who accept the existentialist rejection of meaning
in history do so largely because they prefer an absurd cosmos to
one in which every significant instance of human suffering must
be interpreted as the chastisement visited upon guilty humanity by
an omnipotent and punitive God.

Cox is deeply influenced by Dietrich Bonhoeffer's question of April 30, 1944, ". . . how do we speak of God without
religion?" As I have suggested, I believe the real question should
be *not how we speak of God without religion* but *how we speak
of religion in the time of the death of God.* Even Cox admits that
the names men have constructed for God are somehow without
meaning in our time and that we experience what he regards as
God's absence or eclipse. What the death of God theologians
depict is an indubitable *cultural fact* in our times: God is totally
unavailable as a source of meaning or value. There is no vertical
transcendence. Our problem is not how we shall think of God in
a secular way. It is how men can best share the decisive crises of
life, given the cold, unfeeling, indifferent cosmos that surrounds
us and given the fact that God the Holy Nothingness offers us
only dissolution and death as the way out of the dilemmas of
earthly existence.

It is in this situation that the traditional church and synagogue are most meaningful. We need the religious institution—
the church for Christians and the synagogue for Jews—precisely
because the human condition is unredeemed in the present and
ultimately hopeless in what lies beyond the existential horizon.
The prophetic role of religion as a social catalyst stressed by Cox
is quite secondary. Religion cannot be indifferent to social justice
but neither can its major task be equated with its pursuit. The primary role of religion is priestly. It offers men a ritual and mythic
structure in which the abiding realities of life and death can be
shared. As long as men are born, pass through the crises of transition in life, experience guilt, fail—as fail they must—grow old,
and die, traditional churches and synagogues will be irreplace-

able institutions. It is very difficult for any sensitive intellectual to feel entirely at home in the middle-class churches or synagogues of suburban America. Nevertheless, we ought not to permit our own discomfort to obscure from us the abiding value of these institutions.

Few men who studied under Paul Tillich could be anything but deeply moved by the news of his death. I learned of his passing while visiting Warsaw, Poland. I had just returned from visiting the site of the Warsaw Ghetto for the first time. There was something appropriate in hearing the sad news in that place. An important part of Tillich's greatness was his ability to endow with theological meaning the universal dissolution in two world wars of the old certainties of European civilization. Tillich had known the stability which preceded the breakdown. He had the courage to confront the breakdown and discern within it possibilities of theological renewal.

My sadness was tempered by the knowledge that Tillich's work was, insofar as any man's can be, completed. He had spoken for and to his time, but we have moved beyond that time. I could not help but wonder as I thought about his passing what would be the issues and who would be the men to interpret them in the age of the evolving civilization which looms before us. No theologian could speak effectively to his time during the first half of the twentieth century unless he were deeply cognizant of the terrible facts of the breakdown and its human meaning. The possibility of the renewal of catastrophe has not departed, but hopefully catastrophe will not be our problem in the foreseeable future. Our problems will be those of a mass, urban civilization in an overpopulated world. The new theological sensitivity cannot be indifferent to social structure or what it does to men. Cox's importance as a theologian resides in the fact that he has had the courage and the insight to face some of the problems which must dominate theological discussion in the period immediately before us. *The Secular City* also affords a partial answer to the question, "Who are the men who will come after Tillich?" Cox is one of them, and American theology will be enriched for many years by his brilliance.

Nevertheless, as I read his work, I found myself saying

to him: "Come down from Olympus, Harvey. Stop labeling ways of life foreign to your Free Church background in categories that deprecate their unique relevance. There are many mansions. . . . Living traditions and communities cannot be reduced to abstract categories. Must we go through the debate of Kierkegaard and Hegel all over again?"

In the spring of 1965, Ira Eisenstein of The Reconstructionist *invited me to contribute to his volume* The Varieties of Jewish Belief. *He asked me to join a distinguished group of my colleagues in offering a statement of personal religious belief. I have become convinced that it is impossible to separate religious belief from the religious believer. Theology today is largely an anthropological discipline. It tells of the ways in which men encounter those issues of origin, meaning, and end which concern them most deeply. My response was to write about some of the experiences of my early childhood and adolescence which have helped to shape the religious convictions I now maintain.*

12 / The Making of a Rabbi

I DO NOT KNOW when I began to fear death. I was first aware of my fright when my grandfather died. I was seven at the time. From then on, my childhood fears centered about the fact that I would some day die.

There were times when I assured myself that science would provide a cure for death long before I became an old man. That hope was not destined to last. By my tenth year I understood that though the miracles of science promised much they would never overcome death. Even as a child, I could never entirely escape the nihilism with which I have struggled ever since. I found it impossible to believe in a providential God. I believed that when I died the whole world of my experience would disappear with me. My world would last only as long as I did. It would then disappear as if it had never been. I was convinced that I had arisen out of nothingness and was destined to return to nothingness. All things human were locked in the same fatality. In the final analysis, omnipotent nothingness was lord of all creation. Nothing in the bleak, cold, unfeeling universe was remotely concerned with human aspiration and longing. Even as a rabbi, I have never really departed from my primordial feelings about my place in the cosmos.

Long before I had read the existentialists, I regarded existence as ultimately gratuitous and absurd. I asked myself why I had come to be. I could only answer that I had been cast up in the world absurdly to no ultimate end or purpose. This was coupled with a tragic sense of life which has never left me. Oblivion was the final destiny of all creation. No matter what a man's aspirations, no matter how impressive his accomplishments, all alike were destined to be enveloped in the indifferent nothingness which was our beginning and will be our end. Even if others survived to appreciate our achievements, it mattered not at all to those in the grave, unaware alike of what they had been and what they had wrought.

I had only the most minimal Hebrew education. I attended Hebrew school at Temple Israel in Long Beach, Long Island, where I spent the better part of my childhood years. I do not recall having learned very much or having been especially interested. Hebrew school was part of the Jewish landscape in suburban Long Beach in the thirties. We came to learn how to read the Hebrew prayers so that we could fulfill the Bar Mitzvah ritual. We learned little more than that. It was very rare for anyone to continue his studies after Bar Mitzvah. I was not even to have a Bar Mitzvah.

Our home was not religiously observant. We did observe Rosh Hashanah and Yom Kippur after a fashion, but the rest of the year was devoid of any sense of the majesty of Jewish tradition. We did not keep any of the dietary laws. Ham and bacon were deliberately included in our diet. My mother came from a traditional religious background. Her parents were very religious immigrants from Lithuania. Because of her background, she was incapable of eating meat and dairy products together or of eating pork products. She regarded this as neurotic and wanted to be sure that her children were "free" of such limitations.

Perhaps if I had had a Bar Mitzvah I might never have become seriously interested in Jewish life. I might simply have taken my Jewishness for granted without experiencing the promptings toward rebellion, negation, and reconciliation which were to preoccupy me for so very long. My parents opposed my having a Bar Mitzvah. They rejected the ceremony as superficial and ostentatious. Their refusal was probably more complicated than it seemed at the time. They were both "loners" who did not have a very wide circle of friends. My father's business did not prosper during the thirties. We never quite made it as comfortable

members of the Jewish middle class. However, since my mother
was one of the relatively few Jewish women who had completed
college in the twenties, there really was no other place for her. We
had more culture than money. Mother never adjusted to a world
in which money counted. It did in Jewish Long Beach. She could
never accept the fact that women with far less education invariably made a bigger splash simply because their husbands were doing well. She consoled herself with her superior intellect and
turned unsuccessfully toward writing and literary research. In
my twelfth year we left Long Beach. We moved to the Bronx for a
few months and finally settled in a brownstone apartment on
Manhattan's upper East Side. I was constantly aware of the great
world of luxury which surrounded us but which I could never
enter. I had by this time acquired an overly exaggerated view of
the value of the intellect and a deep sense of not belonging anywhere. Had my parents felt at home in the nascent Jewish suburbia of the thirties, I would have had my Bar Mitzvah and taken
the normal route to a life as a prosperous Jewish doctor, lawyer, or
businessman. By my twelfth year the normal routes were closed
to me, though I did not know it.

My parents' refusal to consent to the Bar Mitzvah shocked
our more traditional relatives and grieved my maternal grand-
mother. They felt that something very important was being with-
held from me. I wanted a Bar Mitzvah badly. I had no understanding of why the ceremony was so important to me. I remember
feeling cheated. I also recall that I was afraid I was no longer
quite like the other boys I knew.

I was given a consolation prize. There was an elaborate
surprise party at a Rockefeller Center restaurant. All of my cousins
came, but it wasn't the same. I had wanted a Bar Mitzvah. My
parents were unable to comply. I had been confirmed neither in
my identity as a man nor as a Jew at the crucial turning point of
adolescence. Had I lived in a community in which the rules of the
game of life were relatively explicit, the identity problem would
have been less urgent. Unfortunately I was growing up in the
heart of Manhattan where people hardly acknowledged their
next-door neighbors.

People joke about the Bar Mitzvah boy's assertion, "Now

I am a man." At least he has some confirmation of who he is at a very important turning point in his life. I had none. This was aggravated by the fact that my mother was the real authority at home. She ran things. She had far more formal education than my father, although, in retrospect, I think he knew more about what was really important. The worst blow to his ego came when he had to accept employment from my mother's brother. I suspect that he didn't feel very competent as a man, as a father, or as a breadwinner. I had been exposed neither to the male puberty rite of Judaism nor to a male model whose example might have offered me a measure of confidence in my own development.

The Bar Mitzvah episode was crucial. Unlike my parents, I could never regard religious ritual as without significance. I eventually came to regard ritual as a historically and psychologically authenticated way of dealing with the crises in the timetable of life. Insofar as religious temperaments are either "Catholic" or "Protestant," mine has been strongly "Catholic." I admire believing Orthodox Jews and Roman Catholics for the structure and order in their lives. They have had it given to them; I have had to find it within myself through great and terrible pain. Bar Mitzvah and the Passover Seder were the first rituals which impressed me. As I matured, other rituals were to become meaningful to me.

My adolescence coincided with the Hitler years and the rise of world-wide anti-Semitism. I grew up in a home milieu in which being Jewish was regarded as old fashioned, outmoded, and perhaps even a bit un-American. We did, however, know that we were Jews. We had the normal range of concern for the condition of Jews throughout the world. I found myself thrust into an era in which the Jewish question could not be ignored but in which I had only the most tenuous sort of Jewish identity. I did not know myself either as a man or as a Jew. Self-acceptance as a man and as a Jew were destined to be linked in my life.

I remember one crucial incident very clearly from my high-school days. I had been to a dance for teen-agers at the Ninety-second Street Y.M.H.A. one Saturday evening and was returning home about midnight. Suddenly I heard some drunken Irishmen screaming from across the street, "God damned dirty

Jews." They weren't yelling at me, but I very foolishly told them to shut up. It was an uneven encounter. The three of them pounced on me and beat me mercilessly with their umbrellas. They left me on the sidewalk thoroughly beaten. My parents called the police, who were Irish and anti-Semitic. Those were the days when Father Coughlin and the Christian Front had a very strong influence on New York's Irish. The police were not the least concerned about the beating. They were interested in establishing the "fact" that I was potentially delinquent because I had been on the street after midnight. That evening I conceived a bitter hatred for the Irish and a distrust of the police which did not dissipate itself until long after I became a rabbi and came to understand some of the problems of Irish history which engendered their bitterness.

Perhaps the most disturbing aspect of the beating was my parents' helplessness in the face of the hostility of the police. I was more disturbed by their lack of political *savoir-faire* and their desire not to make trouble than by the beating itself. At this point Jewishness seemed even emptier and more meaningless than ever. It appeared to me as an incurable hereditary disease from which I had to liberate myself by whatever means I could muster. The personal beating was the analogue of a world-wide condition which became very real to me when I found myself directly affected by it. My first response was flight.

At the time I was a student at New York's Townsend Harris High School, a special school for bright boys. It is now defunct. Over 90 per cent of the student body was Jewish in the late thirties. Moved to rid myself of a seemingly meaningless Jewish burden, I began to study theology with great avidity. I read Gibbon's accounts of the religious conflicts during the decline of the Roman Empire. I spent my afternoons in the local library studying the history and literature of a number of Christian sects. Given my background, it was not surprising that I concluded that Unitarianism was more congruent with my embryonic religious attitudes than any other Christian group. I decided to become a Unitarian.

I did not live far from Manhattan's All Souls' Unitarian Church. I made inquiries and learned that I would be welcome to attend the church's young people's group. I did not have the

courage to join alone. My best friend, in spite of my feelings
about the Irish, was Bob A., a fellow student at Townsend Harris
of Irish background. He was as eager to rid himself of his Irish
Catholic identity as I was to divest myself of my Jewish ties. We
decided to join the Unitarian youth group together. Being *plus
royaliste que le roi,* I became very involved in Unitarian youth
activities. I very quickly decided to become a minister. Beneath my
surface reasons for wanting to become a minister, there was a
pathetic yearning to overcome the curse of a Jewishness I could
neither understand nor accept. I was somewhat unhappy that
Unitarian ministers did not wear clerical collars. Sometimes, as
I sat in a bus or a subway, I envied priests and ministers their
collars. I felt that nobody would mistake me for a Jew if I could
only wear one.

My desire to enter the ministry reached a crisis in my last
year of high school, 1940. There were a number of scholarships
available to candidates for the ministry at the better colleges. I
began to investigate the available scholarships. In the course of
my inquiries I came to know some very helpful Unitarian ministers. One of my new friends suggested that I might stand a
better chance of prospering as a Unitarian minister if I changed
my name to one less obviously Jewish. He insisted that, while Unitarians were close to Reform Jews theologically, there remained
some residual anti-Semitism in Unitarian churches. This made it
advisable for me to choose an Anglo-Saxon name.

His suggestion fit in with my desire for flight. Nevertheless, at a deeper level, something in me rejected both the suggestion and my recently acquired Unitarian affiliation. There were
some things that couldn't be altered. His suggestion made me
understand this. I remain grateful to him to this day. Apparently
there was a limit to the extent to which I could allow myself to
escape the absurd destiny of having been born a Jew in a home in
which Jewishness seemed to have so little meaning. When I
realized that I could purchase entrance into the non-Jewish world
only at the price of a fundamental self-falsification, I refused. In
the archaic sensibility of mankind, few things about a man are as
important as his name. In an adolescent crisis, I discovered that I
could not renounce mine. I had begun my return to Jewish life. At

sixteen I had learned that self-contempt was a far greater burden to bear than the hostility of others.

Unitarians very frequently stress their theological similarities to Reform Judaism. When I realized that Unitarianism involved an impossible self-rejection for me, I turned to Reform Judaism. It seemed at first glance to be a kind of Jewish Unitarianism. For some Jews, Reform has proved to be a way out of Judaism; for me it was to be the way in.

When I think of my original decision to enter the rabbinate, it seems silly and even presumptuous. Realizing the impossibility of becoming a Unitarian minister, I resolved to become a Reform rabbi. I knew almost nothing about Jewish life or literature. I could not read Hebrew. It took some effort for me to become accustomed even to the relatively attenuated Reform service I found at Temple Emanuel. I began to study Hebrew and Jewish history. I was aided by several rabbis who were extremely generous with both their time and their personal encouragement. Without their help it would have been impossible for me to enter the Hebrew Union College in Cincinnati, which I did in 1942.

I became a rabbinical student with the most minimal Jewish knowledge. I could barely read Hebrew. I could not understand the language. It was through an act of generosity and good will that I was admitted to the Hebrew Union College at all. The Judaism I had come to know was classical, anti-Zionist Reform Judaism. In spite of the fact that the bloodiest war in mankind's history was then raging, I believed in the progress and enlightenment of mankind. I regarded liberal Judaism, with its lack of ritual, myth, and religious symbolism, as the most rational and therefore the most enlightened of religions. I especially appreciated classical Reform Judaism's bitter opposition to Zionism and Jewish nationalism. Although a war was being fought in which the vast majority of Europe's Jews were slaughtered, I accepted the belief that Jews differed from their fellow citizens in religious persuasion alone. I shared Reform Judaism's optimism concerning human potentialities and its hope that the education and enlightenment of men would eventually end anti-Semitism. I was most comfortable in a deritualized Judaism in which the language of worship was the only one I understood, English. Unaware of the emotional necessities which had brought me to rabbinical training, I was largely incognizant of the power of the irrational in religion or in myself.

I can remember distinctly the objective issues which brought about my disenchantment with classical Reform and my eventual turning to a more traditional Judaism. By the fall of 1944, the facts about the Nazi death camps had become generally known. Reports of the capture of the camp at Madjdanek, Poland, with its huge piles of ownerless shoes, left an indelible impression upon me. I read about Madjdanek at about the same time I was preparing to serve as a student rabbi for the High Holy days in Tupelo, Mississippi.

The revelation of the death camps caused me to reject the whole optimistic theology of liberal religion. People weren't getting any better, nor did I believe they ever would. The evil rooted in human nature would never entirely disappear. Like the plague in Albert Camus's novel, radical evil might lie dormant for long periods but it remained forever capable of disrupting the pathetically weak fragments of reason and decency with which men have constructed their fragile civilization. My generation might add to the treasury of knowledge, but it was incapable of adding significantly to humanity's store of goodness. Each generation had to confront the choice between good and evil unaided by those who went before.

The death camps spelled the end of my optimism concerning the human condition. Though twenty years have passed, I see little reason to alter my pessimism. I regarded the camps and Nazism as far more than a sport of history. They revealed the full potentiality of the demonic as a permanent aspect of human nature. I was all the more shaken because I began to recognize that the difference between the Germans and other men was not very great. Given similar conditions of political and social stress, most of us could commit very terrible crimes. Moral nihilism had, in any event, been one of the deepest strains in my nature. I had struggled to overcome it from childhood, but the anarchic creature of infantile desire within me had never been put to death. During my years at the Hebrew Union College, it had been suppressed by the regnant liberal optimism. The discovery of the Nazi camps again demonstrated its potency to me. The polite, optimistic religion of a prosperous middle class hardly offered much hope against the deep strains of disorder I saw in the world and in myself.

The shock of the extermination camps was paralleled by the shock of realization of the degree to which both the occupied peoples and even the Allies had, to a degree, cooperated in or assented to the Nazi holocaust. I began to understand the relationship between the Christian theology of history and the deep and abiding hatred of the Jew in the Occident. When the death camps were followed by Britain's refusal to permit the entry of the survivors into Palestine, I came to understand the inadequacy of any definition of Jewish life which rested on religious confession alone. Perhaps the healthiest aspect of my understanding of the ethnic aspect of Jewish life was that I could now see myself and the Jews of eastern Europe as united by ties of common fate and psychology. I had become and remain unimpressed with American Jewish life as a special case.

At about the same time, I became enormously impressed with the Jewish concept of *galuth* or exile. Objectively the destruction of European Jewry and the attempt to establish a new Jewish nation were both expressions of *galuth* as the abiding condition of Jewish life. Liberal Judaism had rejected the notion. Since the war liberal Jewish thinkers have re-examined *galuth* as a meaningful religious category. At the time, many Jewish religious liberals were convinced that we lived in the best of times, in spite of the recent setback, a conviction I found impossible to sustain. I especially remember the blindness with which some of the leaders opposed the establishment of the State of Israel. They insisted that Europe's Jews had an obligation to re-establish themselves and contribute to the liberalism and democracy of their native lands.

The notion of *galuth* seemed to make a great deal of sense both psychologically and existentially. Even in America, I felt that Jews would remain in *galuth* to an extent. *Galuth* had long ceased to be only a Jewish fact. Modern literature is replete with protagonists in real or psychological exile: Kafka's Joseph K., Mann's

Joseph, Camus's Mersault, Sartre's Antoine Rocquentin, Melville's Ahab are a few who come to mind. Neither as a Jew nor as an intellectual would I ever entirely be "in," but then who would be? Existence is exile. We are all superfluous men, whether we know it or not. I was surprised that "old fashioned," "unenlightened," traditional Judaism was more directly on target in its description of both the Jewish and the human condition than was "liberal," "progressive," "modern" Judaism. I began to wonder whether I could in good conscience remain tied to a liberal prayerbook and system of worship which so falsified the human condition by its unwarranted optimism.

Exile expresses theologically much the same reality which underlies the concept of alienation in contemporary social science. It has remained a cornerstone of my religious and psychological perspective. At the level of Jewish-Christian relations, I progressively gave up real hope that the Jew could ever feel entirely at home in the gentile world. This may sound harsher than it is meant to be. There are countless gentiles who have experienced a similar alienation, though it does have a special quality for Jews. We are destined to be strangers and wanderers upon the earth to the end of days. Even the State of Israel cannot escape this destiny, being the Jewish nation in a gentile world. Abraham's destiny would never depart from his progeny.

I also turned to the question of *geulah* or redemption, which is the other side of the coin of exile. Classical Reform Judaism was convinced that the Messiah had already come in the form of German and American enlightenment. As one reads the social and intellectual history of the late nineteenth century, one realizes how hopelessly out of touch the Reformers were. Important social forces were preparing a northern European racial tribalism which would effectively isolate all Jews. My pessimistic reading of twentieth-century Jewish history made me ask the age-old Jewish question, "When will the Messiah come? When will redemption begin?" My real concern was not about a personal Messiah but about the dream of the redemptive alteration of the human condition.

I was very much drawn to the insights of the Jewish mystics on this issue. In the years following the expulsion of the Jewish

community from Spain in 1492, Jewish mystics were agonized by
a problem similar to the one which had seized our times. The catastrophic destruction of Spanish Jewry made the problems of exile
and redemption central to them; the end of European Jewry had
made exile and redemption central to me.

The insights of Rabbi Isaac Luria of Safed, Palestine (d.
1572), and his followers have been especially helpful. They saw
existence itself as alienation. Even God the Creator could exist
only through an act of self-alienation. In their system, the first
creative act was the self-diminution, *tsimtsum,* of the absolutely
simple Ground of existence into Himself, leaving thereby a space
for the created world. According to Luria, the primal act of creation was one in which that which was All, and therefore no discrete limited thing, withdrew into Himself so that both He and
the created world could be limited and defined by each other.
This accorded strangely with my earliest nihilism which saw nothingness as the origin and destiny of all things. I saw God as
the Holy Nothingness. I had exchanged my atheistic nihilism for
a mystical nihilism. To be all that there is, as God was in the beginning and will be in the end, is equivalent to being, so to speak,
absolutely nothing. In the beginning, God dwelt in the womb of
his own omnipotent nothingness. The first act of creation was an
act of self-estrangement whereby the revealed God, in contrast to
the primordial hidden ground, and the created world came into
existence.

Since the world came into existence, so to speak, out of
God's nothingness, all conscious existence is beset by a conflict
between the desire for survival, identity, and individual self-
maintenance and the yearning to return to its source in God's
nothingness. Redemption is return; existence is exile. We purchase identity at the price of estrangement. We know who we are
only insofar as we know who we are not. We both crave and fear
redemption because its reward and its price are the same: disappearance of the individual into the Source whence he came.
This mystical doctrine is not unlike Freud's secularized version
of the same conflict in his late work *Beyond the Pleasure Principle.* Freud posited a lifelong conflict between our instinct for
life and our yearning to return to the quiescence which pre-

ceded our existence. Freud used the metaphor of the *eros-thanatos* conflict. The mystics tended to see the very same conflict in terms of the polarities of the maintenance of the self and the return to the Source. I tended to regard both the mystics and Freud as utilizing different symbolic systems to point to a common reality.

I was particularly struck by the remark a later mystic, Rav Schneur Zalman of Ladi (d. 1813), is reputed to have made. Interrupting his prayers, he declared, "I do not want Your paradise. I do not want Your world to come. I want You and You only."

Eternal separation is eternal exile. The Rav of Ladi yearned ultimately to return. He also knew, insofar as it is given to any human being to know, what it was he was returning to. Shortly before his death he asked his grandson, "Do you see anything?" The boy was astonished. The Rav then said, "All I can see is the Holy Nothingness which gives life to the world."

Life is exile. Evil, pain, suffering can be ended only by ending life. The Jewish situation, like so many Jewish gestures, exaggerates what is common to all men. The Jewish people remain in exile awaiting the redeeming Messiah. The conflict with Christianity is strongest at this point. The good news of the Church is that the Messiah has come, bringing with him actual or potential redemption. There is sadness in the Jewish rejection of the Christian claim. It rests upon a tragic wisdom which asserts the inevitability of pain and evil, along with real moments of joy and fulfillment, as long as life continues. By asserting that the Messiah will come, the Jewish community was also saying of any given *actual era* that his redemption has yet to begin.

There are many Jewish speculations concerning the time of the coming of the Messiah. Isaac Bashevis Singer, the contemporary novelist, has, I believe, penetrated to the heart of the mystical meaning of the hour of the Messiah at the very end of his novel *The Family Moskat*. As Hitler's armies approach the gates of Warsaw, bringing the final destruction of European Jewry with them, one of Singer's characters affirms that the Messiah will come speedily. This affirmation of faith is greeted with astonishment, whereupon Hertz Yanovar clarifies his assertion: "Death is the Messiah. That is the real truth."

Only death perfects life and ends its problems. God can redeem only by slaying. We have nothing to hope for beyond what we are capable of creating in the time we have allotted to us. Of course, this leaves room for much doing and much creating. Nevertheless, in the final analysis all things crumble away into the nothingness which is at the beginning and end of creation.

If existence is ultimately devoid of hope and God offers us absolutely nothing, why bother with religion at all? I must confess that at a significant level I have much sympathy with the contemporary "death of God" Protestant theologians, though many of their concerns are specifically rooted in the ethos of Christianity, which has had to grapple with the meaning of the death of God involved in the crucifixion of Jesus. The question, "Why religion?" probably is meaningless. There are men and women devoid of all illusion who nevertheless regard withdrawal from the religious community as unthinkable. I am one of them. The decision to partake of the life of a community rests upon forces within the psyche which have little to do with rational argument. There is absolutely no reason for those who can do without religion to bother. At a certain tribal level, religion is inescapable in the United States. Our identities are shaped by the religious groups into which we are born. Our religions are less what we profess than what we inherit. There are Protestant, Catholic, and Jewish atheists. Jewish "death of God" theology is very different from its Christian counterpart. At the level of religious philosophy, Jewish and Christian radical theologians make similar denials. Their life styles inevitably reflect the communities they come from. Was it not Santayana who declared that there is no God but Mary is his mother? Nowhere in America can one find abstract men who are Americans without any other qualification.

Inheritance may influence personal identity. It does not necessarily compel religious commitment or affiliation. Undoubtedly the need for a community of manageable proportions to which one can belong and in which one is welcome has had a lot to do with the proliferation of churches and synagogues in middle-class America. For me, another need determined my affiliation. Like the Polish Jew in the East European *Shtedtl*, the tribesman in an African tribe untouched by "civilization," and the Spanish peasant, I cannot dispense with the institution through which I can dramatize, make meaningful, and share the decisive moments of my life. For me that institution is the synagogue; for all men it is the religious community they have inherited. Of course there is something absurd and irrational about this. I did not choose to be Jewish. It has been one of the givens of my nature, but no religious institution other than the synagogue is psychologically and culturally appropriate for my need to celebrate and share the decisive moments of existence. These moments include birth, puberty, marriage, temporary or permanent infirmity, the marking of time irretrievably past, the rearing of children, the need to express and find catharsis for feelings of guilt, the need for personal renewal, and the feeling of awe and wonder which overcomes me when I think about God's nothingness as the ultimate source and the final end.

This may be a highly subjective rationale for synagogue participation, but such subjectivity need not be solipsistic. I suspect other people find the life and liturgy of the synagogue meaningful for similar reasons. Each of the crises I have enumerated tends to be emotionally overdetermined and requires a significant context in which our emotions concerning it can be expressed, objectified, and clarified. Over the years I have come to question the adequacy of non-traditional liturgy for this purpose. The very fact that so much of liberal Jewish liturgy is in the vernacular suggests that it is in the language appropriate to the conscious level of response. There are other levels of response which require drama, grandeur, and mystery. I have found increasingly that the traditional Jewish liturgy, with the fewest possible rationalistic alterations, is the most appropriate vehicle for the expression of both my conscious and my unconscious feelings toward the crises I have enumerated. Myth and ritual are the domains in which we express and project our unconscious feelings concerning the dilemmas of existence. They are indispensable vehicles of expression in an institution in which the decisive moments of existence are to be shared and celebrated at both the conscious and unconscious levels.

I have not said much about the details of my spiritual development after the revelation of the death camps at Madjdanek.

Much has happened of religious importance since then. I left Reform and completed my rabbinical studies at the Jewish Theological Seminary, ultimately finding academic and intellectual work more suitable to my capacities than the congregational rabbinate. Nevertheless, I prefer to conclude the recital of personal details, insofar as they are relevant to my religious development, with Madjdanek. That is as it should be. I am convinced that the problem of God and the death camps is the central problem for Jewish theology in the twentieth century. The one pre-eminent measure of the adequacy of all contemporary Jewish theologies is the seriousness with which they deal with this supreme problem of Jewish history. The fact of the death camps cannot be dismissed or swept under an intellectual rug. It will not be forgotten. On the contrary, we have yet to experience the full religious impact of the terrible happenings of World War II. The catastrophe of 1939–45 represents a psychological and religious time bomb which has yet to explode fully in the midst of Jewish religious life.

Already there are clear and unmistakable symptoms of Jewish reaction to what took place. The birth of Israel is the most obvious. Another has been the massive defection of young Jews from Jewish life in both Europe and the United States. Young Jews tend to be highly intelligent and well educated. They have learned all the lessons of contemporary skepticism. They know how terrible the price of being a Jew can be in an age of murderous technology. Many of them have said to themselves, especially in western Europe, "If being Jewish involves the threat of a future death camp for my children, I will use the respite between the explosions of anti-Semitism to marry outside the Jewish community and give my children a decent chance to escape this fate." Judaism is simply no longer worth the price of martyrdom for far more young Jews than most of us can possibly imagine. One of the results of the age of "broken symbols," as Paul Tillich has called it, is that martyrdom has gone out of fashion among Jews and has been replaced by the possibility of massive defection.

I suspect that many of us remain Jewish because we have concluded that self-contempt and self-falsification are too great a price to pay for safety. I must affirm my identity as a Jew. I have no choice. That is the kind of man I am. Nevertheless, I see no special virtue in my decision. It is simply my pathway to authenticity as a human being. There have been rewards. Self-acceptance as a Jew has made it possible for me to accept myself as a man and to learn how to live, given a decent respect for the necessities of society, in terms of my own needs and my own perspectives. Had I rejected myself as a Jew, I would have had to enthrone the opinions of others as ultimately decisive for my inner life. I could not grant the world that tyranny over me. I am prepared to do many things that society requires of me, granted their consistency with the canons of human decency, but I am not prepared to bestow upon others the right to determine how I shall think of myself or my community. By accepting myself as a Jew, I have liberated myself from the most futile and degrading of servilities, that of forever attempting to appease the irrational mythology that the Christian world has constructed of the Jew. As long as the Christian world regards a Palestinian Jew as God incarnate, it will find it excessively difficult to see Jews in terms devoid of mythic distortion. The only way I can live free of such distortion is through self-acceptance as a Jew.

I believe I have, against surprising odds, found myself insofar as this is possible. The death camps helped me to understand the religious meaning of our era. Ours is the time of the death of God. That time which Nietzsche's madman had said was too far off has come upon us. I understood the meaning of the death of God when I understood the meaning of Auschwitz and Madjdanek. The terrible fact is that the Germans set out to annihilate European Jewry and they succeeded quite well. Most of the participants in the most monstrous crime in history sleep undisturbed in comfortable and even luxurious beds in their newly prosperous fatherland. There has been no real retribution nor will there be. I doubt that there are even real pangs of conscience. On the contrary, when the *Alte Kameraden* gather together to discuss the good old days in the SS, they undoubtedly recall their murders in the same good spirit as hunters regaling each other with tales of the hunt. God really died at Auschwitz. This does not mean that God is not the beginning and will not be the end. It does mean that nothing in human choice, decision, value, or meaning can any longer have vertical reference to transcendent standards. We are alone in a silent, unfeeling cosmos. Our actions are human actions. Their entailments are human entailments. Morality and religion can no longer rest upon the conviction that divinely validated norms offer a measure against which what we do can be judged. As Jean Paul Sartre has shown in *The Flies,* if we are prepared to accept the consequences of our actions, nothing prevents us from carrying out any crime, even matricide. Though most of us will refrain from antisocial behavior, we do so because of the fear of ourselves and others rather than fear of God.

What then of Judaism? It is the way we Jews share our lives in an unfeeling and silent cosmos. It is the flickering candle we have lighted in the dark to enlighten and to warm us. Somehow it will continue for a very long time because there will always be some men who will accept and affirm what they were born to be. Ultimately, as with all things, it will pass away, for omnipotent Nothingness is Lord of All Creation.

This is my earliest theological statement as well as my first attempt to deal with the problem of the death of God in contemporary Jewish theology. It was originally read at Middlebury College, Middlebury, Vermont, at a conference in 1955 on "The Symbolic Content of Religion." It has been partially revised for this book, but it faithfully reflects my thinking when I first attempted to express myself on theological issues.

At the time I was a graduate student at Harvard. I was deeply influenced by Paul Tillich's lectures. His influence is very apparent in the paper. He is, as Thomas Altizer has commented, the father of modern radical theology.

I waited four years before submitting this paper for publication. I was not prepared at the time to risk an exposure of my theological views. In retrospect, I see that it contains in embryo many of the themes in radical theology which I have since enlarged upon.

13 / The Symbols of Judaism and the Death of God

THE GROWTH OF religious institutions and the decline in religious belief have been frequently observed phenomena in postwar America. This development has often puzzled students of religion. A number of scholars have commented especially on the tendency of suburban churches and synagogues to become primarily social institutions. Condemnations by clergymen of the growing religious indifference have been frequent. Yet belief continues to decline, while religious communities continue to expand.

The postwar decline in religious commitment has been very much in evidence in the prospering synagogues of America. While the decline in belief is largely a cultural phenomenon, it does reflect a theological problem which has been covertly understood in religious circles for several decades. The rise of scientific scholarship in the field of religion has been especially threatening to the believing Jew. As a result of the new insights, it has been impossible to accept at face value the myths concerning the authority of traditional Jewish belief and practice. Religious Jews have been compelled either to retreat to a fideistic dogmatism which ignores modern scholarship, or to seek a new rationale for their theological commitments. For many, the problem of finding a new rationale has been aggravated by the death of their personal God. After Auschwitz many Jews did not need Nietzsche to tell them that the old God of Jewish patriarchal monotheism was dead beyond all hope of resurrection.

At the heart of traditional Judaism there is the belief that God, the omnipotent creator of heaven and earth, gave the Jewish people the Torah at Mt. Sinai. This document contained the laws and disciplines by which Jews were obliged to conduct their lives. Traditional Jews believed that they were to fulfill the disciplines of their faith because God had commanded them so to do. Righteousness consisted in obedience to God's will as revealed in the Torah; sin was a want of conformity with His will. Basic to this perspective was the conviction that the Torah was a unitary document which expressed a harmonious point of view. There were some laws in the Torah which seemed to contradict others. The religious Jew believed that such contradictions could be resolved through recourse to the Oral Law, the rabbinic interpretation of the Torah. Since the Torah was a single document emanating from a single source, the discrepancies were more apparent than real. Guided by the interpretations of the rabbis, the religious Jew could rest secure in the knowledge that the conduct of his life was in accordance with God's will.

Biblical scholarship has proven far more threatening to traditional Judaism than to Christianity. The Christian believer is expected to affirm the centrality of the Christ-event for his destiny. Christian faith never rested its ultimate claim on the unitary authorship of the sacred documents of Christian religion. Judaism depended upon the belief in the historical authenticity and the literary unity of the Torah. This text was traditionally regarded as containing an accurate record of God's encounter with Moses. Its interpretation by the rabbis was thought to be faithfully in keeping with its original intent. As a result of modern scholarship, we now understand that the Torah is a collection of many documents with some internal discrepancies of age, environment, and point of view. The documentary hypothesis made it impossible to claim that the Torah was a unitary work containing the record of God's covenant with Israel without contradiction. The traditional believer did not have to face the problem of why he ought to fulfill religious commandments of doubtful origin and authority. We do. The traditional believer was convinced that in obeying the Torah he was fulfilling God's will. We no longer possess that assurance.

When one accepts the new situation, one is forced either to reject Jewish religious practice or to find a new rationale for continuing to fulfill that sector which remains meaningful. As Tillich has suggested, we live in an age of "broken symbols." The problem of the symbolic content of Judaism in our time is to find a viable basis for continuing to maintain Jewish religious practice after its traditional validations have become altogether transparent to us.

While it is no longer possible to accept the traditional justifications of the authority of Judaism, new insights, especially in the social sciences, have made it impossible to dismiss such rituals as entirely meaningless. Edward Gibbon could look upon Notre Dame in Paris as a towering monument to superstition and dismiss it with contempt. Today we see religion as far too deeply rooted in the realities of the human predicament so to reject it.

The insights of depth psychology have been especially helpful in offering us a new understanding of the significance of religion. A century ago the seemingly irrational aspects of religion were either accepted by the faithful without insight or dismissed by the sceptical as meaningless. Today we understand that irrational phenomena in religion, as in other spheres of human activity, are meaningful, purposeful, and goal-directed. They express some of the deepest and most important feelings we experience as human beings. The key to our new understanding lies in a distinction implicit in Freud's work on the interpretation of dreams. I refer to the distinction between the latent and the manifest content of fantasy productions. While the manifest content of dreams frequently lacks coherent meaning, an understanding of the associations the dream symbolism elicits usually reveals that its latent content expresses some unconscious fear or wish of the dreamer.

Freud's insights about dreams were quickly extended to other types of fantasy production, including myths, legends, and religious beliefs. While their manifest content frequently made little sense, their latent content was understood to give expression to unconscious feelings concerning our most significant life-experiences. Freud had spoken of religion as a group neurosis. He tended to regard religious belief as a group phenomenon which paralleled neurotic strivings in the life of the individual. At one level this disparaged religion; at another level, Freud's suggestion pointed to the degree to which religion reflected the deepest fears, aspirations, and yearnings of the individual and the group. As Ernest Jones has commented, although Freud ceased to believe in the *historical* truth of religion, he never ceased to believe in its *psychological* truth. The modern Jew has lost faith in the historical justification of his faith. The psychological justification offers the most fruitful path for a contemporary rationale for Jewish religious belief and practice.

An excellent example of the psychological truth of religious tradition can be seen in the mystical transformation of the Biblical doctrine of *creatio ex nihilo* in the Kabalistic doctrine of R. Isaac Luria, a Palestinian mystic of the latter part of the sixteenth century. In the Biblical doctrine, God creates the world out of a nothingness *external* to His person. In the mystical doctrine, we find one of the most persistent of all myths, the myth of the separation of the world from a primordial sacred ground and the yearning of the separated world ultimately to return to its source. In Luria's myth, *creatio ex nihilo* is taken to mean creation out of the "no thing" which is the primordial Godhead. The primordial ground is understood as beyond substance, above all finitude, and incommensurate with the categories of human discursive reasoning. God in the original plenitude of His being is therefore no thing and, in a sense, nothing. The nothingness of God, in the mystical doctrine, is not the nothingness of absolute privation. It is the nothingness of the absence of all concreteness and "thinghood." God's original nothingness is the nothingness of a superfluity of being. At this stage, one cannot say that God exists. Discrete, quantifiable entities exist. As the distinguished contemporary Jewish mystic, Zalman Schacter, has paradoxically stated, "If there is a God, He doesn't exist." According to this doctrine, God can *exist* only when He becomes less than Himself and ceases to be no thing. This can only happen when God *gives birth to* the world out of His primordial ground. My emphasis on the image of giving birth, though hopelessly inadequate, is nevertheless deliberate.

This mystical doctrine of creation is an attempt to give

mythic structure to the creation of the world through an analogy with the human womb-birth-tomb sequence. Just as the infant discovers its world through severance from its symbiotic relation with the mother, so too in the myth the primordial Godhead becomes God and the world through the self-division or self-diminution of the primal ground of being or *Urgrund*. In Lurianic Kabbalism this process is called *tsimtsum*, the creative self-diminution of the Godhead. The primal Godhead creates both the world and God out of its own no-thingness. The finite persons and things which constitute the created world consist of the divine sparks which have left their primordial source to wander about, only to be regathered at the end of time in the allness which is no-thing. It is also of consequence in this doctrine that the first act of creation is a *fall* or an original catastrophe. The ultimate goal of the created world is the reparation of the catastrophe and a return of all things to God as He was in the beginning. Thomas Altizer has commented that non-Christian religions have as their ultimate goal the recollection of a primordial sacred beginning. His description fits Lurianic Kabbalism. Creation is a catastrophe; creatures are caught between a tendency toward self-maintenance and reabsorption into the primordial ground; the restoration of the original, undisturbed unity of all in God and God as the all-in-all is the final goal.

This is a myth. Nevertheless, it expresses a very concrete reality all can recognize. It is predicated upon the image of man as a finite, alienated creature thrust into existence in a world which cannot entirely satisfy him and in which he is separated from, yet drawn to, the source of his true being in the *Urgrund*. The myth can be read in two ways: In one, the separated and broken character of human finitude is stressed. In the other, man is seen as a fulcrum balancing the forces of life and death, love and hate, organic separateness and inorganic sameness, being and nothingness. The mystics stress the broken character of separated human existence. Freud in *Beyond the Pleasure Principle* stresses the fulcrum character of life which is inextricably bound to the dialectic tensions of *eros* and *thanatos,* and in which *thanatos* is ultimately victorious. There is one vital difference between the mystics and Freud. Freud, and in a sense all of the moderns, would say that the human predicament has "no exit" save death. For the mystic there is always hope for the ultimate reconciliation with God by a return to the ground of being. Nevertheless, the critique of life in the here and now is very much the same in the mystics and the moderns. Both see the human predicament as broken, alienated, and destined to terminate in the nothingness out of which it has arisen.

The same human reality is comprehended by Paul Tillich in *The Courage To Be* in which he describes two types of anxiety. Tillich refers to existential anxiety or *Urangst* and neurotic anxiety. Anxiety is the reaction of the organism to the possibility of loss. According to Tillich existential anxiety is man's ineradicable reaction to the possibility of loss which stems from his condition of finitude and creatureliness: the fact that man is born to grow, see himself decay, and be overwhelmed by an ultimate oblivion against which his own powers offer no hope of rescue. As Tillich uses anxiety, it has a cognitive aspect. It is the non-conceptual, unmediated awareness by man of his own finitude. Unlike neurotic anxiety, existential anxiety is ineradicable. The very condition of human existence makes man forever in danger of ultimate loss, the loss of his own selfhood in death.

Tillich's analysis of anxiety rests on Heidegger and, in the final analysis, on Kierkegaard. Kierkegaard stresses an aspect of anxiety which seems to anticipate Freud. Kierkagaard calls *Angst* a "sympathetic-antipathy," by which he means that we are drawn to the very condition we fear even as anxiety helps us to ward it off. Thus, *Urangst* is not only man's cognition and primordial reaction to his ultimate nothingness, it is also, as in Freud, man's primordial yearning for the same nothingness. The mystic yearning for a return to the Godhead, Tillich, Kierkegaard, and Freud all point to the same existential condition. Man's selfhood is a delicate fulcrum balancing those forces which would restore him to sameness with the cosmos and those forces which preserve his separate individual identity. The same critique of existence is implied in the mystical creation myth that is found in the modern writers. The theme is perennial. The religious myth may lack scientific warrant. Nevertheless, it is, psychologically speaking, very true. As a matter of fact, in its religio-mythic form it calls forth a far greater emotional response than when it is expressed conceptually in its non-religious forms. The unconscious was not invented by Freud. The basic responses of human beings to their condition were dealt with long before the twentieth century. Religious myth expresses many of the most abiding concerns of human beings in every generation in a form that can be understood by people of all levels of intellectual attainment. In all ages religion has addressed itself through myth and ritual to such questions as "What is my origin? What is my destiny? How can I be cleansed of my guilt? What are the meaning and purpose of life?" These are questions of ultimate concern. The fact that myth and religious symbol no longer are regarded as true at the manifest level is entirely irrelevant to their central function, which is to give profound expression to our feelings at the decisive times and crises of life.

It is almost a commonplace that religious myth is deeply congruent with human strivings in our psychologically-oriented culture. It may not be nearly so apparent that religious ritual is also congruent with the most important human strivings. I would not want to suggest that all religious rituals remain worthy of observance. Many have arisen out of obsessional needs which once understood diminish in usefulness. There remains, however, a body of ritual practices so authentically rooted in human need that they are unlikely ever to be dispensed with.

Bar Mitzvah is one such ritual. It is one of the most maligned and vulgarized Jewish religious ceremonies. As practiced in the United States, Bar Mitzvah is especially embarrassing to those who see ritual primarily as a pedagogic instrument through which ethical or moral principles can be dramatized. This embarrassment may be acute when a child, innocent of any knowledge of the Hebrew language, reads for his Bar Mitzvah ceremony a section in Hebrew from the Prophets which contains a bitter denunciation of mechanical ritual devoid of any inner meaning. When the young man is congratulated upon completion of the ceremony for his success in the rote reading of an incomprehensible text, there is a very strong temptation to question the value of the practice. Yet this ceremony continues to have an enormous hold over all denominations within the American Jewish community. Without it it is unlikely that American Jewish adolescents would be motivated to acquire even the modicum of religious training they do receive.

This ritual has a far greater significance than is apparent on the surface. Bar Mitzvah is a *rite de passage*. It allows a young man to formalize his passage from childhood to adolescence and incipient manhood. It confirms him in his newly acquired masculine role. The disappearance of such a ritual would diminish the extent to which the community compels recognition of the new stage the young man has reached in the timetable of life. Since there is something in all of us which would remain an infant if it could, the failure of society to provide ceremonies of passage such as Bar Mitzvah or confirmation can result in the prolongation beyond its time of relevance of the feelings and behavior of the child in the body of a man. There is renunciation of the infantile and acceptance of the reality of the passing of time in the ceremony. Bar Mitzvah reconciles the boy with his father through a reinforcement of identification. The boy passes through the same rite as his father did. He sees his father as encouraging his entrance into manhood rather than impeding it. Not only does the ceremony formalize the child's entry into manhood, it also is the occasion of the parents' entry into middle age. Parents are as much in need of a *rite de passage* as are children. They often "enjoy" Bar Mitzvah more than their children. In short, Bar Mitzvah is a puberty rite.

Sexual identity is one of the deepest sources of conflict and anxiety within American culture. It does not come automatically or with any degree of ease. One of the most effective ways of helping the Jewish male adolescent to achieve an appropriate sexual identity is through this puberty rite. There is much that is primitive and even archaic in the ritual. It is the one in which contemporary Judaism resembles primitive pagan cultures most completely. Here as elsewhere in Judaism the primitive and the archaic prove upon examination to be among the most meaningful aspects of religion. We err when we stress the distance we have traveled from the ways of primitive man. We have been far more successful in mastering the physical world than in dealing with the emotional crises arising out of the developing personalities of individuals in our culture. In such really important aspects of human experience as birth, adolescence, mating, guilt and death, our fundamental experiences tend to remain the same as those of primitive men. If anything, we are at a disadvantage in our secular culture. Primitive man never left the individual to face the crises of life unaided by meaningful myths and rituals as we do. The Bar Mitzvah ceremony is significant because it confirms the young man in his growing identity at a most appropriate time and in a setting of the greatest possible significance. Even without God, this ritual would remain emotionally indispensable for Jews.

Many religious ceremonies dramatize ethical teachings; others possess a definite survival value for the community. Nevertheless, neither the ethical nor the sociological justification of ritual, though entirely valid, is adequate in itself. Where such rationales are stressed, there is an unfortunate tendency to be rid of seemingly irrational rituals which actually play an enormously important role in the development of the personality. One is almost, but not quite, tempted to reassert the doctrine of the divine origin of ritual in that rituals were intuitively created by the community as an unconscious response to its deepest needs. In the time of the death of God, I suspect we need rituals to dramatize and celebrate the crises of life more than ever.

One of the problems which face today's radical theologians is that of formulating an adequate answer to the question, What shall we say of religion in a time of no God? Sooner or later Protestant radical theologians will have to formulate a doctrine of the church if their theology is to have any relevance for Christendom. Similarly, contemporary Jewish theology cannot ignore the question of the meaning of the synagogue in our times.

The synagogue is an extremely problematic institution. All of the tensions felt by Protestant theologians as they confront the conflict between Christianity and Christendom have their analogue in the discomfort felt by contemporary Jewish thinkers as they contemplate the American synagogue. I shall avoid a further rehearsal of the shortcomings of the American synagogue. Enough has been said on that account to make such an effort unnecessary here. Nevertheless, Jewish thinkers know that this inadequate institution in which they can never entirely feel at home is indispensable for Jewish religious life. From Kierkegaard to Bonhoeffer and Cox, Protestant theologians have been fascinated with the problem of a Christianity without the church, a "religionless Christianity." There can be no such thing as a religionless Judaism, a Judaism without the synagogue.

We cannot rest content with asserting the psychological relevance of religious literature, myth and ritual. To do this would be to see these phenomena as no more significant humanly speaking than great literature such as *Antigone, Faust* or *The Brothers Karamazov*. Religion transcends this kind of relevance. Religious symbols cease to be meaningful unless they are appropriated in the shared life of a community. The synagogue is such a community for all of its obvious weaknesses and even vulgarities. It is the institution in which we share not only our inherited rituals and memories but also the human realities which are their ground and content. One need not plead the divine origin of Jewish symbols to understand their special appropriateness to the Jew and Jewish life. There is an interdependent relationship between Jewish identity, Jewish history, and Jewish traditions. Each has helped to create the other. To a very large extent men are the product of the way they bring their memories to bear on their present activities. This is also true of religious communities. History is a decisive determinant of identity in both the individual and the group. As Sartre has suggested, we are our acts. Jewish traditions mirror Jewish identity and Jewish history. No other body of tradition would be appropriate for us. It is part of the givenness of Jewish existence.

The synagogue and the Jewish community retain continuing centrality in Jewish religious life. There can be no Jewish "single one" who turns his back on the community and its traditions and seeks his path to God alone. The mutual need of the individual and the community are perhaps most strongly in evidence in the face of death. No Jew is permitted to mourn the loss of a family member alone. There are few periods in the life of a Jew when the religious community and its traditions mean more to him than at the *shivah* period, the seven days of mourning after the death of a close relative. Judaism possesses no myths of denial by which Jews can pretend that this time is other than tragic. No attempt is made to disguise the emotional impact of death. Every Jewish ritual at the time of mourning forces the Jew to acknowledge the stark reality of what has transpired. Death is not denied; it is affirmed so that the survivors can take up the task of living realistically when the time of healing begins. During the *shivah* period the mourners are not left to themselves. In that crisis in which the individual feels most bereft, the community offers him the presence of his peers to acknowledge and share his terrible burden. *Shivah* is one of the institutions through which Judaism transcends meaning and insight and becomes a sharing of ultimate concern. By use of a common and essentially fixed ritual, we tread a path which others have trod before us. In the face of death we share our predicament with both our peers and those who came before us. The repetition of a common crisis calls for a fixity of form in the rituals with which we confront the experience. This fixity of form is also important for the chain of the generations. It makes for the likelihood that those who follow us will also share with us.

Death, is, of course, the most radical of human necessities. Inevitably it calls forth our freest and most undisguised response to the human predicament. It is for this reason that the synagogue manifests itself here as the community of ultimate concern with the least ambiguity. It would be both untruthful and unhelpful to suggest that the synagogue is normally free of very real impediments to genuine sharing. Usually the need for existential honesty is far less strong. Nevertheless, before we dismiss the conception of the synagogue as the community of ultimate concern altogether, we must ask whether there is any other institution than the church or synagogue in which the existential crises of birth, death, growth, joy, sorrow, pain and mutual support are more meaningfully shared. Both institutions are woefully inadequate because they are, after all, human institutions with very human failings. We possess no better instruments for sharing the decisive events in the timetable of life.

Finally, there is the problem of the God after the death of God. The focus of the synagogue upon the decisive events and seasons of life gives us a clue to the meaning of God in our times. At one level, it is certainly possible to understand God as the primal ground of being out of which we arise and to which we return. I believe such a God is inescapable in the time of the death of God. The God who is the ground of being is not the transcendent, theistic God of Jewish patriarchal monotheism. Though many still believe in that God, they do so ignoring the questions of God and human freedom and God and human evil. For those who face these issues, the Father-God is a dead God. Even the existentialist leap of faith cannot resurrect this dead God after Auschwitz.

Nevertheless, after the death of the Father-God, God remains the central reality against which all partial realities can be measured. I should like to suggest that God can be understood meaningfully not only as ground of being but also as the *focus of ultimate concern*. As such He is not the old theistic Father-God. Nor is He Reconstructionism's "power that makes for salvation in the world." He is the infinite measure against which we can see our own limited finite lives in proper perspective. Before God it is difficult for us to elevate the trivial to the central in our lives. The old Hebraic understanding of the meaning of idolatry is important for an understanding of the meaning of God as the focus of ultimate concern. Idolatry is the confusion of a limited aspect of things with the ground of the totality. This is not the occasion to catalogue the idolatries of our time. That task has been well done by others. If an awareness of God as the ground of being does nothing more than enable us to refrain from endowing a partial and limited concern with the dignity and status reserved for what is of ultimate concern, it will have served the most important of all tasks. The ancient Hebrews regarded idolatry as a special form of enslavement. Nothing in our contemporary idolatries makes them less enslaving than their archaic counterparts. God can truly make us free.

We live in a culture which tends to stress what we can do rather than what we can become. A few examples will suffice to illustrate the encouragements to idolatry and self-deception with which our culture abounds. We are forever encouraged to deny the passing of time in our overestimation of the importance of both being and looking young. One of our greatest needs is to acknowledge our temporality and mortality without illusion. By so doing, we are not defeated by time. We establish the precondition of our *human* mastery over it. As the focus of ultimate concern the timeless God reflects our seriousness before our human temporality.

Another decisive contemporary need is to learn how to dwell within our own bodies. That is not so easy as it may seem. Fewer capacities come harder to Americans than the capacity to dwell within their own bodies with grace, dignity, and gratification. We become caricatures of our human potentialities when we fail to acquire this wisdom. By coming to terms with the biological nature of the timetable of life, we experience an enormous liberation yet develop the capacity for equally great renunciations when necessary. In the presence of God as the focus of ultimate concern, we need no deceptive myths of an immortal soul. We are finite. He is eternal. We shall perish. He remains ever the same. Before Him we confront our human nakedness with truth and honesty. In this venture, our voyage of self-discovery is enormously aided by Judaism's insistence through ritual and tradition on our continuing awareness of where we are in the biological timetable of life. The ancient Gnostics disparaged the God of the Jews as the God of this world. They asserted that all of His commandments were concerned with the conduct of life in this perishing cosmos. They correctly understood Judaism in their hostility. Unlike Gnosticism, Judaism refused to turn the regard of Jews away from the only life they will ever know, the life of the flesh in this world. God as the focus of ultimate concern challenges us to be the only persons we realistically can be, our authentic, finite selves in all of the radical insecurity and potentiality the life of mortal man affords.

One cannot pray to such a God in the hope of achieving an I–Thou relationship. Such a God is not a person over against man. If God is the ground of being, He will not be found in the meeting of I and Thou but in self-discovery. That self-discovery is not necessarily introspective. The whole area of interpersonal relations is the matrix in which meaningful and insightful self-discovery can occur. Nor can the I–Thou relation between God and man be achieved through prayer. This does not do away with worship. It sets worship in proper perspective. Even Buber admits, in his discussion of the eclipse of God, the contemporary failure of personal prayer. While prayer as address and dialogue has ceased to be meaningful, the burden of this paper has been to suggest some of the ways in which religious ritual has retained its significance. Ritual is more important today than prayer save as prayer is interwoven with ritual. Our prayers can no longer be attempts at dialogue with a personal God. They become aspirations shared in depth by the religious community. As aspiration there is hardly a prayer in the liturgy of Judaism which has lost its meaning or its power. Worship is the sharing of ultimate concern by the community before God, the focus of ultimate concern.

Paradoxically God as ground does everything and nothing. He does nothing in that He is not the motive or active power which brings us to personal self-discovery or to the community of shared experience. Yet He does everything because He shatters and makes transparent the patent unreality of every false and inauthentic standard. God, as the ultimate measure of human truth and human potentiality, calls upon each man to face both the limitations and the opportunities of his finite predicament without disguise, illusion or hope.

There remains the question of whether the religion of God as the source and ground of being, the God after the death of God, is truly a religion. Can there be a religion without a belief in a theistic, creator God? Pagan religions have never celebrated such a God. As I have suggested elsewhere, in the time of the death of God a mystical paganism which utilizes the historic forms of Jewish religion offers the most promising approach to religion in our times.[1]

Judaism no longer insists on the affirmation of a special creed. It has long since ceased rejecting its communicants because of ritual neglect. This does not mean that Judaism has descended to the level of a tribal herd bound together by a primitive and externally enforced we-feeling. No religion can exist without a meaningful form of sacrifice. Though it is not always apparent, contemporary Judaism does have its form of sacrifice. It is just as meaningful and in some ways more demanding than the older forms. This form of sacrifice is peculiarly appropriate to our new understanding of the meaning of God and the power of symbols in contemporary Judaism. Our sacrifice is not philanthropy. Nor is it the renunciation of personal autonomy which some traditions

[1] Cf. pp. 93-111.

demand. The sacrifice required of those who would participate in the community of ultimate concern is perhaps one of the most difficult in today's society. It is the sacrifice of that pride through which we see our individual roles, status, attainments, or sophistications as in any way more significant than that of any other human being with regard to the decisive events in the timetable of life. We share in the synagogue what we experience in common from birth to death. These events which we celebrate with the traditions of Judaism are the really decisive events. We can succeed in the world of affairs yet, humanly speaking, be wretched failures in the business of life if we fail to put a goodly measure of energy and attention on the decisive events. The traditions and ritual of the synagogue call upon us for this kind of concentration. That is why the sacrifice of pride in attainments which are not central to the business of life is so essential. I do not wish to disparage worldly attainment or professional competence; I want to suggest the wisdom of Judaism in insisting upon its essential emptiness when the business of life is ignored. Each of us before God as the focus of ultimate concern must regard the real challenges of his personal existence as essentially the same as those of any other human being. Whether we are intellectuals, merchants or laborers, we are born in the same way, need the same love, are capable of the same evil and will die the same death. Concentration on what is of genuine significance in the business of life is the contemporary form of the renunciation of idolatry.

The religious symbol and the God to whom the religious symbol points were never more meaningful than they are today. It is no accident that the twentieth century is characterized by theological excitement and renewal. Our myths and rituals have been stripped of their historic covering. No man can seriously pretend that the literal meanings given to our traditions before our time retain much authority today. Happily, in losing some of the old meanings we have also lost some of the old fears.

God stands before us no longer as the final censor but as the final reality before which and in terms of which all partial realities are to be measured.

The last paradox is that in the time of the death of God we have begun a voyage of discovery wherein we may, hopefully, find the true God.

This paper is the result of two encounters. In November 1965 I was invited to respond to Thomas Altizer at the Conference on America and the Future of Theology held at Emory University. In May 1966, William Hamilton and I were jointly invited to give the Gilkey Lecture at the University of Chicago. We were asked to discuss death of God theology from Jewish and Christian perspectives. These encounters enabled me to formulate explicitly my response to Christian radical theology. That response is embodied in this paper.

14 / Death of God Theology and Judaism

THE NUMBER of men in America who self-consciously regard themselves as theologians is relatively small. During the past decade a few of us have been writing and working on radical themes which have caused us much discomfort. It is not easy to part company with what one has been taught.

Paul Tillich is, as Thomas Altizer has suggested, the father of contemporary radical theology. Every one of today's radical theologians was either Tillich's student or was profoundly influenced by his writing. In the context of much of today's theological writing, Tillich seems almost conservative. Nevertheless, all radical theologians have elaborated on themes which are at least implicit in Tillich. After all, it was Tillich who asserted in *The Courage To Be* that the God whom Nietzsche said was dead was transcended in a "God above the God of theism."

Until recently each of us thought we were working alone on themes which departed radically from the normative theological traditions of our communities. All of us have experienced the condescending disapproval of our official denominational establishments. More often than he may want to admit, the radical theologian has endured frequent crises of self-doubt. There were times when he hoped for a way back to acceptance by his denominational establishment. It was not easy to pursue this work.

A nursery rhyme helped me to continue my writing and research. Whenever I yearned to say the "right thing," I recited:

" 'Humpty-dumpty sat on the wall
Humpty-dumpty had a big fall
All the king's horses and all the king's men
Couldn't put Humpty together again.' "

A breach had been made between the mood and the theological perspectives of our times and those of our predecessors. There was simply no way in which to escape the fact that the second half of the twentieth century was radically different. Our theology would have to be an expression of the way we, rather than those who preceded us, felt about ultimate questions. It was impossible to renounce this work.

About three years ago I first became aware of the fact that other theologians were concerned with the radical profanity and secularity of our times. I received a postcard from Rabbi Abraham Karp of Rochester, New York, telling me of a professor of theology at Colgate-Rochester Divinity School, William Hamilton, who had been reading my theological articles and felt there were some similarities in our insights. I subsequently learned of the work of Professor Thomas J. J. Altizer of Emory University. I began to read whatever I could find by these men.

I experienced something of a crisis upon reading William Hamilton's article "The Death of God Theologies Today" in *The Christian Scholar* for the spring of 1965. I learned to my surprise that Hamilton regarded my writing as an example of death of God theology. My first reaction was one of acute embarrassment. In Judaism God simply doesn't die. The symbolism upon which the metaphor of the death of God rests is of obvious Christian origin. In Christianity Christ, the incarnate Saviour, is both God and man in perfect union. Although the divinity of the Christ is not supposed to have expired on the cross, the age-old anti-Jewish deicide accusation bears witness to the fact that the crucifixion was often regarded as the occasion of the death of God. There are also references in Luther and Hegel to the death of God. Of course, it has always been possible for Christians, in asserting the death of God, to look for a new epiphany of the divine after His death. Though we live in the time of the death of God, even the Christian death of God theologians cannot rule out the possibility of a reappearance of the resurrected God.

For Jews, because of our alienation from the symbolism of the cross, it is impossible to use the words "God is dead." Nevertheless, we must use these words of alien origin and connotation. We share the same cultural universe as the contemporary Christian thinker; we experience the radical secularity of our times as do they. We have been deeply influenced by Freud, Sartre, Hegel, Dostoevski, Melville, and Kierkegaard. Above all, we have been moved by Nietzsche.

If I were asked to cite the text *par excellence* from which I derive the verbal origins of the radical mood, I would follow William Hamilton and unhesitantly point to the chapter in Nietzsche's *Gay Science* entitled "The Madman."[1] In it the Madman proclaims his search for God, asserts that we have murdered Him, and becomes affrighted at the terrible event which has already happened but which is yet too distant to comprehend. The Madman rhetorically asks the question, crucial to Thomas Altizer's apocalyptic theology: "Shall we not ourselves have to become gods merely to be worthy of it?" The Madman then enters a church, which he has declared to be a sepulcher of God, and there sings his *Requiem aeternam deo*. After Nietzsche, it is impossible to avoid his language to express the total absence of God from our experience. Martin Buber felt deeply the profanity of our times. He attempted to soften its harshness by speaking of an "eclipse of God." Buber's formulation would, however, seem to be a compromise. No words are entirely adequate to characterize a historical epoch. Nevertheless, I believe the most adequate theological description of our times is to be found in the assertion that *we live in the time of the death of God*. The vitality of death of God theology is rooted in the fact that it has faced more openly than any other contemporary theological movement the truth of the divine-human encounter in our times. The truth is that it is totally nonexistent. Those theologies which attempt to find the reality of God's presence in the contemporary world manifest a deep insensitivity to the art, literature, and technology of our times. Whatever may be its shortcomings, death of God theology is very much aware of the cultural universe of which it is a very sig-

[1] Cf. William Hamilton, "The Death of God Theologies," *The Christian Scholar* (Spring 1965).

nificant expression. Radical theology is no fad. It will not be replaced by some other theological novelty in the foreseeable future. Too many tendencies in classical theology, philosophy, and literature have intersected in this movement for it to disappear as rapidly as it has gained attention.

Nevertheless, I believe that radical theology errs in its assertion that God is dead. Such an assertion exceeds human knowledge. The statement "God is dead" is only significant in what it reveals about its maker. It imparts information concerning what he believes about God. It reveals nothing about God. I should like to suggest that, since this information has strictly phenomenological import, *we ought to formulate it from the viewpoint of the observer*. It is more precise to assert that *we live in the time of the death of God* than to declare "God is dead." The death of God is a cultural fact. We shall never know whether it is more than that. I am implying that the ultimate relevance of theology is anthropological. Though theology purports to make statements about God, its significance rests on what it reveals about the theologian and his culture. All theologies are inherently subjective. They are statements about the way in which the theologian experiences his world.

The theologian is really closer to the poet or the creative artist than to the physical scientist. The value of artistic creation lies in the fact that a man with a highly sensitive subjectivity is able to communicate something of his own experience which other men recognize as clarifying and enriching their own insights. The theologian, no matter how ecclesiastically oriented he may seem to be, is in reality communicating an inner world he suspects others may share.

The term "God" is very much like the unstructured inkblot used in the Rorschach test. Its very lack of concrete content invites men to express their fears, aspirations, and yearnings concerning their origin, their destiny, and their end. From a technical point of view, theological statements would seem to be most precise when they are enunciated in a phenomenological context. There are indications that this methodological limitation on theological assertion is accepted by Professors Altizer and Hamilton. Nevertheless, there seems to be some lack of clarity concerning whether they speak of what they have experienced or whether they believe God has literally and in fact perished.

Although my first reaction to Professor Hamilton's identification of my writing as death of God theology was one of embarrassment, I am grateful to him for causing me to reconsider my theological moorings. I have concluded that, alien and non-Jewish as the terminology may be, my own theological writing is closer to Christian death of God theology than to any other movement in Christian theology. We are at least agreed upon our analysis of the radical secularity of contemporary culture as a starting point for theological speculation. We concur that ours is the time of the death of God. We are, each in our own way, convinced that both the methods and the conclusions of contemporary theology will reflect the radical hiatus between our world and the traditional communities out of whch we have come.

Nevertheless, there are very great differences between Jewish and Christian radical theology. In the time of the death of God the Jewish radical theologian remains profoundly Jewish as the Christian radical remains profoundly Christian. The old Law-Gospel controversy, which has separated Jew and Christian from the inception of Christianity, continues to separate Jew and Christian in our time. Christian death of God theologians may have lost God, but, as Professor Hamilton has suggested, they have by no means lost the Messiah. Radical Christian theology is profoundly Christocentric; for all Jews Jesus is simply another Jew of no abiding religious significance. Nothing in contemporary radical Jewish theology would elevate Jesus to a higher status than that he has had for Jews for two millennia.

I became aware of the differences between contemporary Jewish and Christian radical theology as a result of first reading, then meeting, Professor Thomas J. J. Altizer of Emory University. I was invited to respond to his paper "Theology and the Contemporary Sensibility" at the Conference on America and the Future of Theology at Emory in November 1965. I was fascinated by Altizer's writings, as I had been with Hamilton's. At a certain level I had the feeling that we were concerned with the same issues and that there were similarities in our theological methods. In spite of profound differences with him, I have enormous respect for him as a co-worker in a common task of contemporary theological exploration. Altizer and Hamilton are investigating the meaning of the time of the death of God for Christianity. I believe I am attempting to understand its meaning for Judaism. Although Professor Altizer speaks of the death of God, he reveals the profound connection between his theology and the classical heritage of Christian theology and mysticism. Although God has died for him, the Christ has become, if anything, more meaningful. His thought is deeply rooted in both dialectic mysticism and its philosophical product, Hegelian philosophy. Professor Altizer views creation as the result of God's kenotic emptying Himself out of His own substance. The view is not unlike the view of Lurianic Kabbalism which I find theologically attractive. The Lurianic view of creation suggests that God, who was originally all-in-all, created the world by an act of self-division and self-diminution. Through this act, the world came into being out of the divine *Urgrund*. Since the divine *Urgrund* lacked all inner division or predication, it was *no-thing*. Creation in the Lurianic scheme was a *creatio ex nihilo*, a creation by God out of His own no-thing-ness. In both the Kabbalistic view and Professor Altizer's theology, creation is an act of self-diminution of the divine ground.

The thrust of Altizer's view is ultimately dependent upon his *either God or man but not both* approach. Altizer is convinced that the slightest trace of the divine is sufficient to impede and thwart the full development of mankind's potentialities. During my recent visit to Poland, a Catholic theologian in Warsaw expressed a scholastic formula somewhat similar in mood to Altizer's basic approach: *"Si Deus est, Petrus non est; si Petrus est, Deus non est."* Altizer suggests that God's greatest love for mankind is reflected in an act of self-riddance. He believes that in the crucifixion God empties Himself out of His own being. It is humanity rather than divinity which is resurrected on Easter Sunday. The real meaning of the cross is the total liberation of mankind as a concomitant of the death of God. It is for this reason that Altizer joyously proclaims the Gospel—the good tidings— of Christian atheism. In the final analysis, the Christian message is mankind's liberation from God.

The deeply Christian inspiration of this radical speculation is obvious. This is a Christian theology, albeit one of both
high daring and originality. The Christian character of Altizer's
thought is also evident in his identification of the God of the Old
Testament as the tyrannical law-giver who enslaves mankind with
his rigid, sin-inducing Law. This interpretation of the Law has a
very respectable theological lineage in Christianity. However, no
Jew, having experienced the Law, could accept it. In Pauline theology, the sacrificial death of the Christ is an atonement capable
of liberating mankind from its bondage to sin and the Law. The
atonement of the Christ, the Second Adam, suffices for all. In
Altizer's thought, it is the Father, source and author of the Law,
who sacrifices Himself through the Son, thereby dissolving the
Law and liberating mankind from sin and repression alike. Altizer sees the time of the death of God in apocalyptic terms. The
death of God is the true meaning of the Christ's sacrifice. The
promise of the Christ is the promise of radical freedom.

There are dialectic affinities between Altizer's theology
and the psycho-sexual hopefulness which pervades Herbert
Marcuse's conclusions in *Eros and Civilization* and Norman O.
Brown's in *Life Against Death*. All three envisage the dialectic
promise of our time as an end to repression and the potentiality
of absolute liberty among men. There are strong overtones of
Nietzsche in his most thoroughly Dionysian mood in Altizer.
Altizer would certainly assent to Nietzsche's Madman's request
that we become gods in place of the dead God. The freedom
envisaged by Altizer is certainly God-like. Altizer would also
agree with Ivan Karamazov's observation: "If there is no God,
all things are permissible." Unless I misread him, Altizer con-
curs that, in the time of the death of God, all things are permissible.

There is, however, an enormous difference between Ivan
Karamazov and Altizer. Dostoevski examined with prophetic
insight the meaning of the death of God almost a century ago.
What he saw gave him no comfort. Smerdyakov, Ivan's bastard
half-brother and *Doppelgänger,* carries Ivan's logic to its extreme: if all things are permissible, parricide is permissible. Ivan
is the thinker; ideas provide the motivation for men of action.

Thinkers are not always happy when the men of action such as Smerdyakov translate apparently impotent ideas into real deeds. The freedom Ivan intuits as the fruit of the death of God ultimately drives him insane. Unlike Orestes in Sartre's *The Flies*, Ivan is not capable of living in the wasteland. I fear Professor Altizer rejoices too soon. The time of the death of God must ultimately become a time of mourning, as it was for the Karamazovs. We shall learn bitterly to regret our loss of innocence.

Altizer's sensitivity to his cultural milieu is especially evident in his self-conscious avowal that America has a theological mission. He is drawn to William Blake's mystical vision of America as the place where the apocalyptic freedom of the Christian will finally be realized. For both Altizer and Blake, America's mission is to reject the past and create a world in which the totally free, autonomous man may flourish for the first time. According to Altizer, America is the land of the future in which the promise of the Gospel will ultimately be achieved. There are obvious similarities of perspective between Altizer's interpretation of America and Harvey Cox's assertion that technopolis is the self-realizing kingdom of God. Cox contrasts "legalistic" tribal and village forms of social organization with the "gospel-like" freedom of the anonymous, highly mobile inhabitants of the secular city; Altizer sees America, cut off from the past and tradition, looking forward only to the future, as a realization of the true meaning of the Gospel. There is a pervasive note of optimism in the work of Altizer, Hamilton, and Cox which reflects the characteristics of American popular culture. All three thinkers exhibit a typically American rejection of history and tradition. Altizer and Cox are especially future-oriented. All three reject tragedy and the tragic sense. The death of God means the end to tragedy. Hamilton has echoed this shared mood in his assertion that, as Americans, we are future-oriented. Deeply sensitive to the various aspects of popular culture, he wisely intuited an element of seriousness in the Beatles' motion picture *A Hard Day's Night*. The final scene of the film in which the Beatles sing, dance, and then depart by rising helicopter from the overly complex world of the television studio is interpreted by Hamilton as a symbol of a new mood of optimism which floats above the despair and alienation of our times. "The death of tragedy," Professor Hamilton claims, "is due to the death of the Christian God."[2]

Altizer's optimism is also rooted in his very exciting attempt to interpret the meaning of "sacred" in Christian and non-Christian religions. Relying heavily on the insights of his teacher, Mircea Eliade, Altizer points out that the oriental mystic follows a path of *anamnesis*—that is, of remembrance and recollection. His goal is the restoration of a lost, paradisaical Beginning. His effort is to return ultimately to the primordial Totality out of which he has come.[3] In contrast to the non-Christian's attempt to make of history a circle restoring the primordial harmony of all things in the nothingness of the *Urgrund,* Altizer sees Christianity as making of the historical process an ascending spiral. For the Christian the posture of faith cannot be the attempt to retrieve an irretrievable past; the Christian must turn his back upon the past, thereby allowing the future dawning of the Kingdom to break in upon the present and penetrate its structures. Altizer is committed to a forward-moving dynamism. He will not commit the error of Lot's wife. The Word came into the world to negate the past; it has become fully flesh; it remains in the world only as long as it abjures nostalgia and continues to negate the past in its movement toward the realization of the Kingdom. Although Altizer believes that the self-negating, self-transcending movement of the Word-become-flesh is developed fully only in Christianity, he does see anticipations of this forward movement in the prophets of ancient Israel and their negation of Israelite priestly religion.

Altizer is radically anti-priestly. He has no doctrine of the church. He is not especially concerned with its ritual and liturgy. He shares this anti-cultic bias with Harvey Cox. The

[2] William Hamilton, "The New Optimism—from Prufrock to Ringo," in William Hamilton and Thomas J. J. Altizer, *Radical Theology and the Death of God* (New York: Bobbs-Merrill, 1966) pp. 164-65.

[3] Cf. Thomas J. J. Altizer, *The Gospel of Christian Atheism* (Philadelphia: The Westminster Press, 1966), pp. 33 ff.; and his "Word and History," in Hamilton and Altizer, *op. cit.,* pp. 121 ff.

tension between the Word and fixed ritual, so necessary for the celebration of the crises of life, has always been more of a problem for Protestantism than for Judaism or Roman Catholicism. Altizer interprets Jewish and Christian priestly religious forms as attempts at *recollection* or a *concrete renewal* of a sacred time in the past.

I would agree with this analysis, though I would prefer to formulate it in psychoanalytic terminology. The rituals of priestly religion are in part akin to *regressions in the service of the ego*. Their purpose is in part to bring us into contact with those sources of *basic trust*, rooted in our earliest childhood, which are indispensable to our meeting the profane, secular world with confidence. That is why the language of parent and child is so necessary in religious rituals. They are significant precisely because they are indispensable attempts at recollection.

Altizer will have none of this *recherche du temps perdu*. For dialectic, Christian, and American reasons he will face only toward the future. Such a dynamic posture means a perpetual negation of what lies at hand. Ultimately the Kingdom will be won by the negation of every link to primordial Beginnings, including God. The Christian, according to Altizer, must not regret the loss of God in our time. He must reject this perilous nostalgia and joyously will His death.

As I read Altizer, I am aware of how radically different our theologies are. I am both amazed and fascinated that I can both comprehend and communicate with him. I suspect it is because we both understand that only a limited number of theological options are available when one deals with the problems of eschatology. I cannot share his rejection of the past, either on existential or on psychoanalytic grounds. How could a Jew ignore history? The basic terms of our encounters with our Christian neighbors were spelled out almost two thousand years ago. The very spectacle of the most august assemblage of Christian leaders of our times, Vatican II, discussing the responsibility of the current generation of Jews for a crime that happened almost two thousand years ago is an indication of how deeply Jews are affected by history. How could Jews follow Professor Altizer's lead and look only to the future? To do so would be to denude our attempts to deal with any degree of competence with our present. All Jews (and Christians, though it is less obvious with them) are at least two thousand years old the day they are born.

Cox, Altizer, and Hamilton all assert that it is American to negate the past and look primarily toward the future. Is there not something adolescent about this denial of roots, something adolescent not only in a future-oriented theology but also in our national popular culture? Europeans probably distrust us Americans more for our failure to understand the abiding impact of history than for any other aspect of our culture. Altizer believes that it is the destiny of America to lead the world away from its past. I suspect that America's real destiny is to become Europeanized as it comes to experience the defeats and the limitations of power which sooner or later history visits upon all nations without exception. We already see anticipatory signs in the Far East. Until the Korean War, we never lost a foreign war. The Korean War ended in a stalemate; no man can predict how the Vietnamese war will terminate. Nor can any man rest certain that America is destined to be victorious in the centuries that lie ahead against every potential adversary or combination of adversaries. Invincibility is simply not an attribute of men or nations.

The optimism of Altizer, Hamilton, and Cox is rooted in the American success story. The real test of America will come only when the going gets rough, when we experience, as has every other nation in history, the bitterness of defeat. It will come; it may not come in our lifetime, but it will assuredly come. Will we have the tragic dignity, the stoicism, and the inner courage to meet the challenge of national disaster?

The American South has produced more than its share of first-rate literature. Perhaps the reason is to be found in the fact that the South is the only part of America which has had defeat engraved on its psyche. William Hamilton denies that the tragic sense of life is possible in our time. If Hamilton is correct, it is not because the death of God means the death of tragedy, as he asserts. It is because we no longer regard human loss as significant. As Aristotle understood, the tragic vision is possible only when something perishes which is of worth and dignity. Everything human must perish. Every life lost is in some sense tragic, provided we regard every life as unique and irreplaceable. If we have lost the tragic sense, it is because an era of mass death has sterilized the impact of death and translated it into a non-human statistic devoid of emotional impact. It is only when we regard human beings as replaceable ciphers whose role is to keep the machinery of technopolis functioning that the tragic sense is lost. The loss of the tragic dimension does not lead to a new optimism but to the depersonalization and dehumanization of life and death alike.

Is it true that if God is dead all things are permissible? I suspect Altizer, following Ivan Karamazov, has taken the myth of God as law-giver much too literally. Although Altizer is acutely aware of such prophets of the death of God in the nineteenth and twentieth centuries as Nietzsche, Dostoevski, Melville, and, in his own way, Kierkegaard, there is one prophet whom he all but ignores, Sigmund Freud. This is especially significant because Freud's myth of the origin of religion begins with a parricide which is almost immediately interpreted as if it had been a deicide. In both *Totem and Taboo* and *Moses and Monotheism* Freud sees God as the first object of human criminality. He postulates that originally men dwelt in primal hordes, dominated by a tyrannical patriarch who had exclusive sexual access to the females of his horde. In order to maintain that prerogative, he drove his sons outside of the group, thus preventing them from having access to his females. Ultimately there came a time when, driven by sexual need, the sons committed an act of cannibalistic parricide to displace the father and possess his women.

According to Freud, their victory over the father was to prove empty and ironic. Having murdered the father, the sons quickly realized that some instrumentality had to be devised whereby sexual need would not disrupt social structure. Freud hypothesizes that the law of exogamy was instituted in order to prevent the group from descending to the level of *bellum omnes contra omnes*. Freud's myth is important because he understood that *reality rather than the father is the author of repression*. The sons impose upon themselves the very restrictions the father had imposed upon them. For our purposes, Freud's etiological myth is not significant as a mode of explaining religious origins; it is important insofar as it lends insight into the indispensability of law and discipline for the social process.

I do not understand what Altizer means by freedom in the time of the death of God. Does he mean sexual freedom? Unless he believes that there will be no giving and taking in marriage, it is unlikely that even our sexually permissive society will tolerate an absolute absence of law in sexual matters. In reality, human freedom is limited the moment the nursing infant is compelled to refrain from utilizing its milk teeth to bite the breast of its mother. The radical limitation inflicted by toilet training leaves its repressive mark upon the individual for the rest of his life. Furthermore, even if the individual had free access to the women of his choice as an adult, they would remain substitute sources of gratification, hardly capable of compensating for the loss of the first and most precious object of love, the mother, unless the individual were to come to terms with his archaic yearnings.

As Freud understood in *Civilization and Its Discontents,* civilization is bought only at the price of an enormous, perhaps an insupportable, degree of repression. Contemporary apocalyptic visions of an end to repression, such as those of Marcuse, Norman Brown, and Altizer, provide no means of altering in adult life those archaic instrumentalities of repression which become operative long before the child is aware of them. Psychoanalysis is non-repressive only insofar as it liberates the individual from neurotic elements of repression which are realistically irrelevant to his adult activities. There is, however, a renunciatory side to psychoanalysis; it arises less from ideology than from a need for realism in meeting the demands of the social process. Psychoanalysis leads to the acceptance of the realistic limitation of infantile yearnings as much as to the rejection of neurotic repression. Altizer must do more than interpret freedom as a dialectic entailment consequent upon the death of the Law-giver. He must spell out what he means by freedom as well as how it becomes operative. At least Cox sees freedom as a potential consequence of the anonymity and mobility of the urban metropolis. However, even Cox refers primarily to adult, conscious freedom of choice. He says little concerning the framework of repression which is built into the human being almost from the moment of birth and which is indispensable in view of the long period of dependence within the bosom of the family required for human nurture and growth. It is simply not true that if God is dead all things are permissible. The structure of human reality is itself inherently limiting and frustrating. If there is to be any kind of society, it will have to be a somewhat renunciatory society. One cannot ignore Freud in searching out the meaning of the death of God.

Can one speak of freedom and the death of God, yet ignore Sartre and Camus? The whole thrust of Sartre's ethical and psychological concern rests upon his exploration of the meaning of freedom after the death of God. Sartre agrees that if God is dead all is permissible, but he does not rejoice in the freedom consequent upon the death of God. He asserts, through one of the characters in his novels, that we are *condemned* to be free. He sees anxiety as a direct concomitant of our freedom. If there is no God, we and we alone are responsible for our actions. Like Dostoevski's Grand Inquisitor, Sartre is deeply skeptical about mankind's ability to accept that responsibility. If there is a characteristic human flaw according to Sartre, it is *mauvaise foi,* bad faith, our incapacity to accept responsibility for the deeds we freely perform. For Sartre, the time of death of God is one of overwhelming irony.

Perhaps no contemporary author has explored the meaning of the freedom of the flesh more insightfully or more beautifully than Albert Camus in his small but overwhelmingly important essay, "Summer in Algiers." Camus's handsome men and women who delight in the sea, the sun, and the flesh on the beaches of Algiers are "gods of this earth." For them as well as for Camus there is neither after life nor personal God; we die and our only kingdom "is of this earth." Camus celebrates his compatriots, a race of men "without a past, without tradition," over whom "no delusive divinity traces the signs of hope or redemption." For the first time in two thousand years the nude body has appeared upon the shores of the Mediterranean. These men and women know only the pleasures of the flesh; there is nothing banished by this pagan race.[4]

These "gods of this earth" are joyous—when they are twenty—but, Camus writes in "Summer in Algiers":

> I know of no more hideous spot than the cemetery on Boulevard Bru, opposite one of the most beautiful landscapes in the world. . . . This race, wholly cast into its present, lives without myths, without solace. It has put all of its possessions on this earth and therefore remains without defense against death.

The world of the death of God is a world devoid of hope and illusion. People grow old, decline, and die. It is relatively simple to celebrate apocalyptic liberation in one's youth, but what of the later years? The death of God does not cancel death. It heightens our sad knowledge that no power, human or divine, can ultimately withstand the dissolving onslaughts of omnipotent Nothingness, the true Lord of all creation. If one penetrates beneath the surface of the joys of the flesh, one finds sadness even in our most precious moments of liberation and gratification. Love and death have been inseparable themes throughout the history of literature. The celebration of the joys of the body carries with it the certain knowledge that this vessel of delight must disappear as if it had never been.

Perhaps the most beautiful place I ever visited was the island of Ibiza in the Balearic Islands. It was a favorite of Camus. Everywhere one turns, one is struck by the richness and beauty of the sea, the sun, the beaches, and human youthfulness. If human beings have found a place where the joys of the flesh can be celebrated most fully, it is beautiful Ibiza. Yet, underneath Ibiza's abiding beauty, perhaps one might better say the other side of her beauty, one meets a tragic sadness. On the hill overlooking the harbor, there is an ancient cathedral sacred to the Virgin. In the museum next door, there is a statue of the Carthaginian goddess Taanith, who was the Holy Mother of this

---

[4] Cf. Germain Brée, *Camus* (New York: Harbinger Books, 1964), pp. 80 ff.

island long before the advent of Christianity. Religions have come and gone, but the adoration of the Mother has never ceased in this place—and with good reason, for She who gives birth announces the hour of death in that very moment. The wise pagans of the ancient Mediterranean unconsciously bequeathed their wisdom to their contemporary descendants. Neither Judaism nor Christianity could entirely suppress the awesome knowledge that Earth is a Mother, a cannibal Mother who gives forth her own children only that she may consume the fruit of her own womb. Almighty Necessity has never ceased Her omnipotent reign. We are born but to perish. We are more than the fools of the gods; we are their food. I do not understand Altizer's optimism. The Kingdom lies ahead of us, but it is not the new reality as he supposes. It is the Nothingness out of which we have come and to which we are inescapably destined to return.

As Christians, Altizer, Hamilton, and Cox cannot reject hope. I would agree that individuals have much reason to hope when they contemplate the possibility of fulfillment in the here and now; there are, however, absolutely no grounds for eschatological hope. Let me again quote Camus's essay. Referring to his Algerian men and women he writes:

> Gods of summer they were at twenty by their enthusiasm for life, and they still are, deprived of all hope. I have seen two of them die. They were full of horror, but silent. It is better thus. *From Pandora's box, where all the ills of humanity swarmed, the Greeks drew out hope after all the others as the most dreadful of all. I know of no more stirring symbol; for contrary to the general belief, hope equals resignation. And to live is not to resign oneself.*[5]   (Italics mine.)

In the time of the death of God, some form of pagan sanity may better accord with the deepest instincts of mankind than does an atheistic Christian apocalypticism. I believe that paganism has in reality triumphed in the hearts of men. Paganism is not a vulgar appeal to what is base in men; it is a wise intuition of man's place in the order of things. In spite of Altizer's hostility

[5] Albert Camus, "Summer in Algiers," in *The Myth of Sisyphus*, tr. Justin O'Brien (New York: Vintage Books, 1961), p. 113.

to priestly religion, priestly religion has won the day in both Judaism and Christianity simply by appropriating their inherited rituals and symbols as instrumentalities whereby the decisive crises of life may be celebrated and shared. What remains of Judaism and Christianity in contemporary America is largely pagan. This phenomenon is by no means an unmitigated disaster. People's instincts are often better than their ideologies. Life has its way of imposing religious demands upon us. Birth, adolescence, marriage, and death demand religious celebration. At such times we are far less interested in prophetic proclamation than in cultic acts. The cultic approach has always had obvious shortcomings; let us not exaggerate them. At least pagan cultic religion is deeply rooted in the realities of human biology and psychology.

Altizer's proclamation of apocalyptic freedom is dependent upon Christianity's conviction that the Gospel liberates man from the Law. As I confront Altizer, and incidentally Harvey Cox, I get the feeling that the ancient debate between the Pharisees and the Christians has not ceased. At the time of the birth of Christianity, Christians asserted that something decisively new had occurred which had the power to transform the human condition. The Pharisees, my spiritual predecessors, hoped for such a transformation as earnestly as did the Christians. They looked both within and around themselves. They sadly concluded that no transformation had occurred. There was no alternative but to remain faithful to the Law. It was and remains a difficult instrument, but it seemed to be the only means by which their society could avoid disintegration and moral chaos. Two thousand years and the time of the death of God have done little to alter that judgment in Jewish eyes. If we must live without God, religious law is more necessary for us than ever. Our temptation to anarchic omnipotence and the total indifference of the cosmos to our deeds call forth the need for a set of guidelines to enable us to apprehend the limits of appropriate behavior. Without God, we need law, tradition, and structure far more than ever before. I grant that these guidelines will not easily be found because of the breach between our culture and its antecedents. We prefer to let people discover their limits through trial and error.

I see no way of altering this preference. I question whether we can in the long run afford to pay the cumulative cost of the inevitable errors which people must make in discovering their limits. In the long run, the trial-and-error method is a costly detour to the acquisition of behavioral norms not unlike those perennially suggested within the religious traditions of mankind.

The problem of the Messiah has separated Judaism and Christianity from the very inception of the Church. Judaism and Christianity remain decisively separated on this issue in the time of the death of God. For Altizer, ours is the Messianic age. Mankind has been liberated from sin and Law through the death of God in the Christ. I would like to suggest a contemporary Jewish doctrine of the Messiah which seems far more descriptive of the actual condition of man than Altizer's apocalyptic enthusiasm. The doctrine derives from an insight on the part of the contemporary Jewish novelist Isaac Bashevis Singer. It is a horrible doctrine. Nevertheless, I think it is the only Messianic doctrine which makes much sense. At the end of his epic novel *The Family Muskat,* Singer portrays the family meeting for the last time as the Germans are at the gates of Warsaw in September 1939. One member of the family makes the assertion that he believes the Messiah will come speedily. The others are astonished at this pronouncement. Hertz Yanovar explains: "Death is the Messiah." The insight is irrefutable. The Messiah traditionally promises an end to the inescapable infirmities and limitations of the human condition. But there is only one way out of the ironies and the dilemmas of existence; that exit is death. The oriental religions understood this in their quest for Nirvana. I have no desire to hasten the end. I would rather pay the price for the continuation of my existence, but I know that payment involves an acceptance of finitude, imperfection, and all of the problematics of the human condition. I cannot accept Altizer's apocalypse because I know that the Messiah's Kingdom is truly not of this world. This world will forever remain a place of pain, suffering, alienation, and ultimate defeat. I recognize that there is much in this world which occasions rejoicing, but true rejoicing is possible only if one remains mindful of the price we must ultimately pay for having entered this world of finitude, temporality, and morality. This is the only world we shall ever know. Our pleasures must be precious in our sight, for we purchase them with our lives. The Messiah will come. He tarrieth not. We need not welcome Him. The world is not large enough for both mankind and its Redeemer.

Altizer does welcome the coming of the Kingdom. He bids the Christian, especially the American Christian, to take upon himself the joyous task of willing the death of God. God must be overcome that the Kingdom may break in upon us. There is an enormously promethean element in this. It draws Altizer to the figure of Captain Ahab in Melville's *Moby Dick*. Ahab hates God and sees the great white whale, "be the white whale agent or be the white whale principal," as the ultimate symbol of that malignant creator-divinity whom he must destroy in order to liberate himself as a man. Altizer and Ahab concur in their judgment: either God or man but not both. In his paper "Theology and the Contemporary Sensibility," Altizer bids us join Ahab in his promethean attempt to bring about the death of God. Ahab is for Altizer the prototype of the new American become "madness maddened" with whom we must move through "this rebirth of the primordial chaos to the dawn of a new and glorious Jerusalem."

I earnestly hope that Ahab is not the prototype of the new American. As Maurice Friedman has said, he is the best example in literature of Kierkegaard's "demonic shut-inness."[6] He forsakes human sanity in a mad quest whose real goal is totally beyond his conscious knowledge. When, toward the end of the book, Starbuck attempts to bring him back to sanity, Ahab tells his mate that he has been on the sea for forty years and that he married only after he was fifty. The woman was more widow than wife. Hardly had he dented the marital pillow before he returned to sea. Undeterred by wife or the normal comforts other men cherish, he would not now be deterred from his quest of the great white whale.

Melville was a master of symbolism. He was by no means unfamiliar with Biblical imagery. His use of forty years as the

[6] Maurice Friedman, *Problematic Rebel—An Image of Modern Man* (New York: Random House, 1963), p. 206.

duration of Ahab's sojourn upon the sea was not accidental. The forty years upon the sea were Ahab's sojourn in the wilderness. *The great whale is the Captain's promised land.* As much as he hates the whale, he yearns unknowingly to be consumed by it. It is not the whale or even God which enrages Ahab. Ahab is maddened by a reality which has frustrated and limited him from the moment he left the womb. Altizer has said that all non-Christian religions seek a way back to primordial beginnings. Ahab assuredly seeks a way back to his blissful origins in the womb. The whale is less a symbol of the malignant father-god than of the all-consuming cannibal mother-goddess. The Captain yearns to return to his source, thereby ending the problematics and the agonies of the human condition. There is more to that slight dent upon the marital bed than meets the eye. Ahab's inability to enter into a real I–Thou relationship, accepting thereby the frustrations and the promise of adult encounter, does not rest upon his insane passion for the whale. His search for the whale is his ultimate confession of his failure to leave the rages of infancy, accept the limitations, but also the opportunities, of adult responsibility, and prove himself a man. Freud has defined the mature individual as the one who has the capacity to *love* and to *work.* Ahab has neither capacity. He remains a petulant infant, totally unable to accept reality, made all the more terrifying by the power he wields over other men.

Instead of regarding Ahab as an anticipation of the new American, I believe he is more accurately seen as the prototype of Adolf Hitler. The same petulant rage at a limiting reality combined with overwhelming power enabled Hitler to carry his ship of state to almost total ruin. When Hitler no longer was capable of bending reality to his anarchic will, he did what he had wanted to do from the very beginning: he put an end through suicide to the frustrations of finitude which had enraged him even in those moments when he had more power than any human being before or since. What troubles Ahab is precisely the fact that we live in a malignant universe, in which human existence is filled with anxiety and despair. There is only one escape. It is certainly not the New Jerusalem. *Moby Dick* does not end with the New Jerusalem; it ends when Ahab returns to the nothingness out of which he has come. What he hates and fears, he also yearns for most deeply.

If, as Altizer suggests, Ahab is the prototypical new American, we shall lack the tolerance for the ambiguity, the irony, the hopelessness, and the inevitable meaninglessness of the time of the death of God. Lacking this tolerance, we will choose self-destruction rather than learn to accept an incomplete and a not altogether satisfying life. Unlike Dr. Altizer, I cannot rejoice in the death of God. If I am a death of God theologian, it is with a cry of agony.

What about religion in the time of the death of God? It is the way in which we share and celebrate, both consciously and unconsciously, through the inherited myths, rituals, and traditions of our communities, the dilemmas and the crises of life and death, good and evil. Religion is the way in which we share our predicament; it is never the way in which we overcome our condition.

I find myself both united with and separated from the Christian believer and his Saviour. I look behind the Saviour and see in this figure the Christian's yearning to overcome guilt and the broken condition of human finitude. I understand that yearning, though I do not believe that the Christ or any power can in fact and in truth redeem men. When I participate in my own Jewish worship, I am sadly aware of the pathetic yearnings of my fellow Jews to make a meaningless life meaningful. This in large measure is the signficance of the religious community, both Jewish and Christian, to me—the absurd, pathetic attempt, for which there can be no substitute, to make a meaningless life meaningful. The attempt is futile but psychologically indispensable.

In conclusion I should like to relate a conversation I had with a Thomistic theologian at the Catholic University of Lublin, Poland, in October 1965. I had just completed a lecture on American theology which reflected many of the same perspectives I have described in this essay. Three days before, I had visited Auschwitz. The Polish theologian asked me, "Do you love God?"

I replied, "I should. We are enjoined to love God 'with

all thy heart, with all thy soul and with all thy might.' But I cannot. I am aware of His holiness. I am struck with wonder and terror before His Nothingness, but I cannot love Him. I am affrighted before Him. Perhaps, in the end, all I have is silence."

He said, "You know, we Catholics believe that God Himself gives us the grace with which we are able to love Him."

"You're really saying the same thing I am," I replied. "It is only because you believe God Himself has enabled you to love Him that you speak as you do. If you didn't believe you have that grace, you couldn't love Him either. On your own, you could not love Him any more than I do."

Here again is the difference between Christian and Jew. The Gospel ends beyond tragedy, on a note of hope. Resurrection is the final word. I wish it were so. But I believe my Pharisaic progenitors were essentially correct two thousand years ago when they sadly concluded that the promise of radical novelty in the human condition was a pathetic, though altogether understandable, illusion, that the old world goes on today as it did yesterday and as it will tomorrow. Against my deepest yearnings, I am compelled to end with their tragic acceptance rather than the eschatological hope that still pervades my Christian brother after the death of God.

It is difficult to serve as a college chaplain without being interested in the "new morality." I first became interested in the Playboy philosophy as a result of an invitation to participate in a two-day symposium on the subject held at Cornell University in April 1965. The highlight of the symposium was a conversation between Hugh Hefner and Harvey Cox.

In the spring of 1966, at Harvey Cox's suggestion, I was invited to participate in another symposium on the new morality scheduled for appearance in Playboy in the fall or winter of 1966. The interview was made in my office for Playboy by Edward Keating, publisher of Ramparts. I taped the interview and edited it. It does not appear in Playboy in the form in which it is presented in this work. Mr. Keating's questions are in italic.

15 / Dialogue on the New Theology and the New Morality

On the basis of your religious persuasion, do you feel that the sexual expression of love should be restricted to marriage?

I believe that the sexual expression of love is most appropriate in the marital situation. However, the conditions of life in our society are not such that sexual love can be expressed only in marriage.

You are a member of the Conservative branch of Judaism, is that correct?

I am a Conservative rabbi, but, as an academician, I am much more involved in the theoretical concerns of theology than the day-to-day work of a congregation. Furthermore, as a university chaplain, I serve all three branches of Judaism.

If I understand the Old Testament clearly, there were very strong strictures in it against adultery, fornication, and so on. Would you say that these strictures still hold?

I am completely in accord with the Biblical strictures against adultery. However, I suspect that the Biblical and rabbinic attitudes concerning premarital sex are somewhat more complex than they seem. According to one statement in the Talmud, when a free man enters a free woman, one neither betrothed nor married, their sexual intercourse is not what the Talmud calls *biath z'nuth,* an intercourse of prostitution. Apparently there was greater sexual expression of love in Talmudic times than we sometimes imagine. My own guess is that other ages dealt with problems somewhat similar to our own. They may have been a little freer than we think.

Do you believe in what we like to call the sanctity of marriage?

I absolutely do.

What are your feelings about divorce?

Divorce is necessary in order that the sanctity of marriage be upheld. When a marriage ceases to be viable, the partners must have a way to terminate it. There is a difference between Judaism and Catholicism on divorce. We believe that marriage is essentially a contractual rather than a sacramental relationship. It can therefore be ended when it ceases to be viable.

Jesus admonished, "Whosoever God has joined together, let no man put asunder." Would that tradition hold in Judaism?

Jesus said this explicitly in opposition to rabbinic teaching. There is a whole section in the Talmud known as *Gittin* dealing with the laws of divorce. Jews have always believed in both the sanctity of marriage and the necessity of a way out should the marriage prove untenable. Divorce is always a tragedy. We don't like to encourage it. We try to avoid it because of the terrible consequences for both the couple and the children. Unfortunately divorce is sometimes the only way out.

In your perspective, can there be premarital sex without a violation of your religion?

The real problem involved in premarital sex is whether those who engage in it are emotionally capable of handling it. As a college chaplain, I would say that most of the young people I know who are so involved are not really emotionally mature. I believe there is much sexual immaturity in our culture. Incidentally, I am convinced it is better to deal with the problem in psychological rather than purely religious terms.

But there is, as I understand it, a strong Judaic belief in the sanctity of the family?

There certainly is.

Premarital sex would violate this concept of the integrity of the family, then?

Not necessarily. The relationship between the young people would be one which, under normal circumstances, would concern only themselves. Basically a sexual relationship is simply a relationship, though one of far greater intimacy than most. Words are the instruments with which we choose to relate to most people. They are surrogates for objects or tactile contacts. In sex, words disappear; the relationship tends to become more concrete. In sex the real question is: Are we prepared for that level of intimacy in dealing with another person? I would guess that many of my students are not so prepared when they enter a sexual relationship.

By the same token, wouldn't you have to conclude that most adults are not prepared for this level of intimacy when they marry?

Quite honestly, I take a somewhat pessimistic view of the maturity of most people entering marriage in our culture. I don't know whether this is the place to say it, but to me the real problem involved in sex is not the question of *quantity* but of *quality:* Are the two people involved in a mutually gratifying relationship, one in which they are confirmed as persons and in which they receive both the psychological and physical gratifications appropriate to their sex? Simply to talk about sexual relations without inquiring about the quality of the relationship is, I think, to miss the mark.

I think you also have to bring out, don't you agree, the principle that any sexual relationship is a social relationship as well?

Yes. What is basically involved is a relationship between persons. The fact that it is a primary relationship which ceases to require words and concepts does not mean that it is a less serious relationship. If anything, it is far more serious because so much of ourselves is involved.

What about the concept of sex as play? I was talking to Dr. H., a Unitarian minister, who is very liberal in many of these areas. He approached sex with great solemnity. He maintained that there should be no frivolity about it, in opposition to the concept of sex as the play of adults. What do you think of the idea of sex as play?

I think sex can be play only when everything is going right, but to see sex primarily as play is to forget what sex is. It is a decisive mode of relating to another human being at a particular moment in our psycho-biological timetable on the road from life to death. The insights of both literature and religion wisely link love and death. Sexual activity is that activity out of which human origins arise. Inescapably, sex reminds us, not only of where we come from, but also of where we are going. There is a tragic sense involved in all sexual acts when they are taken seriously. At the deepest level, we seek a quiescence in sexual gratification which is not entirely unrelated to the terminal expression of quiescence, death. Sandor Ferenczi, one of Freud's pupils, has suggested that one of the most primordial responses of all living organisms is the attempt to be rid of any part of the body which is disturbed by an overaccumulation of excitation. He maintains that a trace of that response remains in human sexual intercourse. The male in placing his organ in the female seeks to end by ejaculation the tension he experiences. At a very deep level, there are traces of a yearning for autocastration in every sexual encounter, as a way of ending a surplus of excitation through being quit of the affected organ. If Ferenczi is correct, and I strongly suspect that he is, there is an inescapable trace of both castration anxiety and the yearning toward autocastration in every male genital activity. Only the most superficial analysis would rest content with the idea of sex as an exemplification of what is popularly regarded as play.

Furthermore, sex is never purely personal and voluntary. In the sex act, we serve forces which are beyond our own individual natures. What we desire transcends ourselves. We serve our most intimate, personal needs, yet we are impelled to do so by universal, elemental forces which transcend our persons.

If two people have formed a good relationship, there can be an element of play in sex. Nevertheless, to accept sex completely is also accept death. Really to accept sex is to accept one's own body which is limited in time. Our bodies ultimately bring with them the price we pay for entering time, death. It would be a mistake to swing over to the other extreme and become morbid or puritanical about sex, but I think one of the signs of our national immaturity is our incapacity to see that we pay for whatever we get and that something as important as sex couldn't possibly be all fun and games. I find the optimism which pervades our sexual attitudes as well as our theologies simply too narrow in perspective. I would agree with Dr. H. There is much that is solemn in and that goes beyond play in sex.

Moreover, all we know about play indicates that it has its serious side. People have an enormous psychological investment in the games they play. Have you watched a good game of tennis lately?

I believe in heartily celebrating the joys of the body. In spite of our so-called "new freedom," there is too little of that in our culture. Nevertheless, if the body is all that we are—and I believe the only life we shall ever know is the life of the body—then the joys which we celebrate have a terminus. It is impossible entirely to separate love and death.

There is a lot of talk about the new sexual morality. Do you believe that there is a new sexual morality in this country?

Quite frankly, yes. I think we are less likely to condemn; we are less likely to see a person involved in nonmarital sex as lost; we are less likely to be judgmental in sexual matters than we used to be. When people do things which used to be regarded as perverse, we are much more likely to see them as sick rather than immoral. I think this is all to the good. There is, however, a regrettable side to the new morality. Young people nowadays tend to find their limits through experiment. Sometimes the experiments leave abiding scars. In more traditional cultures, there were guidelines to help an individual avoid the scars. I don't see how we could reconstitute such a culture in America. Today young people frequently act out infantile strivings which cannot bring them genuine sexual gratification with a partner with whom they can form a lasting relationship.

Don't you think that gratification and fulfillment are less physical than psychological?

They're both physical and psychological. It is the mind that freezes us and prevents us from coming to full orgastic potency. In healthy sex the mind, both conscious and unconscious, as well as the body have to work together. I'm basically a Freudian in my approach to sex. I'm interested in people's being capable of experiencing genital release, but I know that this is not something experienced by the body alone. When everything is going right for the couple, they will experience genital release. If this is not attained, a different partner every day in the week won't bring any real satisfaction.

If there is a new sexual morality, do you think that it is just a theory, something that people talk about, or is it being acted upon?

From where I sit as a college chaplain, I would say that it is being acted upon.

To a very large degree or is it just a peripheral thing?

I would say that premarital sexual relations are far more prevalent on campus today than when I was a college student. However, there is a good deal more responsibility and affection in most of these relationships than some of the more lurid accounts of college sex would suggest.

Do you think that possibly this new acting out—let's put it that way—of the new morality is a reaction to the puritanical attitudes of the last generation and the generation before that, rather than an expression of sexual freedom; perhaps there is an element of reaction against authority and pristine purity?

I unintentionally angered some people at the University of Pittsburgh last year when I was quoted in the *Pitt News* as saying that the *Playboy* philosophy is a Protestant product. What I meant was that I felt much of the *Playboy* philosophy, as well as the career of Hugh Hefner, could only be understood as an attempt at liberation from a repressive, rigid Puritanism. For those of us who were never brought up that way, there has been far less need to negate inherited standards. People who come out of rigidly enclosed primary groups, especially in small towns or farm communities, and find themselves in anonymous, urban communities, either in the big city or in the university, tend to experience a new freedom they did not know at home. As a result, they question inherited standards and assert a freedom they did not know as youngsters. Of course it's a lot harder to get rid of the psychological effects of their early upbringing than some of these people imagine. If they were as free as they say, they'd simply enjoy their newly found sexual freedom and be far less preoccupied with formulating philosophies about it. The decline of religion's power to influence behavior has also contributed to the new freedom. Religious prohibitions no longer derive their authority from a divine sanction. Religious guidelines carry less and less conviction all the time. I am somewhat in sympathy with the Protestant death of God theologians. One of the things they are pointing out is that the thread has been broken between heaven and earth, between God and man. People now ask themselves, "Is this right for me?" rather than "Am I fulfilling God's commandments?" The freedom we experience today is unparalleled in our history.

Are there situations in which you believe premarital sex is permissible or even desirable?

To ask that question is to put the cart before the horse. People become sexually involved when they regard it as appropriate to their needs. They don't ask a clergyman for an opinion. Students usually come to me only after they've gotten into trouble. When they seek help, they are usually disturbed by the relationships they have formed. More often than not, these relationships are extremely neurotic. Nevertheless, for a clergyman to declare, before the fact, that premarital sex is desirable or undesirable would be pointless. People are going to indulge regardless of what opinion a clergyman has. All I can do is try to help people mend things when they seek guidance. I would be most reluctant to pass judgment on the subject of premarital sexual relations. That would be to pass judgment on how other people exercise their freedom.

When you say "mend things"—I believe that is the term you used—do you mean encouraging your counselee to terminate the relationship or do you mean something else?

To "mend" is to help people attain insight into those elements of the relationship which are realistic and those which are neurotic. What impresses me about so many instances of premarital sex, especially among young people, is the degree to which neurosis is involved. To love is to be fully present to another person. If the other person is a surrogate for a parent or sibling and if one makes the partner act in a drama which repeats the conflicts or the unrealistic demands made on a parent or sibling in childhood, that relationship is going to be neurotic. I am impressed by how frequently this takes place.

Do you believe that extramarital relationships should be allowed? If so, why? If not, why not?

People who indulge in extramarital relations aren't going to ask clergymen whether they allow them or not. They will go ahead regardless of clerical opinion. Nevertheless, I believe that extramarital relations are confessions of failure. They are confessions of an inability to form an adequate relationship within marriage. As such, I think they are undesirable. Wherever possible, it is far better for a married couple to seek help so that they can achieve a realistic, adult, gratifying relationship within the marriage. Failing that, I think divorce is preferable to adultery in the long run, even for the children.

What do you think should happen when one spouse is an invalid or is institutionalized or away for a long time? There are situations in which there is no possibility of sexual experience within the framework of the marriage.

I believe that, whenever possible, there ought to be a frank discussion between the parties involved in each instance enumerated. They have to decide for themselves. I find myself unable to pass judgment on what other people do with their lives. However, let us recognize that you have suggested extreme instances which test the limits of a marital relationship.

To prescribe ahead of time what ought to be done is to create a new legalism in place of the old. Each instance you gave me would require a great deal of consideration. In the case of an invalid, the couple would have to decide on the meaning of their relationship under the circumstances. They would have to face the question of the degree to which deceit or mutual consent would be operative. In all of the instances mentioned, there is also the question of whether a mature man or woman would be willing to enter a relationship with a partner who could give only a part of himself or herself because of prior commitment to a marriage. I doubt the adequacy of a relationship involving a person who can commit only a part of himself (because he is still committed within a marital situation). My own guess is that, in the long run, there is only one good way to have healthy sex and that paradoxically is in marriage.

I don't think it's so paradoxical myself. What about masturbation? I don't know about Judaism, but I know that there is a great stigma attached to it in the majority of Christian churches. In the Catholic Church it is considered, by the traditionalists at least, as being a very grievous sin.

I think I understand why Catholicism regards it as a grievous sin. There is a reverence for life in religious tradition. In a sense, in masturbation one pours out one's seed upon the ground, as the Bible suggests. What could be potentially the foundation of new life is wasted. The same prohibition against masturbation is also very strong in Judaism. Personally I see nothing morally wrong with it for a young man or woman who has no other sexual outlet. I do feel that, in the long run, it's bad on psychological grounds. It locks the individual up within himself or herself. An adult who regularly masturbates is, to that degree, psychotic in sexual matters. He is cut off from the reality of the other person. He prefers the safety of his own fantasy life to the challenge and opportunity of sexual encounter with the other person. But, in the case of adolescents, who have no other means of getting rid of their enormous sexual energy, I do not believe that masturbation ought to be condemned.

What about non-total sex, particularly within the marriage situation?

The trouble with non-total sex is that it basically represents an immature compromise. In all instances of non-total sex, one expresses some neurotic fear of the full genital relationship. I believe in a kind of "incarnational" view of sex: the mind and body must be fully at one with each other. They must be united in their total function. On the other hand, I don't see anything immoral about non-total sex. I simply feel that it is incomplete. It represents a fixation at an infantile level of sexual development.

Since most people seem to agree that sex is pleasurable, should sex be engaged in for pleasure alone?

To say that sex is pleasurable is to ignore what sexual pleasure really is. Sexual pleasure is ultimately the diminution

of an unpleasant tension. In sexual activity, there is an element
of the seeking for quiescence whose terminal expression is the
absolute quiescence of death. I am not prepared to say that sex
is just pleasure, as pleasure is popularly understood. As I have
already suggested, I don't see how there can be sexual activity
without some element of anxiety as well. However, insofar as
people enjoy sex for its own sake as a way of relating to each
other and genuinely enjoying each other's presence, I'm all for it.

What's your view of birth control?

I'm absolutely for it. On the other hand, I do understand the doubts of Orthodox Judaism and the Catholic Church
on the subject. If we will what our biology demands, then we
must will the whole process. The sex act is not to be taken out
of the context that it is the means by which children are brought
into the world. Given this perspective, there is some indication
that the desire for procreation is unconsciously involved in all
healthy sex. However, because of the hideous problems which
must arise if we don't face the problem of overpopulation, we
can't afford the luxury of sex without birth control.

Most of the discussion about birth control relates to the
regulation of the size of the family, one, two, three children,
something like that. What is your feeling about the couple who
doesn't want children? They would like to enjoy sex, but they
don't want their activities to result in procreation?

I would certainly question such a couple's maturity and
the kind of love they have for each other. It would seem very
unusual for a couple not to want the ultimate expression of their
union, the birth of a child, especially if they were physically
capable of having children. I have no moral objection to the deliberate choice of a barren marriage. There can be circumstances
under which the decision to avoid children is inescapable—for
example, if the parents are too old or if one is infirm or weak.
But if two healthy young people got married and permanently
avoided having children, I would wonder whether they were
well.

In terms of birth control, I take it you make no distinc-
tion between artificial methods, rhythm, and sterilization.

I would be opposed to sterilization, unless medically prescribed. As far as normal birth control measures are concerned, I would approve of any method which a normal couple found aesthetically appropriate, provided it did not interfere with the full enjoyment of the sexual act.

Do you believe in the principle of abortion?

I am opposed to abortion. The Jewish tradition has a horror of abortion under most circumstances. At the same time, there may be reasons why a medical decision must be taken in favor of abortion. Incidentally, in Judaism a conflict between saving the life of the mother and the life of the child is always decided in favor of the mother. I understand Catholicism gives priority to the child's life. There is also the agonizing problem of illegitimate children. When a child is brought into the world and given up for adoption or raised in an institution, it is deprived of the most important love of all, the love of its mother. I am not at all sure that it is right to bring a child into the world when those are the consequences. In the case of abortion, as with so many other problems in the sexual area, it's very difficult to be very sure what is the right thing to do.

How do you feel about those states which permit abortion on the basis of danger to the physical or mental health of the mother?

I would agree with that.

Suppose there was the danger of a malformed child?

There would have to be pretty good evidence that the child would be malformed. Several years ago a number of children were born deformed because of drugs their mothers took. My feeling was that those births should have been aborted.

Suppose the prospective parents just happen not to want a baby for personal or emotional rather than medical reasons?

That would seem to be the worst possible reason for abortion and one that I would have the greatest difficulty accepting.

In the light of your comments on abortion, do you feel that the abortion laws in the United States should be liberalized or changed in any way?

They are quite primitive. I think one of the best things *Playboy* has done has been to show the hideously archaic character of so many of our laws on sexual matters. One of the things I like least about the *Playboy* philosophy is its tendency to identify the clergy as one of the sources of this archaic legislation. In reality the clergy has, in general, been most sensitive to the terrible problems arising from the archaic laws pertaining to sex. Most matters involving sex are private. The state has no right to extend its domain thereto.

Which leads naturally to the next question, homosexuality. Here I want to emphasize something I think not too many people are aware of, the fact of female as well as male homosexuality. Would you say that homosexuality is a psychological condition or a normality of choice, such as choosing between apples and oranges?

I would say that homosexuality is basically a psychological disease. The homosexual is fixated at a fairly infantile level of sexual expression. He is usually afflicted with what the psychoanalysts call castration anxiety. As a result, he is not capable of having a fulfilling, genital relationship. However, I do not regard homosexuality as immoral, unless it involves the seduction of the innocent. I do not believe that there should be a prohibitory statute in the case of consenting adults. This is a matter of individual choice. On the other hand, I would not want to endow homosexuality with the respectability of consideration as an example of mature sexuality, which it definitely is not. I believe that only an orgastically complete, heterosexual relationship is fully mature and fully gratifying.

Since there are strong laws against homosexual activity, do you think such activity between consenting partners should be permitted?

I think the law should stay out of it; it is no one else's business.

What is the case from your religious perspective?

On occasion I have had students come to me who were involved in homosexual activity. Most of these students sought my help because they experienced considerable conflict. I attempted to get them psychiatric help so that they might eventually attain insight into their fear of a heterosexual relationship.

My counseling goal has always been to enable the student to proceed from what I would regard as an immature homosexual relationship to a more mature and fulfilling heterosexual one.

Normally religious institutions have been hostile toward the homosexual in America. The churches and synagogues tend to focus on the needs of the family. They have no social instrumentality for finding a place for the homosexual. Unfortunately, religion in America has not much understanding of psychological or moral failure. We are too success-oriented even in the sanctuary. As a result, we lack the capacity to handle certain kinds of problems.

Strictly speaking, from a religious point of view, there is absolutely no reason why the homosexual should not have the same entrée into the life of the religious community everyone else does. The church and the synagogue should accept the homosexual as a human being in need of its ministrations. Should the homosexual within the religious community feel that he has conflict about what he's doing, the clergyman ought to seek help for him. I am convinced, however, that the only kind of effective help the homosexual can get is psychoanalytically oriented therapy. I also suspect that the homosexual is made to feel like an outcast partly because every human being has some latent homosexual tendencies. Most people don't want to recognize it in themselves so they turn against the homosexual with a great deal of anger. This anger is really generated by their own insecurity. If any insight of contemporary depth psychology has relevance on this subject, it is that, just as we all possess secondary sexual characteristics, we all are to some degree latently homosexual. The sooner one realizes this about himself, the less likely it will be that he is hostile to a homosexual who has not mastered a problem we all share to a degree. There is a psychoanalytic way of mastering homosexuality. It is through psychological insight. I know of no other.

You talk of giving help to the homosexual. Suppose a student came to you who was an avowed homosexual—would you counsel him or her in such a way as to try to encourage heterosexual interests or would you say to him or her, "The reason

*you came to me is probably because of your guilt feelings"?
Would your goal in counseling be to help the student to come
to terms with remaining a homosexual?*

I would never do that because I am convinced homosexuality represents an infantile mode of encompassing the sexual fact.

But there seems to be a very low percentage of conversion from homosexuality to heterosexuality among those who seek psychiatric assistance. Wouldn't it be better for the clergyman or psychiatrist to help these people achieve peace through acceptance of their problem?

I don't think achieving peace with homosexuality is ever the issue. If a person feels conflict about it, he realizes he's missing something. To the extent that psychiatric help is efficacious, he will find his way. Students who seek counseling have very deep conflicts about homosexuality. They really don't want to be homosexual. Their problem is not learning how to live with their guilt. They want to know how to get to the point at which they can enjoy normal sex. While the homosexual has nothing to feel guilty about, he certainly has a lot to learn about what is possible for him in his own sexual fulfillment.

Yet we give him a great deal to feel guilty about.

I don't.

I mean society.

Society normally doesn't encourage deviant behavior. All that I can do as a clergyman is to accept the homosexual and help him to gain insight through counseling. If he can't get over his problem, I'm not going to condemn him.

Do you think there should be any restrictions on homosexual activities such as "gay bars"?

I've never been to a "gay bar" and I have no idea what these places are like, so I don't know. I would say that in principle I see no reason why homosexuals can't congregate among themselves. I would guess that the social condemnation of homosexuality tends to give these places an aura of sickness, rebellion, and protest. That would tend to make them singularly undesirable places. However, I would not approve of police action against them, provided the innocent aren't taken advantage of.

I've talked with an Episcopal priest about homosexuality in religious terms. He has said, having had a great deal of experience with it, that he has seen love, understanding, and compassion in the homophile community. Therefore, he cannot see that God is absent there.

That seems to be an overly romantic way of putting it. One might say that God is not absent from any place where men are striving.

Just as a matter of curiosity—it just occurred to me—do you know whether there is a lower percentage of homosexuality among Jews or among gentiles?

I have no knowledge of this. I would say that there is a strong insistence in Judaism on the sanctity and the primacy of the family. This would tend to discourage overt homosexuality, but there remains the problem of latent homosexuality. That's a question I can't answer.

Do you believe in censorship?

I don't like censorship and I don't like the kind of people who are normally the censors.

Let's take the old Oliver Wendell Holmes dictum, "The freedom of speech does not include the right to cry 'fire!' in the middle of a crowded theater." Given that sort of comment, would you feel that there should be no censorship prohibitions or some?

I think certain activities ought not to be shown on the screen. For example, I don't believe that the literal depiction of the act of sexual intercourse ought to be exhibited on the screen.

Why not?

Because it tends to make being a spectator more important than the act of participation and relating. On a recent visit to Denmark I attended a motion picture in which something very close to the actual representation of the act of sexual intercourse was on the screen. Denmark is much more liberal than we in matters of censorship. Nevertheless, I couldn't help noticing the embarrassed reaction of the audience. Sex is not a spectator sport. It's a participant relationship. I think there is a point beyond which realism ought not to proceed.

When you object to that sort of thing—and I may be

putting words into your mouth—do you mean that we cannot show the act of love but we can show the act of killing?

Quite frankly, if I had to choose between showing the act of love and the act of killing, I would rather show the act of love on the screen. I think one of the worst aspects of the motion picture industry is its failure to see that there is a pornography of violence as well as a pornography of sex. We would be a lot better off if all that was exhibited on the screen was sexual pornography, but I prefer that neither type of pornography be shown.

Would you carry over that attitude to books, magazines, and things like that?

The value of literature depends upon its capacity to lend insight into some aspect of the human predicament. I see nothing objectionable in the literary presentation of the sexual act. I am opposed to literary censorship. Though I may be inconsistent, my instinct tells me that the depiction of the sexual act on the screen is somewhat different from the depiction of a sexual scene in literature. There is an element of privacy in literature which is absent from the cinema.

If you want to have some kind of regulation of films, books, or magazines, who is going to do it?

You're asking a very difficult question: How can people who are emotionally involved in the human problem dealt with in the cinema or literature be sufficiently objective to be censors? I don't have any good answer to this. I think self-knowledge helps, but most censors have precious little of that. That is one of the reasons why I don't stress censorship. The people who end up doing it are usually political hacks. *Playboy* has performed an important service in pointing out the ugliness of censorship. Of all the things that have appeared in the *Playboy* philosophy, I have liked this best.

You wouldn't call the Catholic Legion of Decency a bunch of political hacks, would you?

No, I wouldn't. I don't want to get involved in an inter-faith debate on the subject of censorship, but I don't always appreciate the Legion of Decency's work. I see nothing wrong with it insofar as its activity is limited to advising Catholics as

to what films to see. However, I've heard it said cynically by
Catholics that sometimes a "C" rating by the Legion is an invitation to view a film. I'm not sure how effective the Legion is even
with Catholics. I would certainly object if the Legion decided to
function as a self-imposed censor for determining what non-
Catholics might see.

*How about the efforts of certain religious groups, par-
ticularly Catholics, who boycott theaters and things like that?*

I think that's their privilege. A religious group that
doesn't approve of a film has the right to encourage its members
to stay away. My own feeling is that the European system of
rating films is a lot more sensible than ours. There is a good
deal less censorship there, but they are pretty strict about not
letting people who are younger than sixteen or eighteen view
"adult" films. If we made a real distinction between films for
adults and films for young people, as they do in England and
France, we would have a much more mature American cinema
than we do now.

*We are all familiar with the principle of the double
standard. Do you believe in it?*

Absolutely not.

*Do you think that the double standard still exists in
this country?*

I think it exists to a lesser degree than it did. I don't
see how in a marriage a real woman could tolerate a man who
felt free to do as he pleased while she remained loyal. I believe
that what's good for one is good for the other. From that point
of view, I reject the double standard.

*Generally speaking, the emphasis in discussing sex seems
to be on the rights, privileges, and immunities of men. What
about the rights, privileges, and immunities of women?*

This is a very important problem. Unless both man and
woman are not being cheated, both sexes will be cheated, each in
its own way. This is something we don't always understand. In
sexual activity an interchange takes place between two people.
It is impossible for one partner to disadvantage the other without bringing unconscious retaliation upon him or herself.
Women frequently have much to be angry about. Let me say a

word about the *Playboy* philosophy. I don't think that a woman
begins to get interesting until she is at least thirty years old.
There is a real difference between women and girls. A woman is
far more compassionate, far more giving, far more responsive,
and far more sexually adequate than a girl. *Playboy* stresses
young women, many of whom are, I suspect, hardly capable of
full genital response. They have yet to experience many of the
ironies of existence. They have a long way to go before they
become mature, compassionate women. My own feeling is that
Playboy's emphasis on nude girls is part of our American immaturity. We look to adolescence as the great time of life. Why
doesn't the magazine feature a forty-five or fifty-year-old Play-
mate? It would seem to me that she would be far more interesting as a woman and probably far more interesting in bed.

But she might not be as attractive visually.

That's precisely the point. She might not be as attractive
visually, but that doesn't necessarily make a woman an inadequate partner, either physically or psychologically. I think this
is where our national immaturity shows. We don't look beneath
the surface. I agree with many of the comments Harvey Cox
makes about the *Playboy* philosophy in *The Secular City*. *Playboy*
doesn't really give women their due. I can't really buy *Playboy's*
conception of masculinity either. A sexually adequate man needs
a woman he can relate to, not a toy he can play with.

*I think it was Harvey who used the term "sexual ob-
jects" rather than "sexual subjects" in terms of this masculine
approach to sexual relationships.*

Well, insofar as a woman is a sexual object, she is not
responding as a sexual partner. If a woman is only something
you look at or go to bed with, rather than a partner in a very
decisive relationship, then she is an object rather than a subject.
Martin Buber's conception of I–Thou is significant in this context. The I–Thou relationship is a spontaneous relationship between two free persons who give of themselves. There's no
constraint; there's no sense that one is an object or is being
manipulated by the other. Both are fully real persons in the relationship. I think that is one of the things Harvey must have
had in mind when he wrote about *Playboy* in *Christianity and*

Crisis and in *The Secular City.* Harvey has made some extremely insightful comments about the *Playboy* philosophy.

Does the psychological nature of a woman inhibit her from such things as premarital or extramarital sex in favor of a permanent relationship based on marriage with the assurance of security for herself and her children?

I believe that any woman who is really a woman and really enjoys sex is going to want marriage, for a very simple reason: The woman understands that the sexual act has real consequences in her body and for the chain of the generations, from the time she is an adolescent girl and experiences her monthly period throughout the rest of her life. She knows that what she commits herself to, in spite of all contraceptive devices, has enormous ramifications and can lead to the birth of new life. Men, on the other hand, seem to see the sexual act as something isolated from the total biological process. They can dissociate themselves with greater ease from what is taking place. Women must insist upon a greater commitment because more of themselves and their progeny is potentially involved. In general, I find women somewhat saner about sex than men.

Does the fact of the pill have any bearing on the attitudes of women toward sex?

A generation ago Walter Lippmann made the point that contraception, because it reduced the fear of pregnancy, was bound to have moral consequences. I doubt that the best contraceptive devices will ever be 100 per cent certain. As a result, women will always have greater anxiety about the consequences of the act than men. Incidentally, one of the most amazing things about sex at the college level is that people who should know about contraceptives don't always use them. I've noticed this as a result of what I have heard in counseling. It would seem to indicate that if a woman has an unconscious desire to have a child, nothing will stop her. This happens with far greater frequency than we often imagine. Here again, I think women understand the consequences of sex far more than men.

One final question: Do you think that the vocation of the ministry is helped or hurt by marriage?

The Jewish answer is that the rabbinic vocation is helped

by marriage. I can't pass judgment on the Catholic priesthood because the Church obviously has another set of standards by which it looks at things. Nevertheless, I believe there is a whole dimension of existence which one can appreciate only by having been a participant. All of the ironies, the tragedies, the sadness, and the joys of marriage must be something a clergyman participates in directly rather than reads about in books. We need this experience for ourselves in order to be able to understand the problems, the dilemmas, and the potentialities of the marriages of the people we serve. Personally I would rather see a married clergy. On the other hand, let's be fair to the Catholic Church. A married clergyman has to face problems a priest doesn't have to meet, such as the support of a family. As Soren Kierkegaard pointed out over 100 years ago, a married clergyman is subject to subtle pressures which can diminish the purity of his religious commitment. The Church may feel that these pressures are extraneous to what it is trying to accomplish. From its point of view, a celibate priesthood may make more sense than a married priesthood. In Judaism we feel the necessity to share this most decisive and important relationship in life.

This isn't on the list but I'm going to try to sum up the idea you seem to expound: that is that the clergy, as well as the laity, must be full participants in life without necessarily passing judgment on things other people do, because most of the time we don't have sufficient insight into the psychological structure or the needs of other people. Would you say that pretty well sums up the idea?

Yes, I think that pretty well sums up how I feel. I believe that no man is exempt from the stresses and strains of life. I believe that what we need is much less judgment and more compassion. We're all hobbling along, trying to make the best we can of lives which are replete with mistakes. God knows, I've made enough in my time. I think we'd be better off if we had a little more compassion in these matters. There isn't a sexual area or a human area in which the possibility of failure isn't enormous. The principal tasks of the clergyman are to be compassionate, to help the troubled individual to achieve insight, and to perform those rituals whereby the individual can safely pass through the decisive crises of life. For my own part, I don't like to be judgmental. As a matter of fact, I distrust people who think God's on their side; those are people I really don't like.

I suspect, then, that you go along with St. Augustine's dictum to "Love and then do as you please."

I would say that St. Augustine's dictum is all right as far as it goes. I would add something inspired by Jean Paul Sartre's existentialist philosophy: "Love, do as you please, but know that whatever you do will have consequences for which you and you alone are responsible."